Regulation and Entry into Telecommunications Markets

This book analyzes telecommunications markets from early to mature competition, filling the gap between the existing economic literature on competition and the real-life application of theory to policy. Paul de Bijl and Martin Peitz focus on both the transitory and the persistent asymmetries between telephone companies, investigating the extent to which price and retail price regulation stimulate both short- and long-term competition. They explore and compare various settings, such as non-linear versus linear pricing, facilities-based versus unbundling-based or carrier-select-based competition, and non-segmented versus segmented markets. On the basis of their analysis, de Bijl and Peitz then formulate guidelines for policy. This book is a valuable resource for academics, regulators, and telecommunications professionals. It is accompanied by simulation programs devised by the authors both to establish and to illustrate their results.

PAUL DE BIJL is Policy Advisor at the Ministry of Finance, The Hague. He has previously published in the *International Journal of Industrial Organization* and *Netnomics*.

MARTIN PEITZ is Heisenberg Fellow of the Deutsche Forschungsgemeinschaft, affiliated to the University of Frankfurt. He has previously published in the *Journal of Economic Theory*, the *Journal of Industrial Economics*, the *Journal of Economics and Management Strategy*, and *Economic Theory*.

Regulation and Entry into Telecommunications Markets

Paul de Bijl

Ministry of Finance, The Hague

Martin Peitz

University of Frankfurt

CAMBRIDGE
UNIVERSITY PRESS

PUBLISHED BY THE PRESS SYNDICATE OF THE UNIVERSITY OF CAMBRIDGE
The Pitt Building, Trumpington Street, Cambridge, United Kingdom

CAMBRIDGE UNIVERSITY PRESS
The Edinburgh Building, Cambridge CB2 2RU, UK
40 West 20th Street, New York, NY 10011–4211, USA
477 Williamstown Road, Port Melbourne, VIC 3207, Australia
Ruiz de Alarcón 13, 28014 Madrid, Spain
Dock House, The Waterfront, Cape Town 8001, South Africa

http://www.cambridge.org

First published 2002

Printed in the United Kingdom at the University Press, Cambridge

Typeface Times 10/12 pt   *System* LATEX 2$_\varepsilon$ [TB]

A catalogue record for this book is available from the British Library

ISBN 0 521 80837 5 hardback

Contents

Figures

Tables

Preface

Perhaps the typical process when writing a book is to start with some papers on a topic and then eventually get ready to do it. However, we did not have any papers to start with. The Dutch telecommunications and post authority, Opta, had asked the CPB Netherlands Bureau for Economic Policy Analysis to undertake a study on competition and regulation in the market for fixed telecommunications. That's how we got involved: Paul as a staff member of CPB, and Martin as an external consultant. In 2000, the project resulted in the CPB publication "Competition and Regulation in Telecommunications Markets," a report primarily aimed at regulators. From the beginning, we could draw on contributions to the literature, in particular by Mark Armstrong, Michael Carter, Jean-Jaques Laffont, Patrick Rey, Jean Tirole, and Julian Wright, who had analyzed competition in telecommunications. Our focus, however, was different from their work in that we were not primarily interested in mature markets, but rather in the process of competition that starts from an asymmetric market environment. This, we found, was what the regulator was particularly concerned with.

In the process of working on the report for Opta, we asked ourselves whether, based on the experience that was gained, we should write something more academic, addressing a wider audience. Put briefly, we decided to write this book.

This book targets academics and Ph.D students interested in telecommunications and, more broadly, in industrial organization, regulation, and applied microeconomics; regulators, competition authorities, and ministries involved in telecommunications; economic consultants; and telecommunications professionals. We also have advanced undergraduate students in mind. To cater to such a wide audience, we kept, on the one hand, the formal analysis in the main text relatively simple (in particular in the more applied chapters 4, 5, 7, and 8). On the other hand, we included several technical appendices, complementing the main text.

We are grateful for many helpful comments by Mark Armstrong, George Norman, Aaron Schiff, Tommaso Valletti, Ingo Vogelsang, and Julian Wright. We would also like to thank Marcel Canoy and Michael Carter for helpful discussions. Furthermore, we would like to thank Jean Tirole for his encouragement and support. We are grateful to CPB and Opta for allowing us to use material from the CPB publication.

Martin thanks the Deutsche Forschungsgemeinschaft for its generous support (in the form of a Heisenberg fellowship) which made it possible for him to work intensively on the book. He also thanks CPB for its hospitality. Paul thanks CPB, and in particular Marcel Canoy and George Gelauff, for their support and making it possible to work on the book. At CPB, he also thanks Kathy Schuitemaker for her help, Arie ten Cate and Erwin Zijleman for computer support, and his colleagues for providing a stimulating work environment. Outside CPB, he thanks the universities of Frankfurt and Alicante for their hospitality. Thanks also to Chris Harrison of Cambridge University Press, who was always very supportive and encouraging, and to Kate Gentles for very effective copy-editing.

This is one of the many books that have affected the private lives of the authors. Paul is grateful to Denise. Martin thanks Ana for all her support and sacrifice, and Elias for his patience.

Frequently used symbols

a, b	linear demand parameters
c_{i1}	per-minute, traffic-dependent cost for operator i of a call that originates and terminates on that operator's network
c_{i2}	per-minute, traffic-dependent cost for operator i of a call that terminates on another operator's network
c_{i3}	per-minute, traffic-dependent cost for operator i of a call that originates from another operator's network
c_{i4}	per-minute, traffic-dependent cost for operator i of a call that originates from and terminates on another operator's network
CS	consumers surplus
f	connection-dependent but traffic-independent cost of the local loop
l	lease price for local loop unbundling
m_i	(monthly) subscription fee of operator i
n	size of the market
p_i	per-minute price of operator i
s_i	market share of operator i
u	direct utility function
u_i^0	fixed utility parameter
v	indirect utility function
W	welfare
x	individual demand function
Z	consumer switching cost parameter
α	probability that carrier-select services fail due to a capacity shortage
α^k	relative size of segment k
β^{kl}	probability that a call which originates on segment k terminates on segment l
δ_i	originating access price to the local loop of operator i

κ	retail price cap on the incumbent's retail services or only on its per-minute price
μ	retail price cap on the incumbent's subscription fee
Π_i	profits of operator i
τ_i	terminating access price to the local loop of operator i

1 Introduction

1.1 Motivation

Telecommunications markets all over the world recently have been, and still are, undergoing drastic changes, fuelled by market reforms and technological progress. State-owned monopolists have been privatized and markets have been liberalized. These transformed markets have attracted entrants in many varieties. Some entrants roll out complete networks, while others build only partial networks or perhaps offer services without having infrastructure themselves but by having access to the networks of incumbent operators.

The move away from regulated monopolies has been made possible by advances in communications technology, which have made the view that markets for fixed telephony are natural monopolies less plausible. The argument in the past was that the cost of connecting end users by digging holes for fixed lines was too high to support more than one operator. Arguably, since the speed at which entrants have been rolling out local networks is perhaps lower than was expected, it is not completely clear to what extent the natural-monopoly argument is no longer valid, in particular in residential and rural segments of the market. However, in the relatively young markets for mobile telephony, voice and data are transmitted over the airwaves so that costly fixed connections are not needed. The argument in favor of competition is therefore more clear cut for mobile telephony. In most national markets in Europe, several network operators have been able to gain substantial customer bases within a couple of years of liberalization taking place.

Telecommunications markets also receive a lot of attention, because they provide the pipes and services that make "convergence" possible, that is, the vertical integration of infrastructure and content, the interchangeability of different types of networks, and the digitalization of different types of information (e.g. voice, data, and video). The growing importance of telecommunications for the functioning of both the "old" and the "new" economy raises the stakes. Hence, regulation in telecommunications markets indirectly affects the whole economy. Against this background of drastic change, which goes together with a lot of uncertainty, it has become vital to develop a thorough understanding of the economic mechanisms at play in telecommunications markets.

This book explores entry in telecommunications markets in a rich set of environments, incorporating details and asymmetries that are relevant in the light of observed market characteristics and regulatory practices. Each of the settings that we analyze focuses on competition between an initially dominant incumbent and an entrant. The settings are different in three dimensions: (i) the type of entrant, e.g. with a complete or a partial network; (ii) the way the operators compete, e.g. in two-part tariffs or in linear prices; and (iii) possible segmentation of the market into different types of customers. In each case we are interested in the possibilities for entry in the market and the extent to which consumers benefit from competition. Each situation may give rise to different possibilities for policy and regulation.

Clearly, in a mature market, there are no reasons for a regulator to treat the incumbent and entrants differently, that is, if there is a level-playing field, then regulation should be symmetric. Our main interest is the impact of regulation in immature markets without a level playing field. In such situations, it is important to explore the potential benefits of asymmetric regulation, possibly favoring entrants on a temporary basis. Large parts of the book are therefore dedicated to *asymmetric regulation in asymmetric markets* – this is a central issue for regulators in the "early" stages of competition in a liberalized market, in other words, in an infant market (as we will call it throughout the book).[1]

We aim at filling a gap between, on the one hand, the economic literature on competition in telecommunications markets, and on the other hand, real-life application of theory to policy and regulation. This book, which is based on models from the theory of industrial organization and techniques of numerical simulation, and the accompanying software, can be seen as a toolbox for economists involved in policy and regulation of telecommunications markets. The simulation programs allow policy makers to perform mock exercises before implementing a certain measure in practice. Testing the effects of policy measures in a simulation model can greatly enhance the understanding of the complicated causalities and interactions in telecommunications markets. Such an understanding makes the existing theory, which is rather abstract, more accessible to policy makers.

At a more general level, applied economists, economic consultants, and telecommunications professionals may find this book useful because it can also be seen as an application of microeconomics to pricing, competitive strategy and regulation. For instance, one can use the simulation programs to experiment with different pricing strategies for the retail market, to work out targeted entry strategies, or to better understand how wholesale prices affect the overall

---

[1] Previous literature on competition in telecommunications hardly addresses this issue.

profitability, which is potentially valuable in negotiations about interconnection agreements. We are convinced that numerical exploration of economic theory by simulation methods adds great value in such applications. Also, it is our experience that numerical simulations are very helpful to communicate general insights and guidelines for policy that can be derived from economic analysis.

1.2   Contribution to existing literature

An important reference on the economics of telecommunications is *Competition in telecommunications* by Jean-Jacques Laffont and Jean Tirole (2000). It is essentially an overview of recent economic theory and its implications for policy and regulation. The main themes in the book are regulation of access to essential facilities, competition between network operators, and universal service provision. Laffont and Tirole make the existing theory of, among others, regulation of access to essential facilities and regulation of markets with competing networks accessible to a broader audience, including policy makers.

Our work builds on and is complementary to Laffont and Tirole's book, and the underlying academic articles on two-way access, in several ways.[2] While recognizing the importance of presenting the central ideas that have emerged in the academic literature, we have experienced in practice that policy makers and regulators still have a need for more direct applications of theory, fine-tuned to the specific problems that they are dealing with. It is because of this need that we have developed a range of models – based on and inspired by existing theory – that can cope with a wide range of policy issues that surface in the real world. Each model clearly demonstrates the main trade-offs that are encountered by policy makers dealing with, for instance, regulation of access prices or retail prices.

Additionally, we merely focus on *entry*. Despite its real-world importance in the light of recent market liberalization, entry is a topic which is relatively unexplored in the literature within the context of telecommunications. In particular, we address how different entry strategies are affected by policy and regulation. More generally, we analyze how regulatory instruments, such as regulation of interconnection tariffs and retail price caps, affect market shares, profit levels, consumers surplus, and so on, as the market gradually matures. We have experienced that policy makers are eager to learn more about the effects of policy instruments in situations of asymmetry between incumbents and entrants. In such asymmetric markets characterized by imperfect competition we explore in detail the virtue of asymmetric regulation. Repeatedly, we find that asymmetric regulation that favors the entrant positively affects consumers

---

[2] See Armstrong (1998) and Laffont, Rey, and Tirole (1998a, b); see also Carter and Wright (1999a).

surplus and entrant's profits. It can thus be seen as a means to promote both short- and long-term gains for consumers.

Another contribution of this book stems from the methods that are deployed. We start with a simple, game-theoretic model that captures the main features of a competitive situation in a telecommunications market. Next, we adapt this model to explore a range of entry strategies, and how market outcomes are affected by regulation, using simulations on a computer. Accordingly, on the one hand a rich and varied set of outcomes is generated, and on the other hand, the standard economic framework provided by game theory gives the reader a good sense of the broad picture.[3]

For problems that are too difficult to solve analytically, simulation is often a method of last resort. Here also, the use of numerical simulations turned out to be useful, and often necessary. This is partly due to the asymmetries between entrant and incumbent that we incorporate in our models. Nevertheless, while some may view numerical methods as inferior to analytical methods, we are convinced that they generate major benefits for the application of economic theory to the practice of policy and regulation – especially for the problems that telecoms professionals are most likely trying to deal with.

1.3   Approach

1.3.1   Game theory and industrial organization

In situations where a relatively small number of firms compete, a sensible analysis of firm behavior and market structure should involve the strategic interaction between firms. Game theory is the mathematical analysis of rational behavior in situations where one player's payoff depends on the actions of other players, that is, the optimal action of one player depends on their belief about the actions the other players are going to take.[4]

Game theory is particularly useful to the telecommunications industry, which is more complex than many product markets. At first glance, one may think that an operator simply sells voice telephony. Nevertheless, sales volume not only contributes to revenues and costs, but also generates traffic between operators. Traffic that goes from one operator's network to another generates access payments between operators. Therefore, the cost and profit structures of an operator are not straightforward. By using a formal model, it becomes easier to understand the operators' incentive structures.

---

[3] De Bijl and Peitz (2000), a study at the request of the Dutch telecommunications authority Opta (the report that led to this book), demonstrates the usefulness for policy purposes of obtaining qualitative insights with numerical methods.

[4] An introductory text book on game theory is Gibbons (1992). A more elaborate reference is Fudenberg and Tirole (1991).

During the last three decades, economists have exerted a lot of effort to apply game-theoretic techniques to problems in industrial economics.[5] The models in this book are applications of the theory of industrial organization. They are based on recent economic theory developed by Armstrong (1998) and Laffont, Rey, and Tirole (1998a, b).

Although models of industrial organization have their limitations just as other theories do, they impose discipline on the researcher to carefully define the boundaries of the problem at hand, and are unique in generating insights into complicated interactions and trade-offs. By itself, game theory is not a theory of firm behavior and market structure, but a set of logical tools that constrain and shape arguments about strategic interaction among firms. The role of game-theoretic models is to deliver insights through structured reasoning. In particular, they build up a system of logic that enables one to recognize flawed reasoning, and provide a common language and framework for analysis.

As a disclaimer, we want to stress that our models do not describe reality in full detail. To analyze strategic interaction in telecommunications markets, one has to solve puzzles in which many pieces are missing. In general, the tools of game theory are not powerful enough to make precise or quantitative predictions about real-world cases, but then neither can other theories. In any case, that is beyond our purposes. As always, one should never rely merely on stylized models but complement them with empirical observations and expert opinion.

1.3.2   Simulation models

As a start, we develop and analyze a stylized, static model of competition, and next, we explore several dynamic extensions of this basic model. Extensions incorporate (i) entry modes; (ii) the nature of price competition; and (iii) possible segmentation of the market.

Both the basic model and its extensions incorporate the fact that operators may initially have different market shares that are "sticky" owing to consumer switching costs. In other words, history matters in the sense that it gives the former monopolist the advantage of a large installed base of customers. In the extensions, we explicitly analyze the speed at which an entrant can gain market share.

The main elements of our approach are the following.
- We assume that its large customer base and reputation for established quality ("track record") gives the incumbent operator a head start. This assumption captures the initial real-world situation in recently liberalized telecommunications markets.

---

[5] See, for example, Tirole (1988), and more recently, on a more basic level, Cabral (2000).

- The evolution of market shares, and the ways they are affected by network investments and regulation, are at the core of the analysis.
- We allow for realistic and interesting asymmetries between incumbent and entrant, in particular with respect to network structures.

To keep the analysis tractable, we assume that in each period operators maximize their per-period profits and consumers maximize their per-period net benefits. Abstracting from intertemporal linkages that would result in a dynamic game, this seems a good starting point for the analysis. We describe operators in their pricing decisions as myopic players who ignore the impact of current market share on future profits when analyzing pricing decisions. Although this assumption is obviously restrictive, at the same time it has some realistic content. For instance, investors sometimes give managers incentives to aim at a fast recovery of investments, hence introducing a bias towards short-run profit maximization. Additionally, a quick turnover of personnel at sales and marketing departments may make it difficult to implement long-term pricing strategies. Finally, we are convinced that this simplification is very useful for the purpose of deriving policy implications, given that one acknowledges its limitations.

The entry situations that we explore cover the most important entry modes observed in most European countries, where the former national monopolist faces different types of competition. For the sake of illustration, we adopt cost and demand parameters that, to a certain extent, depict a small country that resembles the Netherlands. We do not claim that the simulations depict the situation in the Netherlands, though. It is also important to note that within reasonable ranges, the levels of the parameters do not qualitatively affect the policy implications of the models.

The use of numerical methods is becoming more and more standard in economic analysis.[6] We used *Mathematica* software from Wolfram Research to program and analyze numerical simulations on a computer. For the benefit of the reader, we have included one of the main simulation programs in an appendix in this book, while all programs are available at the Cambridge University Press Web site.[7] This allows the reader to perform his or her own simulations under different parameter constellations and regulatory policies.

1.4   Outline

Our book consists of nine chapters. Chapter 2 provides background material on telecommunications technology, markets, institutional settings, and economic

---

[6] For an overview of numerical methods in economics we refer to Judd (1998). For the use of *Mathematica* for numerical analysis in economics see Huang and Crooke (1997) and Varian (1996). Froeb and Werden (1996) and Green (2000) provide applications of numerical analysis to problems in industrial organization.

[7] See http://uk.cambridge.org/resources/0521808375.

concepts. Chapters 3 to 6 analyze competition in a non-segmented market. Chapter 3 describes the basic model and provides some general insights on competition in telecommunications markets. Chapters 4 and 5 analyze three different modes of entry (facilities-based entry, entry based on local loop unbundling, and entry based on "carrier select").[8] In these chapters, we assume that operators compete in two-part tariffs, that is, by setting subscription fees as well as per-minute prices. Chapter 6 explores different pricing strategies, such as linear prices and flat fees. It also analyzes termination-based price discrimination. Chapters 7 and 8 focus on segmented markets and targeted entry (supposing that operators compete in two-part tariffs). Exploring competition in segmented markets at a general level, Chapter 7 concentrates on facilities-based entry in all market segments. Chapter 8 focuses on strategies of targeted entry, where an entrant targets different segments in different ways, or targets only one segment of the market. Throughout Chapters 3 to 8, we highlight the main insights relevant for policy as numbered guidelines. Chapter 9 puts the results and guidelines in perspective by discussing further topics that are relevant for policy from a broader perspective.

Each chapter contains an introduction, laying out in more detail how we proceed. Also, each chapter concludes with a non-technical summary of the main results, allowing the reader to learn the basic insights without going through the analysis. Several chapters contain extensive appendices which contain more technical or supplementary material. Chapters 3 and 6 contain mathematical derivations in the main text. Nevertheless, we have tried to explain them in words, so that readers can skip the mathematics without interrupting the line of reasoning.

We will now describe in more detail the contents of Chapters 3 to 8, the main body of the book. Chapter 3 presents the basic model, the simplest version of our models, which serves as a starting point for the analysis and as a reference point to understand more complicated models. It depicts competition between two operators that are identical except for their installed customer base. In particular, each operator has a network consisting of a long-distance backbone and customer access infrastructure (the "local loop"). Hence this model depicts a situation of "facilities-based competition." We provide a detailed description of its components: operators, consumer demand, consumer switching costs, realized market shares, costs, volumes of on-net and off-net traffic, profit functions, surplus, welfare, and equilibrium concept (Section 3.2). We also relate our model with consumer switching costs to models of differentiated networks. In Section 3.3, preliminary results in a symmetric setting are based on straightforward calculations. Here, we establish equilibrium properties. For asymmetric initial market shares, we use numerical methods which

---

[8] See Chapter 2 for explanations of terminology.

are described in Section 3.4. With the help of simulations we assess the effects of reciprocal terminating access prices and non-reciprocal terminating access prices (Section 3.5). Throughout the book, results are evaluated by looking at prices, market shares, profit levels, consumer surplus, producer surplus, and welfare. In the basic model, the operators compete by setting two-part tariffs (consisting of a subscription fee and a per-minute price). In Section 3.6, we then compare the results derived under two-part tariffs with those under linear prices (consisting of only a per-minute price). Within that context, we discuss the possibility of using the access price as an instrument of tacit collusion. In Section 3.7, we analyze retail price caps on the incumbent's subscription fee and per-minute price.

Whereas Chapter 3 depicts facilities-based competition in a mature market with identical operators and in an infant market with asymmetric operators, Chapter 4 focuses on entry in a dynamic context. The basic model is modified and extended to incorporate market dynamics, as explained in Section 4.2. The subsequent sections investigate access price regulation (we consider cost-based, reciprocal, and non-reciprocal access prices) and retail price regulation by the means of price caps.

In Chapter 5, we explore "local-loop unbundling" and entry by "carrier-select" operators. Section 5.2 analyzes unbundled access to the incumbent's local loop, assuming that the entrant has a long-distance backbone. In order to serve end users, it leases the incumbent's local loop on a per-period and per-customer basis. The lease price then becomes an additional regulatory variable. In Section 5.3, we look at the case where the entrant, having its own backbone but no customer access network, uses originating access to the incumbent's local loop to serve end users. Consumers dial a carrier-select prefix to make calls through the entrant's network. Section 5.4 compares the entry modes explored in Chapters 4 and 5 to discuss entrants' incentives to build a local network. By comparing the entrant's profit levels under different modes of entry for a given regulatory regime, one can assess the effect of the regulatory regime on the entrant's incentives to invest in infrastructure.

The results in Chapters 4 and 5 are based on the assumption that the operators compete with two-part tariffs. Chapter 6 complements those results by considering alternative pricing strategies. In Section 6.2, we have a closer look at linear pricing (i.e., the operators only set per-minute prices). Section 6.3 analyzes flat fees (i.e., the operators only set subscription fees while call minutes are free). Termination-based price differentiation is the subject of Section 6.4: operators are allowed to differentiate the per-minute prices of on-net and off-net calls. This situation applies, for example, to competition between a fixed and a mobile operator.

In the chapters presented so far, the market is assumed to be unsegmented: consumers are homogeneous (with the exception of switching costs). In

Chapters 7 and 8, we consider facilities-based entry in a segmented market. We consider markets with two market segments and assume that either operators can explicitly discriminate between them or that they are subject to a uniform pricing constraint. The typical example of a segmented market is that the market consists of residential and corporate customers, but other interpretations are given as well.

In Chapter 7, the entrant targets both segments of the market; the corresponding model extension is explained in Section 7.2. In Section 7.3, we analyze price discrimination by both operators and, in Section 7.4, we look at price discrimination only by the entrant, and uniform pricing across market segments. Of particular interest is the role of consumers' calling patterns between the segments, that is, their inclination to make relatively more calls to customers in a certain segment.

Chapter 8 complements Chapter 7 by focusing on different modes of targeted entry. Firstly, we look at partial entry, that is, the entrant targets only one segment of the market. We focus on regulation in situations of facilities-based entry (Section 8.2), local loop unbundling (Section 8.3) and carrier-select-based entry (Section 8.4). Secondly, we consider mixed entry, that is, the entrant targets both segments but in different ways (Section 8.5). We consider two cases: a combination of facilities-based entry in one segment and local loop unbundling in the other segment, and a combination of facilities-based entry and carrier-select-based entry. Througout the chapter, we discuss price discrimination as well as uniform pricing across the segments.

The concluding chapter, Chapter 9, addresses further issues, such as efficient entry, regulatory uncertainty, and convergence of markets and technologies. We also discuss the usefulness and limitations of our results.

The appendix contains the simulation program in Mathematica for the model analyzed in Chapter 3. All other programs are available through the Web site of Cambridge University Press.

2 Telecommunications

This chapter provides background material. It first explains the basics of tele-communications technology. It then gives a short account of the developments in the telecommunications industry in Europe and the United States, including regulatory issues. Finally it discusses the characteristics of telecommunications markets and regulatory policy from the viewpoint of the literature on industrial organization and regulation.

2.1 Technology

This section gives a brief overview of the telecommunications technology.[1] It can be skipped by readers who are familiar with telecommunications markets, as the information presented here is of an introductory and descriptive nature. The reader should keep in mind that telecommunications technology is changing very rapidly owing to technological progress and that this section only describes the basic elements.

2.1.1 Circuit-switched networks

This subsection briefly describes the main elements of fixed, "circuit-switched" telecommunications systems. Although other types of networks are gaining importance (see the next subsection), circuit-switched telephony is still the main type of telecommunications service in current, regulated markets.

The traditional telecommunications network, that is, the fixed network to which consumers are connected, is often called the *public switched telephone network* (PSTN). The PSTN is a *circuit-switched* network, that is, each telephone call reserves an end-to-end physical circuit between the calling party and called party during a telephone call. For the duration of a call, this

---

[1] This section is based on, among others, a glossary at Oftel's Web site (http://www.oftel.gov.uk), Glass (1997), and Morgan Stanley Dean Witter (1999). The publisher has used its best endeavors to ensure that the URLs for external websites referred to in this book are correct and active at the time of going to press. However, the publisher has no responsibility for the websites and can make no guarantee that a site will remain live or that the content is or will remain appropriate.

circuit is fully dedicated to that call and is not available to other users of the network.

A telecommunications network permits transmission of information (e.g. voice in the case of basic telephony) between terminal devices (e.g. telephones) of different parties. This is done by establishing a connection, through the telecommunications network, between their devices.

A circuit-switched network consists of:

- *transmission systems*: the means by which information travels through the network, comprising the transmission medium (e.g. copper wire, coaxial cable, fibre-optic cable, wireless radio transmission) and transmission interface equipment (used to convert one type of transmission to another, e.g. from copper wire to wireless).
- *switching systems*: the means by which (temporary) connections between the calling party and the called party are established.
- *signaling systems*: the means by which information about connections that are to be established are conveyed. Examples of information that is typically conveyed by signaling systems are the phone number of the parties involved in the connection (especially the number of the called party), and the nature of the call (e.g. whether the call is toll-free).

At a stylized level, the PSTN consists of two partial transmission systems (or, more generally, partial networks). These are:

- *customer access network* (CAN): the network connecting end users' telephones and local switches (also called local exchanges or central offices) to which end users are connected. An important part of a CAN is the transmission medium between local switches and end users, the local line, in many cases consisting of copper wire. A connection to an end user, often called the "local loop," consists of a local line and a line card (a part of the local switch).
- *long-distance network*: the network enabling calls to be routed between local switches, possibly through several other exchanges, which are called *trunk exchanges*. It is also known as the trunk or backbone portion of the network. Commonly used transmission mediums within the backbone are copper wire, coaxial cable, and fibre.

A simplified network which enables customers to make long-distance calls is depicted in Figure 2.1.

Because of the associated fixed cost, the local line – which is essential to reach end users – is generally perceived as a bottleneck which, in the absence of alternative access, constitutes an essential facility. This is especially true in the case of wireline (i.e., fixed) local loops. The emergence of wireless technology may lower these fixed costs and alleviate the bottleneck problem.

It is instructive to discuss in detail what happens when a consumer makes a telephone call through the PSTN. Lifting the handset causes the telephone

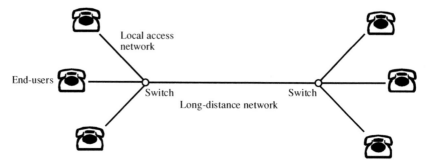

Figure 2.1   A simplified telecommunications network

to send a signal to the local switch to which the calling party is connected, prompting the local switch to provide a dial tone to the telephone. The calling party dials a number, which is also sent to the local switch. Next, the local exchange establishes a connection with the local switch to which the called party is connected. For distant destinations, connection is established through the backbone, possibly via one or more trunk switches (if the calling party and called party happen to live in the same area and have the same local switch, there is no need to use the backbone). The called party's local exchange sends a signal which causes their telephone to ring. If the called party is engaged, a signal is sent back to the calling party, resulting in an "engaged" tone in their handset. Accordingly, one can see how a simple service such as voice telephony makes use of the different network elements, and that more information than only the conversation is transmitted through the network.

2.1.2   *Other networks*

Above we discussed how circuit-switching is currently the main technology for fixed voice telephony. Nevertheless, circuit-switching is not the only way to carry voice through a network, telecommunications networks do not only carry voice but also data, and networks need not be fixed. Data networks, such as the Internet, are usually "packet-switched" networks. Unlike circuit-switched networks, they do not reserve circuits between endpoints. Instead, data is split into a large number of small packets of data. Each packet that belongs to a given data file may be routed differently to arrive at a single destination. Interestingly, packet switching not only works for data communication, but can also be used for voice telephony. Whereas circuit-switched networks, which consist of clear end-to-end paths, are not very prone to delays, a packet-switched network is more efficient in its use, but is much less immune to congestion and delays.

Mobile telephony is based on wireless, geographically flexible links to end users. The PSTN is called a fixed network because geographically fixed links (usually wires) connect user devices to the core of the network. In the case of mobile telephony, mobile phones communicate with the network by using radio signals. Hence, a subscriber to a mobile network can travel around without losing their connection to the network, provided that they do not cross the borders of the area that is covered by the regional base stations (i.e., low power radio transmitters that communicate with the mobile handsets) of the network. The base stations are usually connected by fixed wirelines, possibly part of the backbone of a network that is also used for fixed telephony.

2.1.3   Network interconnection and access to end users

Telephony offers maximum benefits to consumers if network effects are exploited as much as possible, that is, if each consumer can reach as many other users as possible. However, in a liberalized market with entry, it may happen that the calling party and called party do not subscribe to the same network operator. To benefit from network effects in such a situation, separate networks must be linked so that connections can be established. This situation is commonly referred to as *network interconnection*. It is not only relevant when there is more than one fixed network operator, but also in the case of international phone calls, and in the case of calls between different types of networks (such as fixed and mobile networks).

The place at which interconnection takes place is commonly called the *point of interconnect*. Typically, calls that require interconnection are carried on the calling party's network as far as possible before being transferred to the called party's network. By doing so, the calling party's operator can, in general, minimize the payments associated with using a rival operator's network (called access prices and interconnection fees).

An operator with only a small number of users directly connected to its network has an incentive to establish points of interconnection in as many local switches of an operator with a complete network as possible, since this minimizes the portion of calls carried by the other operator. However, because of cost and time considerations, in reality often only a small number of points of interconnection is established, even though this results in more long-distance interconnection payments to the operator of the network where calls are delivered.

Some entrants in recently liberalized markets can reach none or only very few end users, often because they have not (yet) built their own CAN. In such cases, they can use another operator's (typically the former national monopolist) CAN to have access to end users. As an example, consider the situation in which there is an incumbent with a PSTN and an entrant with only a backbone. Thus the entrant has no links of its own to consumers. Any calling party and called party are both connected to the incumbent's network only. Nevertheless, consumers may wish to carry the long-distance portion of their calls over the entrant's network. In such situations, the entrant has to use the incumbent's CAN to provide:

- *originating access*: the provision of a connection between the calling party and the entrant's backbone;
- *terminating access*: the provision of a connection between the entrant's backbone and the called party.

In fact, network interconnection can be seen as a situation of two-way terminating access, that is, terminating access from one network to another and vice versa.

A usual way to establish originating access is *carrier select*, that is, consumers can choose which operator they want to carry a call by dialing a code ("prefix") before the called party's telephone number. They keep their subscription to the incumbent, but pay the per-minute price to the entrant offering carrier-select calls. The entrant pays an originating access price to the incumbent, usually on a per-minute basis. Because consumers cannot subscribe to the entrant, carrier select is a form of indirect access to end users. Note that the entrant, in order to deliver calls to called parties, must have terminating access to end users as well, for which it pays a terminating access fee.

The possibilities for gaining access to end users are greatly enhanced by *local loop unbundling* (LLU), that is, unbundling of the incumbent's customer access network. LLU allows entrants to lease the incumbent's local lines, and hence use the transmission medium to the customer in the incumbent's local loop. An unbundled local loop allows an entrant to operate its "own" transmission system to have direct access to consumers, that is, they can directly subscribe to the entrant.[2] Because of the possibility that consumers subscribe to the entrant, unbundled access to the local loop is an example of direct access to end users, the opposite of carrier select.

Obviously, access payments, that is, the fees that operators have to pay to obtain originating or terminating access to other operators' networks, may have a strong impact on competition and the development of the market. In the case of LLU, this is also true for the lease price of the local loop.

2.2   Telecommunications markets

This section describes the telecommunications market environment, and how it came about during liberalization processes. We put most emphasis on the institutional framework within member states of the European Union. The

---

[2] A common way of LLU is access to the "main distribution frame." Under main distribution frame access, the local line and the linecard are unbundled. Hence an entrant can "plug in" by creating a link from its switch to the incumbent's main distribution frame.

Netherlands is discussed as an example. Since the analysis in this book can also be applied to the situation in the US, we also discuss how the American market was liberalized. We discuss market evolution and important elements of regulatory policy, particularly in relation to network interconnection.[3]

2.2.1   The European Union

Until the 1980s, operators in Europe used to be state owned, vertically integrated monopolists. During the 1980s and 1990s, telecommunications industries went through periods of fundamental change, ignited by privatization of national operators, liberalization of national markets, technological innovations, and, at the European level, convergence of economic policy and institutional structures.[4] This process has not ended yet, as competition is not yet mature in most market segments, especially in the segment of residential customers.

The changes that we have been observing were, at least indirectly, largely driven by technological developments in information technology. Because of the large fixed cost of building a network, telecommunications networks providing voice telephony were traditionally viewed as natural monopolies. Technological progress has generated new transmission systems and decreased the cost of building infrastructure. Therefore, the idea of a natural monopoly in the telecommunications sector was discarded. Since then, most operators have been, or still are, subject to plans to be privatized.

In the member states of the European Union, broad and general rules for liberalization and deregulation have been formulated by the European Commission.[5] In each member state, a national regulatory authority develops these general rules in more detail and then implements them. An important step taken by the Commission was to publish a Green Paper in 1987, which proposed the introduction of competition combined with harmonization measures and application of competition rules. The ultimate result was the liberalization of the markets for all telecommunications networks and services from 1 January 1998. These liberalizations have been accompanied by partial or full privatization of incumbent operators.

The fundamentals of European regulation are defined in the so-called *open network provision* (ONP) framework, which establishes the need for harmonized access conditions in line with principles of objectivity, transparency, and non-discrimination. In practice, these principles entail that operators apply

---

[3] An overview on the practice of interconnection is provided by Noam (2001).

[4] The earliest attempt of liberalization of telecommunications markets in Europe was made by the UK; for an account of UK regulation in the 1980s and early 1990s see, for instance, Armstrong, Cowan, and Vickers (1994). On access pricing in the UK, see Valletti (1999).

[5] For an overview of the recent developments in Europe, see European Commission (2000b); for a description of European legislation, see also European Commission (1999b).

Table 2.1 *Terminating access prices in Europe, March 2000 (in euro cents)*

	Local	Single transit	Double transit
Austria	1.82	1.82	2.40
France	0.63	1.33	2.01
Germany	0.88	1.49–1.89	2.28
Italy	1.00	1.60	2.29
Netherlands	1.05	1.45	1.77
Spain	0.99	1.59	3.07
UK	0.54	0.82	1.71

similar access terms and conditions to all operators offering similar services, including their own activities. Also, interconnection agreements must be available to all interested parties: incumbents are required to meet all reasonable requests for access. In principle, the terms and conditions of access are to be negotiated by the operators. In case of disputes, they can ask the national regulatory authority for help.

An important requirement in the ONP framework is that operators with significant market power (in practice, incumbents) must provide access at cost-oriented tariffs.[6] The aim of this condition is to ensure interconnection of networks and to allow entrants affordable access to various elements of the networks of incumbent operators. The latter is of particular importance, as in the early stages of liberalization new entrants depend on incumbents' networks to offer telephony services to end users.

As an illustration, Table 2.1 shows different types of terminating access prices that were charged by several European incumbent operators (spring 2000). There are significant differences between the countries.[7] These differences are partly due to different costs across countries as well as to different ways of cost accounting. Nevertheless, the European Commission recommended "best current practice" access prices; for 2000, they were between 0.5 and 0.9 euro-cents per minute at the local level, between 0.8 and 1.5 euro-cents per minute for single

[6] According to the Commission, in general an operator has significant market power if the national regulatory authority judges that it has a market share of at least 25 percent in the relevant market. The national regulatory authority may deviate from this rule, however, since factors other than market share may be important (see, for instance, European Commission, 2000b). Initially, significant market power was attributed to all incumbents in the market for fixed public voice telephony.

[7] The table depicts per-minute prices based on a 3-minute call at peak rates, and includes set-up charges where they exist. This information is made available by the European Commission using information from the national regulatory authorities. Prices were effective 1 March 2000. The four distance-related tariff zones in Germany do not correspond directly to the categories of the table (European Commission, 2000d).

transit interconnection (metropolitan level), and between 1.5 and 1.8 euro-cents per minute for double transit interconnection (national level, i.e., more than 200 km), all at peak rates (see European Commission, 2000d; see also European Commission, 2000c).

A consequence of the significant market power requirement of the ONP framework is that, in practice, only incumbents have to offer access at cost-oriented wholesale prices. Hence, access price regulation is, in principle, asymmetric, because entrants are not obliged to charge cost-based access prices. This may change when there is a level playing field, for instance when entrants have become sufficiently strong and are judged to have significant market power as well.

Whereas the guidelines for access in the ONP framework are primarily aimed at reducing entry barriers, and thus at improving efficiency in the market, political considerations are included as well. The Commission acknowledges the importance of affordability of telephony services for all citizens. Thus, European legislation defines *universal service* as a minimum number of services (including voice telephony) of a certain quality, available to all consumers no matter where they live. It requires that the national regulatory authorities in the member states make sure that in each geographic area, at least one operator provides basic services. In the monopoly situation of the past, cross-subsidies were used to guarantee affordable prices for different telephony services. For example, local calls were subsidized by higher revenues from long-distance and international calls. In the current situation, national regulatory authorities can put mechanisms in place for sharing the costs associated with the provision of universal service among market players, if they find that the universal service obligation represents an "unfair" burden.[8]

For consumers, the principle of affordability may have important implications for retail prices, since consumers need to be protected from monopoly prices in those market segments where there is not yet effective competition (and the accompanying downward price pressure). In such situations, retail price caps and uniform pricing constraints are means to guarantee affordability of telephony services.

The national regulatory authorities in the member states have a certain degree of discretion while implementing European legislation. In fact, the national regulatory authorities are doing most of the work of the implementation process. The speed and effectiveness of liberalization is not the same for the different countries within the EU (see European Commission, 2000e). The regulatory regimes in Germany, the Netherlands, and the UK are usually viewed as

---

[8] For example, the UK regulator Oftel (as well as most other European regulators) has found that the universal service obligation does not represent an unfair burden, so neither transfers need to be made nor does a universal service fund have to be established. Oftel also imposes uniform pricing across geographic areas. See Oftel (2000c, 2001c).

relatively pro-competitive in the sense that they put strong pressure on incumbents. In some cases, there is no total separation of regulatory functions and state ownership of the incumbent (e.g. Belgium and France). It is sometimes argued that the French regulator is somewhat biased in favor of the incumbent. In Italy, regulation has come about only very recently. Nevertheless, the Commission tries to establish consistency across countries with respect to their regulatory regimes.

Market liberalization has led to entry on a large scale by all sorts of network operators and providers of telecommunications services. Among the new fixed-line players in the European market one can distinguish:

- *network operators*: operators that install and operate their own transmission systems to provide public telephony or network services;
- *service providers*: operators that offer services primarily through third-party networks by leasing capacity;
- *resellers*: operators dealing exclusively with resale (including call-back or calling-card operators) or engaged only in marketing and billing activities.

Typically, entrants are not hampered by possibly obsolete infrastructure and associated cost structures, or by bureaucratic organizations and associated operational practices. Hence, the former monopolists are facing a fundamental challenge to redefine their value propositions and strategies, and to reorganize their business practices. Also, because of universal service obligations, incumbents may still have to provide telephony services in remote areas, perhaps as a loss-making activity.

In the late 1990s, the main strategies and tactics of incumbent operators to cope with the drastic changes in the industry included the following:

- internal restructuring to increase efficiency, flexibility, quality of service, and responsiveness to customers' wishes;
- diversification (e.g. mobile telephony, Internet access provision), consolidation and internationalization (e.g. foreign acquisitions, international alliances and mergers) to compensate for the expected loss of domestic market share in the market for fixed voice telephony;
- innovation (e.g. high-bandwidth transmission systems, intelligent applications in the network).

Somewhat later, in the early 2000s, one can observe that the uncertainty about new technologies and new markets may have been underestimated. Alliances broke apart, merger negotiations failed, auctions for third-generation mobile telephony increased operators' indebtedness, and incumbents sometimes even withdrew from freshly entered markets abroad. As this book is being written, the uncertainty has not yet resolved. Some incumbents have been struggling to adapt not only their organizations, but also their financial structures, to cope with heavy debt burdens. Despite investments in new technology and in foreign countries, the traditional activity in the domestic market for fixed voice telephony will remain a source of revenue (and debt repayment) for some time.

Parallel to changes taking place in the industry, regulatory policy is being overhauled. In 1999, the European Commission proposed a new framework with the purpose of accelerating the process of economic and structural reform in the European Union by lowering access prices and reinforcing competition (the "Review" by the European Commission, 1999a). According to the Commission, the European market is still fragmented and dominated by incumbent operators, even though entry has been substantial and retail prices have decreased.[9] While the existing framework was designed to cope with the transition process to competition, the new framework seeks to reinforce competition, especially in market segments at the local level. Moreover, it will have to cater for the rapid technological change and unpredictability of telecommunications markets.

The Review identifies several important developments in the telecommunications market. A prominent one is globalization (e.g. mergers, acquisitions, and alliances at the European and global level). Also, the Internet blurs the distinction between voice and data communication and may quickly overturn traditional market structures. Communications technologies are being improved, resulting in lower costs and increased capacity of networks (driven by the computer industry). Finally, wireless applications as well as technologies within the media sector (e.g. digital TV and video on demand) are becoming more and more important. Accordingly, it is acknowledged that the telecommunications industry is taking part in a development usually referred to as "convergence."[10]

In the Review, the Commission proposes a "light" regulatory approach for new services markets, while ensuring that market power is not abused by dominant firms. As competition matures, regulation can gradually be reduced. A central proposal is that the new framework would cover all electronic communications infrastructure and services (e.g. voice, data, and also television signals, which may be transmitted through PSTN, Internet, cable, wireless, etc.).

Some key elements in the policy proposals by the Commission that are highly relevant for fixed voice telephony are the following:

• common principles for regulation of access and interconnection across all types of networks, so that entrants can compete with incumbent operators by using any transmission system, thereby minimizing bottleneck problems;

• high priority to establish competition in the local loop, either through existing networks or new infrastructure (e.g. local loop unbundling, cable networks, wireless local loop).

---

[9] Some regulators provide information on retail prices and other data. For instance, the British regulator publishes detailed quarterly data (see Oftel, 2001b).

[10] See Chapter 9 for a further discussion of convergence. A structured approach of the rather vague notion of convergence and the changes in the industry can be found in Fransman (2001). See also European Commission (1997).

The policy proposals in the Review were motivated by the fact that incumbent operators have managed to keep their strong positions in certain segments. Not all market segments have been effectively exposed to entry. Incumbent operators may still benefit from monopoly positions in market segments that are sometimes viewed as less profitable, given the fixed cost of rolling out local networks. This is especially the case in the residential market segment, and hence for local telephony services.[11]

In 2000, the Commission proposed a new package of measures for a new regulatory framework for electronic communications networks and services (European Commission, 2000g; see also European Commission, 2000f). In line with the Review of 1999 (European Commission, 1999a), all electronic communications networks and services are within the scope of this package, to provide consistency across different networks. In particular, it covers all satellite and terrestrial networks (fixed or wireless), including the public switched telephone network, networks using Internet protocol (IP), cable TV networks and broadcast networks. The proposal provides a lighter regulatory touch if the condition is satisfied that there is effective competition while certain services are available to all users at affordable prices.

An updated definition of significant market power in the new package moves closer to the notion of dominance in competition law, and therefore raises the threshold for *ex ante* regulation (see European Commission, 2001). Unbundled access to "metallic" local loops (i.e., based on twisted metallic pair circuits and not on, for instance, optical fibre) is mandated only to operators that have been designated by their national regulatory authority as having significant market power in the fixed PSTN (see European Parliament and Council, 2000; see also European Commission, 2000a). The provision of local loops based on optical fibre is seen as a specific market to which different conditions apply (aiming at the stimulation of investments). Moreover, existing universal service obligations will be maintained, while introducing a procedure to review and revise the scope of universal service if that becomes necessary in the future.

Overall, in Europe, the emphasis is shifting from opening up traditional markets for telecommunications to stimulating effective competition in the longer run. Hence, the focus is gradually changing from creating healthy conditions in infant markets, to promoting and reinforcing competition in more mature markets.

---

[11] At present, there are some alternatives to voice telephony through the incumbent operator's local access network. The wireless local loop is an obvious example, while another example is cable telephony. Nevertheless, these alternatives are not yet widely available. In the future, local access through electricity networks may also become available.

2.2.2   An example: the Netherlands

It is interesting to see how national markets were affected by liberalization. We will therefore discuss, as an example, how the market developed in the Netherlands.[12]

The Dutch incumbent operator, KPN Telecom, was a state monopolist until 1989, when it became a public limited liability company, although still fully owned by the state. The government sold 30 percent of its shares in 1994, and another 25 percent in 1995. When competition was introduced in 1996 on the basis of the so-called "interim legislation," two entrants, Enertel and Telfort, obtained licenses for national, fixed telecommunications infrastructure.

Enertel, currently called Energis, was formed by Dutch energy companies and cable companies. Later it became a 100 percent daughter of Energis in the UK, while it developed a long-distance backbone of more than 1200 km in the Netherlands. It has two switches, located in Amsterdam and Rotterdam. Energis serves only the corporate market, by offering voice and data services and Internet access, although it can indirectly reach about 70 percent of all households in the Netherlands. It has a cable link between the Netherlands and the UK on the bottom of the North Sea.

The other entrant in 1996, Telfort, was formed by the Dutch Railways and British Telecom. Its fixed infrastructure is based on the network alongside the main railways in the Netherlands, consisting of more than 1000 km of glass fiber, with a connection to BT's international network. The network has access to most of the business areas in the larger cities. Telfort is active in both the residential market (carrier select) and corporate market (voice and data services and Internet access). It has not built a customer access network to serve the residential market. In addition, Telfort is operating a license for mobile telephony.

The independent post and telecommunications authority in the Netherlands, Opta, came into existence in August 1997. Right from the start, Opta had to deal with the allocation of costs for interconnection and special access, issues that arose in a conflict between incumbent KPN Telecom and entrant Telfort.[13] Policy in the Netherlands is based on the principle that general competition policy will be sufficient as soon as the market (i.e., competition) functions effectively. The government aims to reach this situation as soon as possible. Reflecting this principle, the Dutch regulator Opta will be

---

[12] See Van Damme (1999, Chapter 5) and Cave et al. (2001) for an overview of developments in policy and regulation in the Netherlands since 1997. Most of the facts presented below are derived from DGTP (2000).

[13] As the ONP directive stating that KPN had to offer "special" access to entrants had not yet been incorporated into national law, it was still possible that the cost of the local loop was allocated completely to originating access and not to terminating access. Telfort, in need of originating access, claimed that this would make local calls a loss-making activity. See Van Damme (1999).

brought under the Dutch competition authority as an independent division in 2005.

The Dutch market was completely liberalized in 1998 with the new Telecommunications Act, in line with European Union policy on liberalization. Since full liberalization in 1998, several more entrants have appeared in the Dutch market. Some of them operate their own fixed network, as illustrated by the following examples. Colt (from the UK) has built a long-distance backbone, four fibre "city rings" in Amsterdam and its surroundings, and one in Rotterdam. GTS has a European backbone and a point of interconnection in Amsterdam. It took over the Dutch networks of Hermes Europe Railtel and Esprit, and is building a city ring in Amsterdam. MCI Worldcom has its own backbone and networks in Amsterdam and Rotterdam, and intends building networks in The Hague and Utrecht as well. Another example is Versatel, which, in November 1999, had built more than 800 km fibre in the Benelux, including a ring between the major cities in the Netherlands. It is able to serve about 40 percent of the Dutch corporate market with local broadband access (DSL). Versatel is building a network of 2200 km, enabling the firm to serve more than 80 percent of the market.

Other entrants, especially carrier-select operators, may be active with minimal network investments. A case in point is Tele2, a carrier-select operator that has had only a single switch for some time. By competing with KPN Telecom on marketing and administrative operations (e.g. billing), Tele2 has followed a resale-based entry strategy.

Besides the entrants discussed above, cable operators have entered the market. An operator with a substantial number of connections in the Amsterdam area is Priority Telecom, previously known as A2000 and now owned by UPC. However, most of the cable networks in the Netherlands still have to be upgraded to allow for two-way communication.

In the meantime, incumbent KPN Telecom has been active with reorganizations, mergers and acquisitions, diversification (e.g. mobile telephony, Internet provision, and Internet banking), and joint ventures (with US firm Qwest, building a pan-European, IP-based fibre network). Although entry in the Dutch market has been substantial, KPN still has large shares in several markets. For instance, KPN's market share in 1999 was 80 to 95 percent in the markets for national telephony and calls from fixed phones to mobile phones, 90 to 99 percent in the market for local telephony, and 85 percent in the consumer market for international telephony. At present, KPN's customer access network is still an essential facility in most parts of the country, certainly with respect to residential customers and small businesses. The firm is trying to cope with its heavy debt burden (partly caused by its high bids in frequency auctions for third-generation mobile telephony).

Obviously, there is a lot of uncertainty in the development of the Dutch market. As in other countries, share prices of telecommunications operators have fallen sharply. Local loop unbundling has not been very successful so far, although the regulatory framework has been in place for some time. The incumbent has been trying to oppose unbundled access at cost-based lease prices by using legal procedures. Entrants' profits have been harmed by "price squeezes" (see Chapter 5). The government has had plans to license auctions for wireless local loops, but so far these plans have not resulted in auctions (because of legal complications and procedures). Entrants active in the residential segment seem to be more interested in offering broadband services through xDSL (a technology that upgrades fixed lines to make them suitable for fast Internet access) than in offering voice telephony.

At this point in time, it is still hard to say whether local loop unbundling or facilities-based entry will result in competition in the local segment, despite the optimism that reigned when liberalization was set in motion. The picture of the Netherlands sketched above contains two messages, which apply not only to the Netherlands. Firstly, the telecommunications industry matures more slowly than expected in the recent past, and not necessarily in the envisaged direction. Secondly, there is still a lot of uncertainty regarding the future success of established as well as new operators.

2.2.3   The United States

In the United States, the first step to break the monopoly position of AT&T, the original incumbent operator, was to allow entry in the long-distance market. In the 1970s, MCI and Sprint entered this market segment. A subsequent milestone was the government-mandated breakup of AT&T in 1984. The breakup resulted in seven regional "Baby Bells" (also called RBOCs, that is, Regional Bell Operating Companies), providing local telephony services without facing entry in their segment.[14] Mother company "Ma Bell" (AT&T) was left to operate as a long-distance provider. The underlying idea of the breakup was that only local telephony was a natural monopoly. Effectively, the market structure for access to the local loop (upstream) and long-distance calls (downstream) became vertically separated.

After the breakup of AT&T, the growth of long-distance operators like MCI, Sprint, and Rochester Telephone, strongly reduced long-distance rates. Besides four long-distance operators with their own networks, there is also a large number of resellers, which are buying wholesale capacity from facilities-based operators such as AT&T and selling services to consumers. Arguably, however, the decline in prices was not as large as was made possible by technological change and cost decreases (see Economides, 2000). Also, the Baby Bells were allowed to charge high access prices to the long-distance operators for terminating

---

[14] Ameritech, Bell Atlantic, Bell South, NYNEX, Pacific Bell, Southwestern Bell, and US West.

calls on their networks. These high access charges were meant to contribute to the provision of universal service. The local operators were not allowed to enter the long-distance market, however, as they did not face high access prices themselves, since they own the local loops. Thus, measures were taken to prevent anti-competitive abuses of the essential facility of the local access networks.[15]

The Telecommunications Act was introduced in 1996 as a major restructuring of the telecommunications sector, and primarily aimed at introducing competition in the local loop, which was still a bottleneck controlled by local operators. Thus, the idea was to establish competition not only in the long-distance segment but also in the market for local telephony. In particular, the Act orders the Baby Bells to unbundle the local loop and to lease parts of their networks to newcomers in the market. In addition, it orders that any service can be bought for resale at a wholesale discount. The Act also required that competition be present in local markets before the Baby Bells are allowed to enter the long-distance segment.

The Act contains provisions that define universal service and implement universal service obligations. It states that "consumers in all regions of the Nation, including low-income consumers and those in rural, insular, and high-cost areas, should have access to telecommunications and information services, including interexchange services and advanced telecommunications and information services, that are reasonably comparable to those services provided in urban areas and that are available at rates that are reasonably comparable to rates charged for similar services in urban areas." (Telecommunications Act of 1996, Sec. 254 (b)(3)). Because of the industry structure in the US some local operators have to be compensated for providing universal service and a complicated mechanism for universal service funds is implemented.[16]

Opening up the local operators' networks as envisaged by the 1996 Act has been problematic, though, because of legal and implementation constraints. Arbitration processes turned out to take a long time, for instance, because incumbents continued to raise legal obstacles. To circumvent these problems, long-distance companies have been looking for other ways to access end users. For example, AT&T started acquiring cable television companies in order to offer local telephony through existing coaxial cables. The success of the conversion of cable networks to allow for two-way communication services (not only telephony, but also Internet access and video services) still seems uncertain to some extent, however, because of uncertainty about costs and technological possibilities.

The Baby Bells themselves, planning for the moment that they could enter the long-distance market, have been going through a merger wave. For instance,

---

[15] An elaborate source on competition and the local loop in the United States is Vogelsang and Mitchell (1997).

[16] On the universal sevice obligation and its implications in the US, see Riordan (2001).

Southwestern Bell acquired Pacific Bell, and Bell Atlantic acquired NYNEX. It is uncertain what the consequences for the effectiveness of competition will be, though, as combined local operators may have better opportunities for price squeezes (i.e., increasing access charges in order to reduce the price-to-cost ratio of long-distance competitors) and cross-subsidization. The debate in the US about the alleged success of the 1996 Act has led to a strong criticism of some of its provisions (see Economides, 1999). Whatever the defects of regulation, however, in some segments of the market we have seen more mature competition than in the countries of the European Union.[17]

To conclude, in the US there was a different initial situation at the beginning of the 1990s, compared with Europe, primarily because in the US long-distance telephony and access to the local telephony had been vertically separated for a long time and competition in the long-distance market had been effective. To a large extent, however, current regulatory challenges in the US are similar to those in Europe. For instance, in Europe local telephony also remains a burden, since entrants have hardly started to roll out customer access networks in residential areas. Therefore, an important challenge both in the US and in Europe is the potential impact on local competition – and the difficult implementation process – of unbundled access to the local loop.

2.3   Insights from the economics literature

2.3.1   *Market structure and competition in telecommunications*

General description   Telecommunications markets can be seen as complex systems of markets for goods and services which are in substitute or complementary relationships with other goods and services provided by that industry. Many prominent topics of the industrial organizations literature can be found in these markets, such as sunk costs, switching costs, product differentiation, non-linear pricing, product bundling, and vertical relationships, to name just a few.[18] Also, several aspects of the antitrust literature, such as predation and foreclosure, have been explored in the context of the telecommunications industry. Furthermore, due to fast technological progress accompanied by changes in the regulatory environment, the relevant framework for parts of the industry is transforming from a protected monopoly, via a market with monopoly segments and imperfectly competitive segments, to a market characterized by imperfect competition.[19]

---

[17] The FCC makes information on prices and other data publicly available (see FCC, 2001).

[18] Some of the topics on pricing discussed in this section are also covered by Mitchell and Vogelsang (1991, part II).

[19] Other segments may be well described by a dominant firm model, in which one firm with market power competes with a competitive fringe (see Armstrong 2001); we do not consider such models in this book.

Clearly, in such an industry several modeling tools of industrial organization have been used to gain insights in abstract models of competition. The most distinctive characteristic of telecommunications, and several other industries such as electricity, water, and railroads, is the network element, which is absent in most other industries.

In the past, a monopolist served all consumers of a given geographical area and was subject to some sort of regulation. A protected monopoly (with multiple products) does not give too many modeling choices, so that building a theory of the market is not very problematic. In such an environment, the standard economics literature on regulation is relevant; see Subsection 2.3.2. In contrast, the dominant firm environment is possibly approximated by the former monopolist being the only strategic decision maker, where reactions of new competitors follow supply curves and related concepts of a competitive environment. Since competitors must have access to parts of the monopoly segment the terms of access are essential for the success of competitors in the liberalized market segment. Here, regulation has to make sure that, among other things, these competitors are not at a disadvantage relative to the former monopolist which is also active in the competitive segment. This leads to access price regulation in situations of one-way access.

Further down the road, there is imperfect competition among several network owners which have to grant access to each other; see Subsection 2.3.3. A priori, it is not clear if intervention by a regulator is needed or if the existing rules and institutions to enforce competition policy are sufficient to guarantee a proper functioning of the market. In particular, the economics literature has identified situations in which access price regulation seems desirable, even in the case of mature competition in network industries.

Before entering the specifics of telecommunications markets, it is useful to discuss selected topics which telecommunications markets share with some other markets. As a starting point, we suppose that operators compete by setting prices. Operators enjoy some market power, so that the price undercutting argument that is inherent to the Bertrand paradox is not relevant in the markets that we consider (see Tirole, 1988, Chapter 5).

Sunk costs   In many segments of telecommunications markets, sunk costs of entry are an important element of market structure. A firm entering such a market incurs an initial cost which it cannot recover when leaving the market. As emphasized in the seminal book by Sutton (1991), it is essential for results on market structure to distinguish between exogenous and endogenous sunk costs. Exogenous sunk costs refer to sunk costs which cannot be affected by the actions of competitors. An example of exogenous sunk costs is provided by a cable operator which starts a business in telephony by upgrading its network (to make it suitable for two-way communication). Also, a firm which decides to enter the market by building its own long-distance backbone, incurs a setup cost of cables and switches for this network. This cost is exogenous and likely to be partially sunk (it is partially sunk if the firm cannot fully recover it by selling out to a competitor).[20]

Sunk costs are endogenous if they depend on the actions of the competitors. License payments which are independent of the customer base constitute an endogenous sunk cost of entry. Also, advertising campaigns to launch a new product or service are sunk costs which are often endogenous, for example if the advertising intensity for existing services affects the costs of advertising for the newcomer. An incumbent firm can take such actions as an entry deterrence strategy.

An incumbent's action that makes entry more difficult does not necessarily lead to endogenous sunk costs. As an example, take contracts which bind consumers to an incumbent operator for a specified period. This makes it more difficult to gain consumers but does not represent a cost of entry. Also payments for a license on a per-consumer base do not constitute sunk costs of entry.

In some cases, the government decides on whether entry costs are endogenous or exogenous. For instance, a mobile operator has to obtain a frequency which involves a payment to the government. This payment may be fixed and some rationing may occur or the payment may be determined by the competitors via an auction. In the former case the entry cost is exogenous, whereas in the latter it is endogenous. If in an auction, some licenses are reserved for newcomers, the fact that entry costs become endogenous may be neutral to competition (and only affect side payments from firms to the government). In their absence, the fact that under an auction entry costs are endogenous may negatively affect entry of new firms.[21]

Consumer switching costs   In telecommunications markets, as in many other markets, the subscription of a consumer is valuable beyond the profits stemming from that consumer in the current period, because there are lock-in effects. Namely, a consumer suffers a monetary or non-monetary disutility from

[20] For instance the UK regulator, Oftel, states that "Sunk costs are particularly relevant to telecommunications because a very large investment is needed to create an efficient telecommunications network and it is likely that little of this could be recovered if the entrant later decided to leave the market. This is likely to be exacerbated by the significant economies of scale and density which characterise telecommunications networks. These mean that a large network is always likely to have lower costs than a smaller one, with the result that an entrant would need to take a large share of the market if it was to be able to compete. But in order to gain such a large market share, it is likely to have to price well below the incumbent, which would make it more difficult to recover sunk costs. Therefore barriers to entry by competing network operators are likely to be high" (Oftel, 2001a, p. 36).

[21] As an example, take the German spectrum auction for third-generation mobile telephony as contrasted to the UK auction which reserved slots for newcomers. As a matter of fact, newcomers succeeded in obtaining licenses in both countries.

switching service providers.[22] Such consumer switching costs are an important source of imperfect competition and create an asymmetry between early and late arrivals in an industry, because initial market share is valuable. Since the presence of consumer switching costs might lead to higher profits, they are not necessarily detrimental to entry (see Wang and Wen, 1998). However, as with other sources of imperfect competition, they may lead to inefficient entry.

Firms possibly anticipate consumers' lock-in when they make their present pricing decisions. This type of pricing behavior makes a strategic analysis of models of consumer switching costs relevant (see also the discussion on this topic in Chapter 3). For an overview of this strand of literature, see Klemperer (1995). If consumers are aware of the lock-in effect, firms possibly have to attract consumers by initially lower prices.

Note that consumers are valuable for firms independently of whether the former are aware of the lock-in effect. If one assumes that consumers are ignorant about lock-in effects, firms have an incentive to build up market share as soon as possible because this allows them to extract profits better from these consumers.

Product differentiation   Independent of the date of entry and the installed customer base, product differentiation arising from different characteristics over which consumers have different opinions or preferences – consumers may disagree over the more favorable characteristic (horizontal product differentiation) or some evaluate quality improvements higher than others (vertical differentiation) – creates imperfect competition among firms. The industrial organization literature has developed models with great detail which describe the effects of product differentiation on entry and competition. Models of mature competition in telephony use simple models of horizontal product differentiation to capture the less than perfect competition in a mature market.

Other market characteristics, such as capacity constraints, can also be a source of market imperfection which seems to be relevant in some telecommunications markets. It can usually be thought of as a quality characteristic of a service, for instance the probability that a call will go through.

---

[22] The UK regulator, Oftel, remarks on consumer switching costs that "many markets will have some barriers to switching, for example, due to the prevalence of long-term contracts or supplier-specific equipment. It may also be that a number of barriers specific to telecommunications have discouraged consumers from switching operator. These may include the disruption caused by changing the physical connection between the premises and the network when switching access supplier (e.g. to a cable company)... In the past, the need to change number when changing access supplier... may have been further barriers to switching, but these have now been addressed by the availability of number portability" (Oftel, 2001a, p. 16). A survey on consumer switching behavior in the UK suggests that one of the main barriers to switching relates to the lack of consumer information (Oftel, 2000b). In this respect, consumer switching costs can be interpreted as costs to acquire relevant information on alternative operators.

Non-linear pricing When the price per unit depends on the quantity demanded one speaks of non-linear pricing. An example is two-part tariffs which are typical for the telecommunications market, consisting of a per-minute price and a subscription fee. The economics textbook example for optimal two-part tariff pricing by a monopolist is an amusement park, where a two-part tariff can consist of an entry fee and a charge per ride inside the park. It is optimal for the park to fully capture consumers surplus through the entry fee, and set the price per ride equal to its marginal cost. Without a fixed fee, the monopoly price is above marginal cost, resulting in a loss of total surplus (the "dead-weight loss"). This is due to the fact that a price above marginal cost results in too little consumption, compared to the social optimum. Using a two-part tariff and setting the usage price equal to marginal cost allows the monopolist to create and capture maximal surplus. If charging the per-minute price is costly (because of metering costs) it might even be optimal to set the usage price equal to zero, in spite of a positive marginal cost; for this consumer preferences have to be satiated (see Nahata, Ostaszewski, and Sahoo, 1999). The flat fee offered by several Internet providers may be explained by this.

Two-part tariffs also differ substantially from linear pricing in an oligopolistic setup, as will be explored in Chapter 3 (see also Laffont, Rey, and Tirole, 1998a). Other non-linear prices observed in real life include fixed initial quantities purchased on a monthly base, combined with a per-minute price for higher quantities, as is the case with many Internet providers, as well as some tariffs offered by fixed and mobile operators. Often, operators offer a whole menu of non-linear prices, which is used as a price discrimination device between heavy and light users.[23]

Product bundling Product bundling consists of selling several goods and/or services at one price. If only such bundles are offered one speaks of pure bundling; if, in addition, goods or services are offered unbundled one speaks of mixed bundling. In telecommunications markets, one can observe that Internet providers offer a package of services such as Internet access, e-mail, home banking, chat groups, and content together. Another example is contracts with Deutsche Telekom for ISDN lines which include several services and a free subscription to T-Online, the Internet provider of Deutsche Telekom. Also, some operators offer mixed bundles that consist of fixed line and mobile telephony.

Consumer benefits from product bundling might stem from the desire of consumers not to shop around for a collection of goods and services, but rather to have just one contract, as is likely to be the case with Internet providers.

---

[23] For an analysis of non-linear pricing under imperfect competition, see Armstrong and Vickers (2001), Rochet and Stole (2002), and Stole (1995); a general reference on non-linear pricing is Wilson (1993).

Also, there may be potential complementarities between services which can be captured if the product bundle is designed appropriately.

Offering mixed bundles can be beneficial for a firm, as shown, for instance, by McAfee, McMillan, and Whinston (1989). The reason is that firms can use such mixed bundles as price discrimination strategies.

Note that pure product bundling might also occur when complementarities between services do not exist. As Nalebuff (1999) has shown, an incumbent firm with a monopoly segment can gain from pure product bundling even if evaluations across products of the bundle are unrelated, whereas an entrant loses. Even if entry can occur in more than one segment, bundling can be used as an entry deterrence strategy (Choi and Stefanides, 2001). Bundling as an entry deterrence strategy is potentially of concern for telecommunications markets.

However, using the same argument as Nalebuff (1999), one can argue that product bundling can be a potentially successful *entry* strategy in telecommunications markets. That is, firms with a monopoly segment in some other market may enter certain market segments in telecommunications with bundled offers.

As an additional aspect of product bundling, note that product bundling can be seen as a differentiation strategy. For instance, it offers the possibility of product differentiation between operators for fixed line telephony by offering differentiated, added services. Namely, even if basic fixed line telephony can be seen as a homogeneous good, operators gain market power through tied-in additional differentiated services.

Vertical relationships   If the final product for a consumer is obtained through a combined effort of different firms, we can speak of a vertical relationship, where the downstream firms usually fix the retail price, which is the final product price that consumers pay. Other firms offer inputs so that there exists a vertical relationship between the downstream and upstream firms. For instance, if a local cable operator offers local and long-distance telephony there has to exist a vertical relationship with an operator with a long-distance backbone, unless the regulatory regime forces operators with a long-distance backbone to give access at a price fixed by the regulator.

In the context of vertical relationships, the pricing issue known as double marginalization arises.[24] This problem is known from situations with a non-integrated chain of monopolies (ranging from upstream to downstream producers). Each monopolist maximizes its own profits by adding its own markup, inflating the price of the final good. The problem does not occur if all producers coordinate their pricing decisions, as in the case of a vertically integrated producer. Therefore, in telecommunications markets, negotiation instead

---

[24] On double marginalization, see for instance Tirole (1988, pp. 174–175).

of competitive setting of access prices may allow operators to eliminate the double marginalization problem.

Another important issue in the context of vertical relationships is an antitrust consideration, because some of the incumbent's facilities, such as the local loop, may be essential for entrants to be able to compete (see Rey and Tirole, 1998). Not only may owners of an essential facility try to make entry difficult, they may also try to leverage their market power in one segment into other segments.

Network externalities and compatibility A network consists of several components which are complementary to each other. For instance, in order to make a long-distance call a consumer has to use the local loop that connects their line to a local switch, the long-distance backbone, and the local loop which connects to the person they want to call. Telecommunications networks are two-way networks because the roles of caller and receiver can be distinguished.

The economics literature on networks is concerned with many issues which are outside the focus of this book (see Economides, 1996; Shy, 2000). Here, we only touch on the important concept of network externalities (see also Katz and Shapiro, 1994). Demand exhibits network externalities if it depends on the (expected) size of the network or, more generally, on the number of users of the same or compatible products. Such externalities arise if the marginal willingness to pay of a consumer in a given network depends on the total number of consumers subscribed to this network. This holds in particular if the total number of subscribers determines the number of bundled services that are made available to consumers. Demand is derived such that consumers' expectations of the network size are fulfilled.

If more than one firm operates in a network industry, the question of whether to choose compatibility arises (see Katz and Shapiro, 1985). Consider the possibility of two networks, each of them only offering calls that stay on their network (on-net calls). This corresponds to two incompatible networks. If, on the other hand, on-net and off-net calls are available to consumers for the same price then the two networks are fully compatible. The increased demand under compatibility works in favor of compatibility, whereas compatibility often leads to more intense competition which reduces profit levels. Hence, if the second effect is relatively strong, firms have an incentive to choose incompatibility.[25] Incompatibility corresponds to an infinite access price whereas compatibility corresponds to non-differentiated pricing. An intermediate case is to look at termination-based price discrimination, that is, price discrimination

[25] Possibly, firms in an industry offer not a single product but differentiated components, so that compatibility can reduce the incentive to set lower prices. For particular industries with differentiated components, Economides (1989) and Matutes and Regibeau (1988) show that firms always choose compatibility.

between on-net and off-net calls as observed in mobile telephony.[26] If, under compatibility, only the joint size of the network is relevant in a telecommunications market, and total participation is independent of prices (on a certain range of prices), no network externalities are present.

Typically, a dominant firm has an incentive to choose incompatibility because this makes entry more difficult; this suggests that compatibility should be enforced by the regulator. Nevertheless, for innovative services incompatibility may be desirable, because this can increase the incentives for engaging in innovative activities in the first place. Hence, for established, "old" technologies, regulatory intervention may be desirable, whereas for more innovative services, it may be socially optimal for firms to be free to choose incompatibility.[27]

2.3.2   Regulation and one-way access

Incentive regulation   A large body of literature on regulation is concerned with the regulation of a monopolist when there is asymmetric information between the monopolist and the regulator (see, for instance, Laffont and Tirole, 1993). Such regulatory issues remain relevant when entry is weak, so that the former monopolist is subject to a similar regulatory environment as before. Before entering into the particularities of the telecommunications industry, it is worthwhile to recapitulate some general lessons from incentive regulation. In particular, given the importance of asymmetric information in the real world, when abstracting from asymmetric information between firm and regulator, results have to be interpreted carefully.

Cost-based regulation depends on the quality of information that the regulator has. As two classes of problems of asymmetric information, one can distinguish between adverse selection and moral hazard. The regulator confronts an adverse selection problem if the incumbent is better informed than the regulator about variables beyond the firm's control. For instance, the firm has better information about exogenous technological characteristics that influence its actual cost level than the regulator observes. If the informational asymmetry is only due to this type of hidden information, from the viewpoint of the regulator this hidden information is a random factor that influences the firm's cost level. Should the regulator ask the firm about its cost level, the firm has incentives to manipulate its private information if reported cost reductions result in a decrease in the regulated price. Possibly, there are ways to partially resolve this uncertainty by using information from other geographical areas, but hidden information is likely to remain an important problem for the regulator.

---

[26] As discussed below, Laffont, Rey, and Tirole (1998b) analyze termination-based price discrimination.

[27] Applied to telecommunications markets, this means that in the case of basic fixed telephony, interconnection is mandatory and termination-based price discrimination is prohibited, whereas in the case of mobile telephony termination-based price discrimination is allowed.

The regulator confronts a moral hazard problem if it cannot observe variables within the firm's sphere of influence that affect its cost level. This is, for example, the case if the regulator cannot observe and verify how much effort the firm exerts in cost reduction. If the firm is made residual claimant for cost savings it has incentives to reduce costs. Clearly, if a firm knows that its efforts in cost reduction will lead the regulator to enforce lower prices, its incentives to engage in such cost reduction efforts will be reduced or even eliminated.

Hence, in a world of asymmetric information between an incumbent and a regulator, the latter faces a trade-off between the goal of limiting the monopolist's profits and the goal of efficiency. The first calls for *low-powered incentives*, whereas the second calls for *high-powered incentives*:

- low-powered incentives give the incumbent weak incentives for efficiency but limit the incumbent's informational rents and therefore its profits;
- high-powered incentives give the incumbent strong incentives to reduce costs but grants the incumbent informational rents resulting in substantial profits.

A combination of adverse selection and moral hazard means that the realized costs which can be observed by the regulator are affected by the firm's effort and random factors which influence technology, both of them unobservable to the regulator. Suppose that a firm is either of a high-cost or a low-cost type (which simplifies the adverse selection problem). The first-best outcome would be that the high-cost and the low-cost type choose the efficient effort level and that they are reimbursed for their costs. In a second-best world, efficiency can be reached by a price cap such that the high-cost type breaks even given the efficient effort level. Under such a contract, a low-cost type extracts the full informational rent. Alternatively, the regulator can design a menu of simple contracts as a screening or self-selection device: it offers a price cap to the low-cost type such that it breaks even under efficient effort, and a cost reimbursement to the high-cost type. None of the two types can gain by deviating from any of the proposed contracts so that self-selection obtains (meaning that each type chooses the contract designed for it). The elimination of rent extraction has a price: the high-cost type does not have an incentive to engage in efficient effort. The general lesson from this example is that *ex ante* more efficient types choose high-powered incentives, whereas *ex ante* less efficient types choose low-powered incentives (see Laffont and Tirole, 2000).

Under high-powered incentive schemes, firms are rewarded for low costs. High-powered incentive schemes include pure price caps.[28] The use of high-powered incentive schemes is, however, limited to the extent that the regulator

[28] The price cap takes the form of a global price cap which includes wholesale and retail prices; see Laffont and Tirole (1994). An alternative to price cap regulation would be rate-of-return regulation. However, rate-of-return regulation is seen as inferior in several respects. Among several disadvantages, it provides less incentives for cost reduction; for a theoretical analysis see, for instance, Cabral and Riordan (1989). Also, in a dynamic context with technological progress, it leads to less efficient capital replacement, see Biglaiser and Riordan (2000). However, uncertainty with respect to future costs may make periodic revisions of price cap regimes desirable

may not be able to commit to reward cost savings in the future. If, for instance, price caps are revised based on past cost reductions, then the incentive to undertake these cost savings in the first place is partially destroyed.

Ramsey pricing and price caps   Consider a multi-product telecommunications operator, which is a monopolist. Implementing the first-best outcome in any market requires marginal cost pricing. If government subsidies to cover fixed costs are not feasible or desirable, the regulator cannot enforce marginal cost pricing since the participation constraint of the telephone operator would be violated (it cannot recover the fixed cost). In order to keep distortions as small as possible, the regulator has to take cost and demand parameters into account when maximizing welfare under the constraint that the monopolist makes non-negative profits. Prices which satisfy this condition are called Ramsey prices, resulting in an optimal welfare in a second-best world (Ramsey, 1927; Boiteux, 1956). The problem can then be rewritten into profit maximization, subject to the constraint that welfare is at least equal to the second-best optimal welfare level. If the cross elasticities for the different products are zero, Ramsey prices are inversely proportional to demand elasticities.[29] This implies that relative prices between any product of the monopolist are the same as in the case of an unregulated monopoly. If cross elasticities are non-zero, allowing for products being complements or substitutes, Ramsey prices are downsized prices of an unregulated monopolist.

In order to implement Ramsey prices directly, the regulator needs to know demand functions and costs. In the absence of such precise knowledge, pricing can be decentralized to the monopolist by making profit maximization subject to a global price cap, that is, prices p_i have to satisfy $\sum_i \lambda_i p_i \leq \kappa$ where λ_i are weights and κ is an average price cap (see Laffont and Tirole, 2000). If the weights are proportional to realized quantities, profit maximization under a price cap leads to Ramsey prices in structure. The choice of κ then determines whether the monopolist makes profit. In order to choose weights λ_i and cap κ, the regulator would still need to know costs and demand functions. However, lacking such precise information, an educated guess should give prices close to the Ramsey prices, thus close to the minimal distortions in the market.

(see Schmalensee, 1989); this, in effect, means that some (delayed) cost-plus component is also present in price cap regimes. For example, the UK regulator Oftel makes periodic adjustments of its RPI-X rule. For a discussion of rate-of-return regulation and price cap regulation see, for instance, Liston (1993). While, in practice, the difference between price cap and rate-of-return regulation is somewhat blurred there remain differences with respect to the information used and the timing of reviews; see, for instance, Pint (1992). For a review of incentive regulation and its application to telecommunications markets, see Sappington (2001); see also Sappington and Weisman (1996).

[29] To be precise, $(p_i - c_i)/p_i = \rho/\varepsilon_i$, where p_i is the price for product i, c_i its marginal cost, ρ a constant factor, and ε_i the price elasticity of demand.

The Ramsey model can also be applied to non-linear prices (see Laffont and Tirole, 1993; Wilson, 1993). Decentralization via price caps is straightforward in the case of two-part tariffs. The subscription fee can be seen as being paid for the service of being able to have a connection and to be called, whereas the per-minute price is the price for the actual use of the line.

Regulation of an essential facility: one-way access   In the early days of the liberalization of telecommunications, there was no competition in the local loop and easy access to the incumbent's local loop was essential to stimulate entry. By charging a sufficiently high access price, the incumbent can keep potential competitors out of the market. It is commonly recognized that the access price plays a crucial role in regulatory policy.

Suppose that originating and terminating access on the incumbent's local loop generates the same costs c_3 for the incumbent so that the total cost of the local loop of a long-distance call is $2c_3$. The purely cost-based access charge would be $\tau = 2c_3$, in which case the incumbent would not recover any part of the fixed cost incurred by operating the local loop.

Suppose that an entrant makes zero profits. Then a welfare-maximizing regulator sets a global price cap on the incumbent which just allows the incumbent to break even. Under such a price cap the incumbent chooses the access price, giving it some margin over its marginal costs. With such a policy the regulator can decentralize Ramsey prices, which take into account cross elasticities between the different goods (retail and wholesale). Weights have to be chosen to reflect "expected" demand, allowing the second-best outcome to be implemented (see Laffont and Tirole, 2000).[30]

In this context, suppose that retail prices are fixed and that the regulator chooses the access price so as to maximize welfare. This then gives rise to the efficient component pricing rule (ECPR). It has been proposed by Willig (1979) and Baumol (1983), and has received a lot of attention (for a discussion of the ECPR under one-way access, see Armstrong, 2001). The ECPR says that the access charge should be equal to the cost of providing access: demand for providing access times the average costs of providing access (that is, $2c_3$), plus a correction term which reflects the second-best nature. This correction term can be thought of as a tax for the entrant which ensures that entry is efficient. Under the assumption that incumbent and entrant offer the same product, the entrant should provide the product if it has lower costs than the incumbent. For this purpose, the entrant's tax has to be equal to the incumbent's lost profits caused by providing access to the entrant. Hence, the ECPR can alternatively be interpreted as follows: the access charge should be equal to the cost of providing access plus the incumbent's lost profits.

---

[30] In practice, a global price cap is applied in the United States (see, for instance, FCC, 1999) but not in the European Union (see below).

Suppose that the incumbent's retail price is fixed at p_1. If one call minute by the entrant replaces one call minute by the incumbent, the ECPR reduces to $\tau = 2c_3 + (p_1 - c_1)$, where c_1 stands for the incumbent's costs of a call minute if its local loop and its backbone are used. Denote the cost of using the backbone with c_4. Then a call minute on the incumbent's network costs $2c_3 + c_4 \equiv c_1$. Hence, the ECPR becomes the "margin rule":

$$\tau = p_1 - c_4.$$

If the retail price was fixed at the price that an unregulated monopolist would choose, the access price would be equal to the price–cost margin of a monopolist in the retail market.

What happens if the incumbent's and entrant's service are not perfect substitutes? In this case, the above relationship between Ramsey pricing and ECPR breaks down (see Armstrong 2001).

In the absence of retail price regulation, the access price is the only regulatory instrument. Under perfect competition, access should be priced at marginal costs if entry is efficient, otherwise it should be priced below. In such a market, the ECPR only serves to maintain monopoly profits for the incumbent (see Tye and Lapuerta, 1996). In general, it is difficult to determine the optimal level of the access price (see Armstrong, 2001). Only in special cases is it optimal to price access equal to marginal costs. However, a general insight is that a higher access price pushes retail prices up. Hence, to the extent that the aim of regulation is to achieve low retail prices, access prices should be low.

Furthermore, if the regulator is concerned less with welfare in the short term, but rather with facilitating entry, it will want to set a low access price. To avoid an excessive exploitation of consumers in the short term it may, in addition, impose a retail price cap on the incumbent (see Section 3.7). Such a pragmatic regulatory policy, which is not explicitly based on solving a planner's problem (although it obviously has in mind some long-run maximization of social welfare), has been used, for instance, by the UK regulator Oftel (see Oftel, 2000a).[31]

2.3.3   Access price regulation: two-way access

In a mature telecommunications market with several operators, access prices may be chosen individually by each operator. Alternatively, a reciprocal access price may be freely negotiated between existing operators with some provision for an arbiter if operators cannot agree. As a third option, the regulator may step in and fix the access price. As we proceed in the book, some results of the literature that are discussed below will be explored in detail.

---

[31] On the combination of ECPR and price caps, see Laffont and Tirole (1996).

Linear pricing   Under linear pricing, Armstrong (1998), Carter and Wright (1999a), and Laffont, Rey, and Tirole (1998a) have shown that the access price can be used as a collusive device to sustain higher retail prices. If operators set access prices non-cooperatively (before setting retail prices), they set them above the level which supports collusive retail prices because the situation corresponds to one of double marginalization. Cost-based access price regulation eliminates tacit collusion. (See also Sections 3.6 and 6.2.)

Two-part tariffs and non-linear prices   Contrary to the case of linear pricing, tacitly colluding through the access price is not possible under two-part tariffs (see Laffont, Rey, and Tirole, 1998a; see also Dessein, 1999a, and Hahn 1999). Here, the subscription fee is used to attract consumers. If operators set access prices non-cooperatively, they set access prices above marginal costs. However, if they negotiate a reciprocal access price they will not gain by setting an access price different from the corresponding marginal cost. (See also Section 3.3.)

In particular, Dessein (1999a, 2000) has shown that this result is robust to heterogeneous consumers who are offered a menu of non-linear prices (see also Hahn, 1999). Therefore, it remains an issue of debate whether regulation is needed under mature competition. Note, however, that second-degree price discrimination (with a menu of non-linear prices) affects the way in which networks compete with each other. Dessein (2000) has shown that for certain parameter constellations, the incentive constraint of light users is binding, and that light users select a tariff in which they pay an (implicit) per-minute price below perceived marginal costs. Operators do not make as much profit on light as on heavy users (see Dessein, 1999a).

Termination-based price discrimination   Returning to two-part tariffs with a single consumer type, if operators can set different prices for on-net and off-net calls, a high access price raises the rival's cost of an off-net call (see Laffont, Rey, and Tirole, 1998b). This makes it willing to compete more fiercely for market share. If operators negotiate reciprocal access prices, they will agree on an access price below marginal costs because this softens competition for consumers, thus generating profits from higher subscription fees (see Gans and King, 2001).

3   The basic model

3.1   Introduction

This chapter presents a concise model of facilities-based competition for fixed telephony between two operators.[1] The model has been made as simple as possible. The purposes of presenting such a model here are:

- to provide a framework for more detailed, realistic and case-specific analysis (an investigation of a rather simple, stylized model will make it easier to understand the models presented in later chapters);
- to make the reader familiar with the type of assumptions needed to get meaningful results;
- to introduce and explain important economic indicators (in particular profits, consumers surplus, and welfare);
- to explain the notion of an equilibrium;
- to develop a basic understanding of strategic interaction among operators and causal effects of parameter changes.

Although the static model itself provides several interesting insights, it is too stylized to address more specific policy issues. To make the analysis more realistic, some assumptions will be dropped later, and extensions will be made in different directions. This will be done in later chapters, for instance by incorporating entrants that offer services through carrier select or lease the incumbent's unbundled local loop, by distinguishing different types of customers (e.g. residential and corporate customers), and by allowing for alternative forms of price competition (e.g. termination-based price discrimination).[2]

---

[1] In this chapter and most parts of the book we hardly touch on mobile telephony, for two main reasons. From a modeling point of view, the assumption of price inelastic subscriptions is acceptable for fixed telephony but not for mobile telephony (see below). From a more conceptual point of view, incumbency advantages are less pronounced in mobile telephony and regulatory intervention can be less prominent. Finally, it seems appropriate, when dealing with fixed telephony only, to abstract from interactions between mobile and fixed telephony: fixed and mobile telephony are currently seen mainly as complements and not as substitutes (see Oftel, 2000d; see also Oftel 2001a). For an analysis of mobile telephony with access from fixed networks, see Wright (2000). See also Gans and King (2000) and Armstrong (2001).

[2] The model in this chapter, and some of the models in later chapters, were first explored in de Bijl and Peitz (2000).

Section 3.2 presents the static model. In Section 3.3, some preliminary and basic results are derived and interpreted. Section 3.4 contains a description of the simulation methods and the standard parameter configuration. Simulations are then provided in the regulatory framework of access price regulation for the case that the incumbent operator initially serves the whole market. This is done for two-part tariffs in Section 3.5, which also contains further analytical results on the effect of terminating access prices. Section 3.6 contains results on linear pricing; we will come back to linear pricing in Chapter 6. Finally, Section 3.7 is devoted to the analysis of retail price caps in telecommunications.[3] Section 3.8 summarizes our findings.

3.2   Description of the model

We present the model in different modules: operators; demand, switching costs, and realized market shares; costs, traffic volumes, and profit functions; surplus and welfare; and equilibrium concept. Most of the notation for the book is introduced in this section. For the notation of mathematical functions we adopt the convention that we use square brackets for the argument of a function. For example, $g[x]$ denotes a function g with argument x.[4]

3.2.1   Operators

We consider a telecommunications market with two operators, an incumbent (labeled as operator 1) and an entrant (labeled as operator 2).[5] Their initial market shares in terms of subscribed consumers, denoted by s_1^0 and s_2^0, are given and satisfy $s_1^0 + s_2^0 = 1$. Typically, we assume that $s_1^0 > s_2^0$, that is, initially the incumbent has a larger market share than the entrant. We are particularly interested in the situation in which the incumbent previously was a monopolist, that is, $s_1^0 = 1$ or 100 percent.

Each operator has a full-coverage network that consists of a long-distance backbone, a local access network, and switches; this means that the model depicts facilities-based competition. The symmetry of the physical networks makes the exposition of our model more transparent.

In the retail market, each operator i chooses a price per minute p_i and a (monthly) subscription fee m_i. Accordingly, the operators compete in two-part tariffs. The market shares of firms 1 and 2 resulting from competition and

---

[3] We elaborate on the results of Sections 3.5 and 3.7 in Chapter 4.

[4] This is in accordance with the convention used in *Mathematica* software, and also makes it easier to distinguish functions from other expressions.

[5] The literature on competition in telecommunications markets generally considers duopolies. We claim that our main insights obtained in such duopoly models carry over to adequately specified models with more than one entrant. For example, one may use a multi-dimensional logit specification to analyze a market with more than two operators.

consumers' choices are denoted by $s_1[p_1, p_2, m_1, m_2]$ and $s_2[p_1, p_2, m_1, m_2]$, respectively. Accordingly, realized market shares depend on all retail prices. In particular, since the operators offer substitutes, we will see later that, for instance, if operator 1 increases its subscription fee, then operator 2's market share increases. We will write s_1 and s_2 in most cases for the sake of notational simplicity. By definition, it must be that $s_1 + s_2 = 1$. Note that market shares possibly depend on access prices; our formulation captures market shares for given access prices.

We analyze markets with a single type of call; here one can think of a long-distance call, which may be intra-state or inter-state. Enriching the model by allowing for different types of calls (e.g. long-distance and local calls) would complicate the analysis so much that we decided not to consider such an extension in this book.[6]

3.2.2   Demand, switching costs, and realized market shares

The consumer side consists of a number n of individual consumers who all are subscribed to either one or the other network.[7] We express the market share of operator i as the number of consumers subscribed to it divided by the total number of consumers. Each consumer has only one subscription (a consumer's demand for a connection is inelastic). Given a price per minute equal to p_i, each consumer has an individual demand of $x[p_i]$ call minutes, and derives utility $u[x]$ from calling for x minutes. Since individual demand of a subscriber to operator i is obtained by:

$$x[p_i] = \arg\max_x \{u[x] - x\, p_i\},$$

individual demand is derived by solving the first-order condition for utility maximization $u'[x] = p$.

In addition to the utility from calling, each consumer derives a fixed (and possibly operator-specific) utility level u_i^0 from subscribing to network i, independent of the number of telephone calls that are made, which may come from, for example:

- brand preference (e.g. due to an operator's corporate image);
- services offered in addition to voice telephony (e.g. wake-up services, voice mail);
- the quality of the network and services delivered;
- having a telephone connection in the case of unforeseen events (e.g. emergencies);

---

[6] Most of the insights gained in our model carry over into a model with various types of calls. However, we do not claim that one cannot gain additional insights by enriching the model. For an analysis with local and long-distance telephony, see Carter and Wright (1999b).
[7] Formally, in the model there is a continuum of consumers with mass n.

Table 3.1 *An example with linear demand function*

Function	Description	Example
$u[x]$	Utility from calling x minutes	$ax - \frac{1}{2}bx^2$ $(a, b > 0)$
u_i^0	Fixed utility from a connection	Non-negative constant
$x[p_i]$	Demand for call minutes	$(a - p_i)/b$
$v_i[p_i, m_i]$	Total net utility	$u_i^0 + \frac{1}{2}(p_i - a)^2/b - m_i$
$\varepsilon[p_i]$	Elasticity of demand	$-p_i/(a - p_i)$

- the possibility to make free calls (800-numbers in the US);
- last but not least, the possibility of being reached by friends and relatives.

The latter three may be thought of as being operator-independent. We postulate that the fixed utility u_i^0 is the same for all consumers, that is, all consumers coincide in the willingness to pay for the characteristics of a network as summarized in u_i^0.

The total net utility of a subscriber to network i, who optimally chooses their calling time, is denoted by an indirect utility function which takes values $v_i[p_i, m_i]$. Assuming that utility levels are expressed in monetary units and can be added up, conditional indirect utility can be written as:

$$v_i[p_i, m_i] = u_i^0 + u[x[p_i]] - p_i x[p_i] - m_i.$$

Net utility consists of a traffic-independent part, $u_i^0 - m_i$, and a traffic-dependent part, $u[x[p_i]] - p_i x[p_i]$. The latter only depends on the calls made and not on the calls received.[8]

Naturally, a consumer's net utility level is decreasing in prices:

$$\frac{\partial v_i[p_i, m_i]}{\partial p_i} = -x[p_i], \quad \text{and} \quad \frac{\partial v_i[p_i, m_i]}{\partial m_i} = -1.$$

To guarantee that consumers want to participate in the market, net utility level $v_i[p_i, m_i]$ has to be positive. Our parameter choices will therefore be such that participation constraints of consumers do not bind. This seems to be a reasonable assumption for fixed telephony in developed countries.[9]

Table 3.1 presents a concrete example of demand and utility functions. These are also the specifications that will be used throughout the analysis and simulations.

---

[8] Most of the literature assumes that consumers do not derive a positive utility from receiving calls. An exception is Jeon, Laffont, and Tirole (2001), who consider a mature telecommunications market in which consumers also obtain utilities from the calls they receive. They analyze the determination of receiver charges (regulated or market determined).

[9] For instance, the UK regulator has made a residential survey which indicates that subscription for fixed-line telephony is rather inelastic (see Oftel, 2000d).

The linear demand function that we use can be seen as an approximation of a non-linear demand function: information on price elasticity at a particular point allows for a linear specification which works well in a neighborhood around this point. Therefore, it is important to have reliable information on demand for a range of prices from which operators are likely to choose.

Consumers choose their subscriptions when they observe the operators' prices. The most straightforward way to model the subscription decision would be to have consumers choose the highest utility level among $v_1[p_1, m_1]$ and $v_2[p_2, m_2]$. The consequence would be that extremely small price differences (resulting in extremely small utility differences), would tilt the balance towards the operator offering the highest net utility. This operator would then instantaneously gain a market share of 100 percent. In reality, however, we do not observe such "bang-bang" outcomes. Instead, market shares exhibit a certain extent of stickiness, and change in a rather smooth fashion. In particular, gaining market share from a well-known, established firm with a large installed consumer base requires great marketing efforts and substantially better price–quality combinations by a new competitor.

In order to allow for a realistic transition of market shares over time, we introduce consumer switching costs (not to be confused with the costs of switches in networks).[10] Suppose a certain consumer, identified by a parameter z, initially subscribes to the incumbent's network. They will end their subscription and switch to the entrant if and only if:

$$v_2[p_2, m_2] - z > v_1[p_1, m_1],$$

where z is the cost of switching from one operator to another. Parameter z will be assumed to be different across consumers (see below).

We assume that no new consumers are entering the market. This avoids the situation where a small undercutting of the competing network drastically increases market share. New consumers could be incorporated into the analysis without creating such drastic changes in market share if we assumed that networks are to some extent differentiated in the eyes of those new consumers.

For simplicity, we assume that consumers who were initially subscribed to network i are uniformly distributed on the interval $[0, Zs_i^0]$, where $Z > 0$ is a given constant.[11] Since the total mass of consumers is n, it follows that:

$$\int_0^{Zs_1^0} \frac{n}{Z}\, dz + \int_0^{Zs_2^0} \frac{n}{Z}\, dz = \frac{n}{Z}\left(Zs_1^0 + Zs_2^0\right) = n.$$

[10] Switching costs are clearly relevant in telecommunications markets, see Section 2.3. In our model, switching costs are heterogeneous across consumers to allow for smooth market demand functions.

[11] A uniformity distribution greatly facilitates the analysis. Also, the distribution can be constructed as follows: consider a uniform distribution of *potential* switching costs on $[0, Z]$. A consumer's effective switching cost equals the product of their potential switching cost and the initial market share of the network they were subscribed to.

The simplest formulation which expresses a positive relationship between switching costs and initial market share of the network s_i^0 is the multiplicative form $Z s_i^0$. This formulation has the important benefit that it leads to continuously differentiable profit functions, which greatly facilitates the analysis.

Parameter Z can be said to measure the stickiness of market demand. Later we will see how different values of this parameter affect competition. It can also be interpreted analogous to the extent of product differentiation (see below), or the strength of the consumer lock-in effect.

There are several aspects relating to the interpretation of the distribution of consumers:

- An operator's customer base ranges from consumers who are easily willing to switch (characterized by z close to 0) to consumers who need substantially lower prices to be encouraged to switch (characterized by z close to $Z s_i^0$).
- All consumer types in the range are equally likely (because of the uniform distribution).
- The larger an operator's initial market share s_i^0, the more customers the operator has with higher switching costs; in other words, market share is valuable (see below for interpretations).

The assumption that effective switching costs depend on initial market shares can be motivated in several ways. Firstly, a consumer is unlikely to switch to a small network that has only a few consumers who have experienced the network's quality. If on the other hand a network is large, this facilitates the consumer learning from others about the quality of service and connections (for a model in this spirit see, for example, Smallwood and Conlisk, 1979). Secondly, to the extent that network size and brand recognition go hand in hand, a stronger established brand makes attracting consumers more difficult for a new competitor. Thirdly, a small competitor may suffer from some probability of quality breakdown which makes switching less attractive.

Similar to the incorporation of switching costs into the model, one can make assumptions about fixed utility levels u_1^0 and u_2^0 that depend on market share or on the number of periods that the entrant has been active in the market. We will come back to this in Chapter 4.

The consumer switching costs affect the way market shares are realized. Let the operators' prices be given and suppose that $v_2[p_2, m_2] > v_1[p_1, m_1]$. Then there is a certain customer of the incumbent, characterized by switching cost parameter z_0, who is indifferent between staying with operator 1 and switching to operator 2. Equivalently, z_0 satisfies:

$$v_2[p_2, m_2] - z_0 = v_1[p_1, m_1].$$

Accordingly:

- current customers of operator 1 with $z \in [0, z_0]$ switch to operator 2, and with $z \in [z_0, Z s_1^0]$ stay with operator 1;
- all current customers of operator 2 stay with operator 2.

Since $z_0 = v_2[p_2, m_2] - v_1[p_1, m_1]$, the fraction of firm 1's consumer base that switches to operator 2 equals:

$$\frac{v_2[p_2, m_2] - v_1[p_1, m_1]}{Zs_1^0}.$$

The fraction of operator 1's original customers that maintain their subscription is equal to:

$$\frac{Zs_1^0 - (v_2[p_2, m_2] - v_1[p_1, m_1])}{Zs_1^0}.$$

It follows that the realized market share of operator i is equal to:

$$s_i[p_1, p_2, m_1, m_2] = s_i^0 + \frac{v_i[p_i, m_i] - v_j[p_j, m_j]}{Z}.$$

Intuitively, an operator's market share increases if the operator offers a relatively larger level of net utility to consumers, and decreases otherwise. Recall that parameter Z was earlier interpreted as a measure of competitiveness. One can observe that larger values of Z make it more difficult to gain market share. In other words, the less competitive the market is, the lower an entrant has to set its prices if it wants to capture market share.

Our analysis is also useful for markets in which the distribution of consumer switching costs is not uniform. For the proper choice of parameter Z, note that consumers switch at a rate $1/Z$ from one operator to the other. In order to use the uniform distribution as a proxy for a non-uniform distribution, one has to choose Z such that it approximates the non-uniform density for those consumers who are indifferent between the two operators at prices which have found their equilibrium values.

Assuming, without loss of generality, that $v_2[p_2, m_2] > v_1[p_1, m_1]$, the customer switching costs incurred by all consumers that switch are equal to:

$$\int_0^{v_2[p_2, m_2] - v_1[p_1, m_1]} z\left(\frac{n}{Z}\right) dz = n\frac{(v_2[p_2, m_2] - v_1[p_1, m_1])^2}{2Z}.$$

Notice that for given prices an increase in Z leads to a decrease of the incurred switching costs. The reason is that a higher Z results in fewer consumers switching because they are less sensitive to price changes. Nevertheless, this effect does not necessarily appear in equilibrium outcomes. The reason is that operators adjust prices in equilibrium, which reflects that changes in Z lead to changes in the competitive pressure that they experience.

To complement the discussion on switching costs, we want to emphasize that the interpretation of our model with asymmetric, differentiated networks is equally valid (see Appendix 3.3 to this chapter; see also de Bijl and Peitz, 2001a). The latter interpretation makes it clear that our specification introduces a network externality, which is not present in the models by Armstrong (1998) and Laffont, Rey, and Tirole (1998a).[12] Our specification says that market share is valuable in the future because it makes a network more "attractive" for consumers.

3.2.3   Costs, traffic volumes, and profits

Following recent theory on competition in telecommunications (e.g. Laffont, Rey, and Tirole, 1998a, b) we distinguish between different sorts of costs:[13]
- fixed costs which are independent of traffic and the number of consumers served;
- connection-dependent but traffic-independent costs (the fixed cost of the local loop);
- traffic-dependent costs.

The fixed costs in the classification above include all costs that depend neither on traffic nor on the number of connections to end users. Such costs include, for instance, the costs of building a backbone, and are typically sunk when pricing decisions are taken. Throughout this chapter, we will abstract from this type of fixed costs, as we take investment decisions as given.

Some costs may be fixed with regard to traffic, but nevertheless depend on the number of connections. We therefore introduce connection-dependent but traffic-independent costs in the model, or the per-period and per-connection fixed cost of the local access network (the fixed cost of the local loop). This cost captures, for instance, the maintenance cost of the local loop, and, in reality, may also include the investment cost that has to be recovered per customer. Operator i's fixed cost of the local loop is denoted by f_i.

Connection-dependent but traffic-independent costs affect the gain per consumer and therefore operators' pricing decisions. If subscription fees can be freely adjusted, such costs only affect subscription fees and not per-minute prices.

When considering traffic-dependent costs, the marginal cost of telephony calls is practically zero, if one strictly applies the definition of marginal costs. It would roughly equal the cost per time unit of the electricity that is needed to transmit signals through a network. Note that it is very difficult to measure marginal costs; firms may not even know them themselves. In reality, operators typically impute fixed costs to telephony traffic, enabling them to define a reference point for prices (this may happen despite the fact that these costs are either sunk once a network has been built or do not directly depend on traffic).

---

[12] This network externality does not affect the formal analysis because its size depends on initial, not current, market size of a particular operator.

[13] For a concise description of the cost structure of a telecommunications network, see, for instance, Falch (1997).

Table 3.2 *Traffic-dependent costs*

Call type	Operator 1	Operator 2
On-net call	c_{11}	c_{21}
Off-net call	$c_{12} + \tau_2$	$c_{22} + \tau_1$
Incoming call	$c_{13} - \tau_1$	$c_{23} - \tau_2$

One then refers to "marginal costs" as the costs that a sales/marketing department attributes to traffic when making pricing decisions.[14]

Costs which are also perceived as traffic-dependent are traffic-dependent charges for interconnection and access. Total traffic-dependent costs therefore include an operator's marginal cost as defined in the previous paragraph, plus per-minute charges paid to other operators for interconnection and access.

Some notation is needed to define the traffic-dependent (i.e., marginal) costs of telephone calls. Let c_{ik} denote operator i's traffic-dependent cost per minute associated with a telephone call of type k. We distinguish three types of telephone calls:

- *on-net calls*: calls that originate and terminate on a single operator's network ($k = 1$);
- *off-net calls*: calls that terminate on another operator's network ($k = 2$);
- *incoming calls*: calls that originate from another operator's network ($k = 3$).

In most parts of our analysis, we consider symmetric cost structures and we write:

$$c_k \equiv c_{1k} = c_{2k}.$$

In our analysis, we will follow the convention in the literature, where it is typically assumed that the marginal cost of the local loop is the same for originating and terminating traffic. In addition:

$$c_{i1} - c_{i2} = c_{i3}.$$

In the case of off-net calls and incoming calls, the operator of the network where the call originates pays a per-minute terminating access price to the operator of the network where the call terminates. The terminating access price paid to operator i is denoted by τ_i. These wholesale prices affect the operators' traffic-dependent cost levels, as depicted in Table 3.2.

Before profit functions can be derived, we have to specify calling patterns. We assume that, when a consumer makes a telephone call, the receiving consumer

[14] To obtain clear guidelines for regulation, we implicitly assume in our analysis that in the calculation of marginal costs, no traffic-independent costs are included.

Table 3.3 *Net revenues*

Source	Operator 1	Operator 2
On-net traffic	$n\, s_1 s_1 x[p_1](p_1 - c_{11})$	$n\, s_2 s_2 x[p_2](p_2 - c_{21})$
Off-net traffic	$n\, s_1 s_2 x[p_1](p_1 - c_{12} - \tau_2)$	$n\, s_2 s_1 x[p_2](p_2 - c_{22} - \tau_1)$
Incoming traffic	$n\, s_2 s_1 x[p_2](\tau_1 - c_{13})$	$n\, s_1 s_2 x[p_1](\tau_2 - c_{23})$
Subscriptions	$n\, s_1 (m_1 - f_1)$	$n\, s_2 (m_2 - f_2)$

may be any other consumer with equal probability, independent of the network they are subscribed to. This implies that the numbers of on-net and off-net calls of an operator are proportionate to market shares, that is, the *calling patterns are balanced*. For instance, given prices and realized market shares, the total volume of call minutes that originates on network 1 is equal to $n\, s_1 x[p_1]$. If calling patterns are balanced, then a fraction s_1 of this volume, that is, $n\, s_1 s_1 x[p_1]$, terminates on network 1. Similarly, the traffic volume terminating on network 2 is $n\, s_2 s_1 x[p_1]$. Because all consumers have the same individual demand functions x, and on-net and off-net calls have the same price, the assumption of balanced calling patterns seems a natural assumption to make. In models with heterogeneous consumers and/or price differences between on-net and off-net calls this assumption is more restrictive (see Chapters 6 and 7).

For given prices, and using the assumption of balanced calling patterns, revenues dependent on and independent of traffic contribute to profits of operator i as shown in Table 3.3.

For later use we define the access revenues from incoming calls net of variable costs for operator i by:

$$AR_i = n\, s_i s_j x[p_j](\tau_i - c_{i3}).$$

We now define operator i's total profits $\Pi_i[p_1, p_2, m_1, m_2]$ as the sum of all the elements in the corresponding row for i in Table 3.3. Formally:

$$\begin{aligned}
\Pi_i[p_1, p_2, m_1, m_2] = &\ n\, s_i s_i x[p_i](p_i - c_{i1}) \\
&+ n\, s_i s_j x[p_i](p_i - c_{i2} - \tau_j) \\
&+ n\, s_i s_j x[p_j](\tau_i - c_{i3}) \\
&+ n\, s_i (m_i - f_i).
\end{aligned}$$

Profits are a function of both operators' prices, which reflects that the operators strategically interact with each other. As remarked earlier, fixed and sunk costs not attributed to traffic or connections are not included in the profit functions. Although they clearly affect realized profit levels, they do not influence pricing decisions.

3.2.4   Surplus and welfare

The effects of competition and regulation can be evaluated by assessing:
- consumers surplus (consumers aggregate net utility);
- producers surplus (total industry profits);
- welfare (total surplus in the industry, i.e., the sum of consumers and producers surplus).

It may sometimes be important to consider more than one measure of surplus, since one should not rule out the possibility that a regulatory measure increases welfare, but at the same time is detrimental to consumers surplus.[15] Also, a regulator wishing to ensure that consumers benefit from entry and competition, may be interested in maximizing consumers surplus, while taking explicitly into account that operators make enough profits to have incentives to invest in infrastructure and quality.[16]

We will now define the three measures of surplus within the context of the model. Producers surplus PS is defined as the sum of profits in the industry, that is:

$$PS = \Pi_1[p_1, p_2, m_1, m_2] + \Pi_2[p_1, p_2, m_1, m_2],$$

and consumers surplus CS, defined as the consumers' aggregate net utility, is equal to:

$$CS = n \left(s_1 \cdot v_1[p_1, m_1] + s_2 \cdot v_2[p_2, m_2] - \frac{(v_1[p_1, m_1] - v_2[p_2, m_2])^2}{2Z} \right).$$

Notice that consumers surplus is defined net of the costs of switching between operators; the third term in brackets represents the switching cost incurred on average by consumers. Finally, welfare W is equal to the total surplus that is realized in the market, that is:

$$W = PS + CS.$$

Throughout this chapter, and partly in later chapters, we follow existing literature and assume that both operators' networks have similar characteristics in terms of costs and fixed utility levels:

$$c_k \equiv c_{1k} = c_{2k}, \quad k = 1, 2, 3;$$
$$f \equiv f_1 = f_2; \quad \text{and}$$
$$u_1^0 = u_2^0.$$

---

[15] A discussion of the use of a weighted total surplus is contained in Mitchell and Vogelsang (1991, pp. 31–34).
[16] For example, the telecommunications authority in the Netherlands, Opta, tends to follow such an approach.

Before analyzing the model, we would like to point out some of its first-best properties. In the first-best outcome, per-minute prices are equal to true marginal costs of production, in our notation $p_i = c_1$. (In the case of network congestion, the social costs of using the network has to be included in the per-minute price.) Because we assume that all consumers participate in the market, the level of the subscription fee has no impact on welfare. The assumption that all consumers participate seems a good approximation if subscription fees are sufficiently low (and initial connection costs, which we do not consider, are small). In our first-best analysis, we therefore consider the case in which the subscription fee is equal to the cost of a connection, that is, $m_i = f_i$.

Because of recent liberalizations in telecommunications markets, it is interesting to compare a monopoly and a duopoly situation (with a facilities-based entrant). A monopoly with first-best prices has several advantages over a duopoly: connection-independent fixed costs are not duplicated. In particular, the fixed cost of duplicating a network is avoided, and consumer switching costs are not incurred. Note that duplication of fixed costs of infrastructure can, at least to a certain extent, be avoided by stimulating carrier-select-based or unbundling-based entry. They can be completely avoided if all of the network owner's services are for resale.

One can make two observations concerning the evaluation of the costs of duplicating and operating networks. Firstly, the cost of building a new network has decreased due to technological progress so that historical costs exaggerate the costs of duplication. Secondly, a protected monopolist usually has less incentive to operate efficiently (there are so-called X-inefficiencies).[17]

In the discussion above we have ignored the fact that competition may have important effects apart from production costs. Indeed, the cost of regulation may well be higher in a monopoly situation than under (regulated) competition. Another positive aspect of competition is that consumers may benefit from increased choice and variety in a liberalized market (see also de Bijl and Peitz, 2001a).

Considerations of this type have led governments to assess that the introduction of competition is beneficial for consumers, at least in the long run. Accordingly, we perform our analysis under the hypothesis that some form of competition is superior to a regulated monopoly.

3.2.5 Equilibrium concept

To conclude the description of the model, we recapitulate the structure of the game. At the outset, initial market shares s_1^0 and s_2^0 are given. Terminating access

---

[17] Another question is whether the protected monopolist has less incentive to invest in innovation, which, if true, is harmful for dynamic efficiency.

prices τ_1 and τ_2 are given as well. The operators simultaneously choose per-minute prices p_1 and p_2, and subscription fees m_1 and m_2. Consumers observe these prices, choose where to subscribe and make their telephone calls. Market shares s_1 and s_2 and demand levels for call minutes are realized, resulting in profit levels $\Pi_1[p_1, p_2, m_1, m_2]$ and $\Pi_2[p_1, p_2, m_1, m_2]$.

At this point, we assume that terminating access prices are given. In reality, they may be the outcome of negotiations between operators, or be subject to regulation without necessarily fixing the access prices. The optimal level of these tariffs by a regulator is one of the main concerns of our analysis. Attention will also be paid to negotiation by operators.

We assume that the operators behave rationally, in the sense that each of them chooses prices to maximize profits. Moreover, each operator sets prices while taking the prices chosen by its rival firm as given. Equilibrium values of functions and variables will be marked with a superscript $*$. For example, operator 1's per-minute price in equilibrium is denoted by p_1^*.

Formally, an equilibrium (to be precise, a Nash equilibrium) characterized by prices $(p_1^*, p_2^*, m_1^*, m_2^*)$ is defined by the following conditions:

• Each operator's prices p_i^* and m_i^* maximize its profits given the other operator's prices p_j^* and m_j^*, for $i = 1, 2$, where $i \neq j$.
• Consumers choose a network and a quantity of call minutes to maximize net utility, and the operators take this behavior into account while choosing prices.

In equilibrium, none of the operators has an incentive to deviate from its pricing strategy (p_i^*, m_i^*), formally:

$$\Pi_1[p_1^*, p_2^*, m_1^*, m_2^*] \geq \Pi_1[p_1, p_2^*, m_1, m_2^*] \quad \text{and}$$
$$\Pi_2[p_1^*, p_2^*, m_1^*, m_2^*] \geq \Pi_2[p_1^*, p_2, m_1^*, m_2]$$

for all admissible p_1, p_2, m_1, m_2. Hence a Nash equilibrium can be described as a situation that is strategically stable, and therefore seems the appropriate prediction of the market outcome (presuming that a unique equilibrium exists).[18]

One can derive a necessary condition for an equilibrium as follows: given p_j and m_j, each operator i maximizes profits by choosing p_i and m_i. When both firms have a positive market share, the slope of the profit function has to be zero in a maximum. This translates into first-order conditions:

$$\partial \Pi_i[p_1, p_2, m_1, m_2]/\partial p_i = 0,$$
$$\partial \Pi_i[p_1, p_2, m_1, m_2]/\partial m_i = 0.$$

Later, we will check that the operators are indeed maximizing profits by checking that the solution to the system of first-order conditions is a global maximizer.

---

[18] Profit-maximizing prices of operator i given the prices of operator j can be called the best reply of i to the prices of j. Mutual best replies then constitute a Nash equilibrium.

3.3   Basic results

3.3.1   Equilibrium properties

Before discussing whether an equilibrium exists in the first place, we briefly consider some properties of prices in an equilibrium outcome.

With two-part tariffs each operator has two "instruments" at its disposal that affect revenues and profit levels: the per-minute price, which can be used to generate voice traffic, and the subscription fee, which can be seen as an instrument to build market share; see also Laffont and Tirole (2000, p. 207). To see in more detail how this takes place, it is helpful to take a closer look at the conditions for profit maximization. By manipulating operator i's first-order conditions, one can show that profit-maximizing prices of operator i, when operator j's prices are given, satisfy in equilibrium:

$$p_i^* = s_i^* c_{i1} + s_j^* (c_{i2} + \tau_j), \tag{3.1}$$

$$m_i^* = f_i + s_i^* Z - s_i^* x[p_i^*](c_{i2} + \tau_j - c_{i1})$$
$$+ (s_i^* - s_j^*) x[p_j^*](\tau_i - c_{i3}). \tag{3.2}$$

One can make the following observations:

- An operator's optimal strategy (as a best response) involves choosing a price per minute equal to its *perceived marginal costs*. Given the traffic flows on and between the networks, the perceived marginal cost reflects all traffic-dependent costs and payments that are incurred by that operator and that are directly affected by its prices. We refer to this observation as the *marginal cost pricing principle*.
- An increase in Z, which can be interpreted as less intense competition, directly pushes subscription fees upwards if one ignores indirect effects through market shares.

Furthermore, it is straightforward to show that, if an operator sets its per-minute price equal to perceived marginal cost, it makes zero profits from its total volume of on-net and off-net traffic. The reason is that equation (3.1) is equivalent to:

$$s_i^* s_i^* x[p_i^*](p_i^* - c_{i1}) + s_i^* s_j^* x[p_i^*](p_i^* - c_{i2} - \tau_j) = 0.$$

Intuitively, an operator's marginal costs relevant for its own pricing are the traffic-dependent costs associated with the traffic that its own customers generate. Incoming traffic, generated by its competitor's customers, cannot be directly affected by an operator and therefore does not contribute to its perceived marginal costs. A consequence of this observation is that equilibrium profits can be simplified and written as:

$$\Pi_i^* = n\, s_j^* s_i^* x[p_j^*](\tau_i - c_{i3}) + s_i^* (m_i^* - f_i)$$
$$= n\, (s_i^*)^2 (Z - x[p_i^*](\tau_j - c_{i3}) + x[p_j^*](\tau_i - c_{i3})).$$

If the terminating access price is equal to the symmetric marginal cost of terminating access, that is, $\tau_i = c_3, i = 1, 2$, then $p_i^* = c_{i1}$ and $m_i^* = f_i + s_i^* Z$. In this case, the operators do not make any profits from traffic so that all profits are generated by subscription fees. Moreover, from solving:

$$s_i^* = s_i^0 + \frac{v_i[c_{i1}, f_i + s_i^* Z] - v_j[c_{j1}, f_j + s_j^* Z]}{Z},$$

that is, market share in equilibrium is equal to market share realized at equilibrium prices, it follows that:

$$s_i^* = \frac{1 + s_i^0}{3} - \frac{1}{3Z}(f_i - f_j - u[x[c_{i1}]] + u[x[c_{j1}]] - u_i^0 + u_j^0 + c_{i1}x[c_{i1}] - c_{j1}x[c_{j1}]).$$

One can see from the expression above that if the operators are identical except with respect to initial market shares (which we in fact assume throughout this chapter), then their market shares in an equilibrium are determined only by the initial division of the market, as given by s_1^0 and s_2^0. For instance, if the incumbent initially covers the whole market, that is, $s_1^0 = 1$, then the entrant's realized market share after competing in prices is $s_2^* = \frac{1}{3}$.

3.3.2   Equilibrium existence and uniqueness; profit neutrality

So far we have not addressed the issue of whether an equilibrium exists, nor whether it is unique. The following proposition shows existence and uniqueness of equilibrium under a restriction on terminating access prices or the intensity of competition. The result is both an adaptation and a generalization of Proposition 7 in Laffont, Rey, and Tirole (1998a). We adapt their result to a situation with consumer switching costs, and generalize it to allow for asymmetric operators (defined by different initial market shares) and to allow for asymmetric terminating access prices (instead of reciprocal access prices).

> **Proposition 1** Suppose that, in equilibrium, both operators have strictly positive market shares. If demand for subscription is sufficiently sticky (i.e., Z is sufficiently large) or access prices are relatively close to the marginal cost of the local loop (i.e., $\tau_i - c_3$, $i = 1, 2$, is sufficiently small), then there exists a unique equilibrium.

The formal proof of this result is relegated to Appendix 3.1. Let us here only remark that the proof consists of: (i) a demonstration that at most one equilibrium exists, that is, if an equilibrium exists then it must be unique; and (ii) a demonstration that there indeed exists an equilibrium. Moreover, note that the restriction to interior solutions is quite reasonable, given that in later chapters, we are mostly interested in situations in which the entrant gradually gains market share over time. For a discussion of corner solutions, see Subsection 3.3.3.

Under reciprocal access pricing, that is $\tau \equiv \tau_1 = \tau_2$, and using our earlier assumption about cost symmetry, equations (3.1) and (3.2) reduce to:

$$p_i^* = c_1 + s_j^*(\tau - c_3),$$
$$m_i^* = f + s_i^* Z - (s_i^* x[p_i^*] + (s_j^* - s_i^*) x[p_j^*])(\tau - c_3).$$

Equilibrium profits can be simplified to:

$$\Pi_i^* = n\,(s_i^*)^2 (Z + (x[p_j^*] - x[p_i^*])(\tau - c_3)).$$

Clearly, if networks are identical and have initial shares of $\frac{1}{2}$ one can show that in the unique, symmetric equilibrium (see Proposition 1) profits are $\Pi_i^* = n\,Z/4$. Such a situation corresponds to a mature market in which all asymmetries have disappeared over time.[19] In this case, higher switching costs (measured by Z) translate into more market power, which is beneficial for both operators. Equilibrium prices are then equal to:

$$p_1^* = p_2^* = \tfrac{1}{2}(c_1 + c_2 + \tau),$$
$$m_1^* = m_2^* = f + \frac{Z}{2} + \frac{1}{4b}\left(2ac_1 - c_1^2 - 2ac_2 + c_2^2 - 2a\tau + 2c_2\tau + \tau^2\right).$$

In a situation of price competition, a firm can only gain market share by increasing consumers' net benefits through reducing its price. This downward pressure on prices forces the operators to set the usage price equal to marginal cost. Market power, resulting from brand loyalty or consumer switching costs, is exercised through fixed fees. In particular, profit levels in a symmetric equilibrium are independent of terminating access prices.

Proposition 2 Suppose that $s_1^0 = s_2^0 = \frac{1}{2}$. Then terminating access prices do not affect profit levels in an equilibrium.

Proposition 2 is the profit neutrality result for two-part tariffs, which was already shown by Laffont, Rey, and Tirole (1998a). To understand this result, notice that a higher access price implies that operators make more profits from incoming calls. Since prices are equal to perceived marginal costs, each operator's net revenues from traffic generated by its own customers is zero. Operators do not make higher profits because higher per-minute prices are exactly offset by lower subscription fees.

---

[19] We speak of a mature market if initial and realized market shares coincide.

The profit neutrality result implies that, in a mature market (characterized by identical operators with identical market shares), operators do not have an incentive to tacitly collude by agreeing on markups in access prices. The result can be interpreted to mean that regulatory intervention is not needed except for mandating interconnection; the operators do not have an incentive to deviate from cost-based reciprocal access prices.

The profit neutrality result depends on the fact that operators compete in two-part tariffs (and not in linear prices, see Section 3.6), and will be reassessed in more complex and realistic market environments in later chapters.

> **Guideline 3.1:** Consider facilities-based entry. Suppose that operators compete in two-part tariffs. In a mature market, profit levels do not depend on the level of the reciprocal access price.

Finally, notice that access prices above marginal costs increase per-minute prices and hence lead to a reduction of consumers surplus.

3.3.3   Corner solutions

The fact that we focus on interior solutions (see Proposition 1), that is, equilibrium outcomes in which both operators have positive market shares, is not as restrictive as it may seem. Firstly, it is a natural restriction given that we are mainly interested in the development of the entrant's market share over time. Secondly, an equilibrium outcome in which one operator serves the whole market (a "corner solution") is possible in theory, but would occur under rather strong assumptions. One can obtain a corner outcome by assuming, for instance, that one operator is substantially more efficient and offers a substantially higher fixed utility level than the other operator. It may in theory even happen that the more efficient operator is unconstrained by the presence of a competitor, so that two-part tariffs are set as in the standard monopoly situation.

If the incumbent is constrained by the entrant, we would expect in a standard oligopoly model that there exists a corner outcome such that, in equilibrium, the less efficient operator j sets prices at cost levels, that is, a per-minute price $p_j = c_1 + (\tau_i - c_3)$ and subscription fee $m_j = f$. The more efficient operator i chooses as a best reply with per-minute price $p_i = c_1$ and subscription fee m_i allowing it to capture the whole market. To see that this constitutes an equilibrium under cost-based access prices, meaning that unilateral deviations are not profitable, note that each operator can only attract consumers by offering a higher net surplus to consumers. By a deviation from the proposed two-part tariff, operator j, that already prices at cost levels, cannot increase its profits.

For certain parameter values, neither can the incumbent operator gain by a unilateral deviation.

Consider now the case of a reciprocal access markup. Notice that the perceived marginal cost of operator j is increasing in p_j if $\tau_i - c_3$ is strictly positive (this is due to the fact that s_i is increasing in p_j). Can the strategies above constitute an equilibrium? This is not possible because the entrant has an incentive to offer a higher net utility to consumers.[20] Therefore, under a reciprocal access price markup (and, more generally if $\tau_i, \tau_j > c_3$), there cannot exist a Nash equilibrium, provided that the incumbent's pricing is constrained due to the presence of the entrant.

3.4   Numerical simulation

3.4.1   Equilibrium and Newton's method

When two operators compete in two-part tariffs, the system of first-order conditions that has to be solved to obtain equilibrium prices, consists of four equations. This system can be reduced to two equations which only depend on m_1 and m_2. Even in the case where unequal initial market shares are the only asymmetry in the market these equations contain polynomials of degree 3 with mixed terms and we could not obtain an analytical solution. Without complete symmetry, in particular with asymmetric initial shares, we therefore use numerical methods to solve the system of first-order conditions.[21]

We use Newton's method to solve the system of first-order conditions; for details see Appendix 3.2. In general, to find a solution to an equation of the form $g[x] = 0$, Newton's method tries to approach its solution on a step-by-step basis by sequentially calculating $x_n = x_{n-1} - g[x_{n-1}]/g'[x_{n-1}]$, given a starting point x_0. It is best to choose a well-educated guess as a starting point. Iterations stop either if a predefined level of accuracy has been reached, that is, $g[x_n]$ is sufficiently close to zero, or, alternatively, if the maximum number of steps has been reached. In the latter case, no solution has been found.[22] In order to use Newton's method in our model, the operators' profit functions have to be twice differentiable. This condition is satisfied.

Given a parameter constellation, we obtain a system of first-order conditions and apply the following step-by-step procedure:

---

[20] At the corner, the entrant's reduced profit function $\widehat{\Pi}_j$ (as defined in part 2 of Appendix 3.1) is increasing in the net utility of consumers when evaluated at the prices above.

[21] The appendix at the end of the book contains the *Mathematica* notebook of the simulation program for the model of facilities-based competition in two-part tariffs, with the possibility of setting separate price caps on the per-minute price and the subscription fee.

[22] Alternatively, we could have used the secant method, which starts with two starting points and approaches a solution from two sides.

1. Choose appropriate starting values for Newton's method. Determine the maximum number of steps that is allowed. Apply Newton's method with the FindRoot procedure in *Mathematica* (see Appendix 3.2). Supposing that the desired accuracy is reached within the maximum number of steps, this will result in a candidate solution (p_1, p_2, m_1, m_2). If no candidate solution is obtained, choose a different starting point or increase the maximum number of iterations.
2. Check if the candidate solution is a local maximum by evaluating second-order conditions. This is done by checking that at the candidate solution, the following conditions are satisfied:

$$\partial^2 \Pi_i / \partial p_i^2 < 0,$$
$$\partial^2 \Pi_i / \partial m_i^2 < 0,$$
$$\left(\partial^2 \Pi_i / \partial p_i^2\right)\left(\partial^2 \Pi_i / \partial m_i^2\right) > (\partial^2 \Pi_i / \partial p_i \partial m_i)^2,$$

for $i = 1, 2$. If this is not the case, choose a different starting point and start again.
3. Check if the candidate solution is a global maximum.[23] That is, check whether $\Pi_i[\cdot, \cdot, p_j^*, m_j^*]$ is maximized at p_i^*, m_i^*. This is equivalent to checking whether $\hat{\Pi}_i[\cdot, v_j^*]$ is maximized at consumers' net utility v_i^*, given p_j^* (for the definition of $\hat{\Pi}_i$ see Part 3 of Appendix 3.1). We do this by plotting the respective functions. Alternatively one can check if the candidate is a global maximum by drawing plots of profits $\Pi_i[\cdot, \cdot, p_j^*, m_j^*]$ as a function of p_i and m_i for all feasible price levels.

If the procedure is successful we obtain a Nash equilibrium.

3.4.2 *Parameter values*

To obtain a numerical solution, one must give appropriate values to the parameters. Some parameters, such as access prices, may be observable in the real world. Other parameters, such as marginal costs and demand parameters, can be estimated by using, for instance, expert judgment or market research.

Checks performed by running the model under a variety of parameter constellations showed that the levels of cost and demand parameters, if chosen within reasonable ranges, do not affect the qualitative implications of the model, although naturally the outcomes change quantitatively. Therefore it is safe to choose the parameters for purposes other than real-world accuracy, in particular if the main purpose is to understand how market interactions causally depend on the regulatory regime.

---

[23] Clearly, this implies that the solution is a local maximum; that is, the check in step 2 is successful.

Table 3.4 *Standard parameter configuration*

Category	Parameter	Value
Demand parameters	a	20 euro-cents
	b	0.016 euro-cents
	Z	6000 euro-cents
	$u_1^0 = u_2^0$	5000 euro-cents
	n	8000000
	s_1^0	1
Cost parameters	$c_1 \equiv c_{11} = c_{21}$	2 euro-cents
	$c_2 \equiv c_{12} = c_{22}$	1.5 euro-cents
	$c_3 \equiv c_{13} = c_{23}$	0.5 euro-cents
	$f \equiv f_1 = f_2$	2000 euro-cents

We will choose rather simple, "nice" numbers, which, to a certain extent, resemble cost and demand structures in a relatively small-sized country such as the Netherlands. One should keep in mind, though, that the structure and assumptions of the model are such that our outcomes are not meant to describe the actual situation in the Netherlands. Nevertheless, we try to obtain outcomes of the right order of magnitude.

The main asymmetry between the operators that we allow in this chapter is that the incumbent starts with an initial market share of 100 percent. Thus, the operators are identical except for parameters s_1^0 and s_2^0. In subsequent chapters, we will incorporate additional asymmetries, such as different fixed utility parameters u_1^0 and u_2^0.

According to KPN (1999), the average consumer called 13 minutes per day in 1998. This number is the product of the call rate (number of calls per day), equal to 3.86, and the call duration, equal to 3.37 minutes. Compared to the year before, the call rate had grown by 3.9 percent, and the call duration by 3.0 percent. Assuming that these growth rates are constant throughout the following years, the estimated call rate in 2002 is 4.50, and the estimated call duration 3.79 minutes. Thus the average consumer calls 17.06 minutes per day in 2002. In a period of two months (sixty-one days), which constitutes a single period in our model, a rough estimate of individual demand is $x = 1041$ call minutes (at prices which are assumed to be constant over time).

A rough estimate for the average per-minute price in 1998 is $p = 3.0$ euro-cents (average of local, national, peak and off-peak calls; see de Bijl and Peitz, 2000). An estimate of the average price elasticity is $\varepsilon = -0.18$ (average of local, national, residential and business calls; Nera, 1999). Since $\varepsilon = -p/(a - p)$, it follows that $a = p(\varepsilon - 1)/\varepsilon = 20$. The demand equation $x = (a - p)/b$ results in $b = (a - p)/x = 0.016$.

We summarize the standard parameter configuration in Table 3.4.

Table 3.5 *Units of output variables*

Category	Variable	Unit
Prices	p_1, p_2	Euro cents
	m_1, m_2	Euro cents
		In figures: euros
Profits	Π_1, Π_2	Million euros
	AR_1, AR_2	Million euros
Surplus	PS	Million euros
	CS	Million euros
	W	Million euros

Table 3.5 summarizes the units in which outcomes are depicted throughout this book.

3.5   Access price regulation and entry

In this section, we explore the effects of terminating access prices in a market that is not mature in the sense that operators do not have the same initial market shares. In Subsection 3.5.1, we consider general levels of initial market shares s_1^0 and s_2^0. In later subsections, we assume that the incumbent starts with a market share of 100 percent, that is, $s_1^0 = 1$ and $s_2^0 = 0$. We call such a market an infant market because entry has "just" occurred and the freshly liberalized market still has to develop. In such an asymmetric market we are, in particular, interested in reciprocal and asymmetric access price regulation. As a starting point, we consider cost-based access prices.

3.5.1   Cost-based access prices

We have already seen that in equilibrium, operators set per-minute prices equal to perceived marginal costs. If terminating access prices are equal to the marginal cost of local connections, that is, $\tau_1 = \tau_2 = c_1$, then per-minute prices in equilibrium equal $p_i^* = c_1$ and subscription fees equal:

$$m_i^* = f + \frac{1 + s_i^0}{3} Z + \frac{u_i^0 - u_j^0}{3}, \quad i = 1, 2. \tag{3.3}$$

Given our assumptions on symmetry between the operators, it follows that $m_i^* = f + (1 + s_i^0)Z/3$. The operators' market shares are $s_i^* = \frac{1}{3}(1 + s_i^0)$. Profits in equilibrium are $\pi_i^* = (1 + s_i^0)^2 Z/9$. If the incumbent starts with a market share of 100 percent, then $m_1^* = f + \frac{2}{3}Z$ and $m_2^* = f + \frac{1}{3}Z$. The entrant then obtains a market share of $\frac{1}{3}$.

Table 3.6 *Reciprocal access prices in an infant market*

τ	0.25	0.5	0.75	1.0	2	5
p_1	1.92	2	2.08	2.17	2.50	3.44
p_2	1.83	2	2.17	2.33	3.00	5.06
m_1	6094	6000	5906	5813	5447	4419
m_2	4189	4000	3814	3692	2912	907
s_1	0.667	0.667	0.667	0.667	0.668	0.679
Π_1	213.31	213.33	213.31	213.24	212.49	204.73
Π_2	53.33	53.33	53.33	53.33	53.33	53.11
AR_1	−5.05	0	4.95	9.81	28.27	73.25
AR_2	−5.02	0	4.98	9.91	29.11	81.16
CS	756.66	756.67	756.66	756.64	756.48	756.45
W	1023.30	1023.33	1023.30	1023.22	1022.30	1014.28

The equilibrium outcome has a number of intuitive properties. In particular, an installed consumer base is valuable, that is, $\partial \pi_i^*(s_i^0)/\partial s_i^0 > 0$. Also, in a more "sticky" market, both operators obtain higher profits, since $\partial \pi_i^*(Z)/\partial Z > 0$. If we allow for different fixed utility levels, that is, $u_1^0 \neq u_2^0$, then operator i's profit is increasing in utility difference $u_i^0 - u_j^0$. We will explore the joint effect of installed consumer base and fixed utility asymmetry in Chapter 4.

Note that with cost-based access prices, perceived marginal costs are constant so that the per-minute prices that are chosen in equilibrium do not depend on market shares. Hence, for the sake of exposition, we can ignore per-minute prices and focus on subscription fees. In particular, one can observe that subscription fees are strategic complements, in the sense that an operator's marginal profits are increasing in the subscription fee of the rival operator; formally, $\partial^2 \pi_i/\partial m_i \partial m_j = n\, \partial s_i/\partial m_j > 0$. This implies that best-response functions are upward sloping: an operator's best reply to an increase in its rival's subscription fee is to increase its subscription fee as well.

3.5.2   Reciprocal access prices

In this subsection we explore how different levels of terminating access prices affect market outcomes. We consider reciprocal access prices so that $\tau \equiv \tau_1 = \tau_2$. We set the entrant's initial market share to 0, that is, we consider an infant market in which the entrant completely lacks installed consumer base.

Consider Table 3.6, where cost-based access price regulation refers to the column where $\tau = 0.5$. The simulation confirms our earlier analytical results. In particular, per-minute prices are equal to perceived marginal costs. Since the incumbent maintains more than the majority of consumers its perceived marginal costs are lower than those of the entrant. Although the entrant charges a higher per-minute price when the access price is above the marginal costs of the local loop, it can attract consumers by offering a significantly lower subscription fee.

One can observe from the table that market shares are rather insensitive to changes in the access price, so that changes in the reciprocal access price do not significantly help the entrant to gain additional consumers. In the simulation, profits are also hardly affected by the access price. This means that the competitive positions of the operators remain more or less intact, although a higher access markup implies that the entrant faces higher perceived marginal costs than the incumbent, putting it at a disadvantage. Our simulation suggests that a reciprocal access markup does not seem to be a good tool for creating a level playing field (see also Section 4.4).

Furthermore, observe that consumer surplus is hardly affected. If market share did not change, the only effect on consumers surplus would come from per-minute prices. Recall however that consumers surplus is net of aggregate consumer switching costs, so that in this respect a higher market share of the incumbent is good for consumers. Overall, the welfare effect seems negligible.

Interestingly, both operators have an incentive to ask for cost-based access price regulation if access prices have to be reciprocal. This suggests that if a regulator is committed to reciprocal access prices, it might as well allow, for instance, the operators to agree on reciprocal access prices or the incumbent to set reciprocal access prices. With such a decision the regulator can avoid the overheads associated with acquiring information about marginal costs (note that we have assumed cost symmetry).[24]

Guideline 3.2: Consider facilities-based entry. Suppose that operators compete in two-part tariffs. In an infant market, a reciprocal access markup reduces consumers surplus and the entrant's profits. In a mature market, it does not affect profits but again it introduces a deadweight loss in welfare and hence a reduction of consumers surplus. Accordingly, if reciprocity of access prices is a requirement, then they should be cost-based.

To address the robustness of our results, we will vary some parameters of the model, in particular the switching cost parameter Z, individual demand

---

[24] Independently, Carter and Wright (2001) have elaborated on reciprocal access pricing in an asymmetric market. In their model, they show that the incumbent always prefers cost-based access prices to any other reciprocal access prices. The preference of the smaller operator depends on the asymmetry of the market. Nevertheless, we do not claim that the property that the incumbent's profits decrease in the reciprocal access price (above costs) is a general property that holds in *any* model. See also Section 4.4.

Table 3.7 *Reciprocal access prices in a "less sticky" infant market*

τ	0.25	0.5	0.75	1.0	2.0
p_1	1.92	2	2.08	2.17	2.50
p_2	1.83	2	2.17	2.33	3.00
m_1	4094	4000	3906	3814	3449
m_2	3189	3000	2814	2629	1909
s_1	0.667	0.667	0.667	0.667	0.669
Π_1	106.64	106.67	106.64	106.57	105.81
Π_2	26.67	26.67	26.67	26.67	26.66
AR_1	−5.05	0	4.95	9.81	28.21
AR_2	−5.02	0	4.98	9.90	29.06
CS	903.33	903.33	903.33	903.31	903.16
W	1036.64	1036.67	1036.64	1036.55	1035.63

parameters a and b, and the shape of the demand function. To start with, consider changes in the stickiness of the market.

Reducing the switching cost parameter to $Z = 3000$ results in more intense competition (see Table 3.7). This intensified competition is reflected in lower subscription fees, lower profits of the two operators and higher consumer surplus. Since the incurred switching costs decrease on average, welfare is higher if the market is less sticky. We have seen that this can be easily shown analytically under cost-based regulation, but it also holds under reciprocal access price regulation more generally. For a higher value of access prices, a higher Z results in a smaller share of consumers who switch to the entrant.

Concerning the individual demand parameters, it is straightforward to demonstrate that the results do not critically depend on demand parameters a and b. To confirm this, we considered three alternative scenarios, varying our estimate of an average consumer's demand for calls and the reference per-minute price. The values of (a, b) that we looked at were $(20, 0.019)$, $(26, 0.021)$, $(26, 0.024)$; they leave the values for subscription fees, market shares, and profits almost unchanged. Consumers surplus and welfare react strongly to these parameter changes without affecting any of our comparative statics exercises.

We also tested the sensitivity of the numerical outcomes by incorporating an alternative utility function with constant-elastic demand of the form:

$$u[x] = \frac{(\alpha x)^{1+\frac{1}{\varepsilon}}}{1 + \frac{1}{\varepsilon}} + \beta,$$

where ε is the (constant) elasticity of demand and α, β are constants. These parameters were chosen such that utility and demand correspond to the values in the linear demand specification at a per-minute price of 3 euro cents (compare the parameter constellation in Section 3.4.2). In our simulations with access price regulation of the form analyzed above, the outcome with constant elastic demand strongly resembles the outcome with our linear demand specification.[25] We therefore stick to the linear demand specification without referring to the corresponding results under constant-elastic demand.

3.5.3   Asymmetric access prices

Asymmetric access price regulation allows for the possibility of setting different access prices for the incumbent and the entrant.[26] In order to favor the entrant the regulator can, for instance, impose an access price equal to marginal costs for using the local loop of the incumbent and above marginal costs for using the local loop of the entrant.

Suppose the regulator implements the asymmetric access price regulation that favors the entrant. This increases the perceived marginal cost of the incumbent, thus leading to an increase in its per-minute price. The incumbent has to pay more for access to the entrant's network, and therefore is more eager to maintain its market share. Also the entrant gains more from a larger market share, because this generates access revenues (and possibly saves access payments). Accordingly, competition becomes more intense.[27]

Table 3.8 depicts simulation outcomes for a range of access price combinations (mainly asymmetric). In the first part, only the entrant is allowed to charge an access markup. In the second part, both operators include markups in their access prices.

As one can see from the first part of Table 3.8, in equilibrium, the entrant operator is pricing more aggressively if its access markup increases. The market environment is changed in its favor and its profits increase: the loss in subscription revenues due to more intense competition is more than offset by the increase in access revenues. The incumbent is worse off: its profits decrease as terminating access to the entrant's network becomes more expensive.

Again we see that market shares only weakly respond to changes in access prices. For instance, although an increase in τ_2 induces the incumbent to increase its per-minute price, it also leads to downward pressure on subscription fees. Overall, market shares are hardly affected.

---

[25] This also holds for the simulations with asymmetric access prices. Nevertheless, if per-minute prices are far away from 3, demand reacts quite differently in the two specifications, so that the outcome of simulations with linear pricing is more sensitive to the prevailing demand specification. Again, this does not affect our qualitative results.

[26] This and additional asymmetries in regulation are addressed throughout the book. An introduction to asymmetric access price regulation is provided by de Bijl and Peitz (2001b). Perrucci and Cimatoribus (1997) describe some of the additional asymmetries in regulation in telecommunications markets.

[27] For an example of asymmetric access price regulation in the Netherlands see Section 4.5.

Table 3.8 *Asymmetric access prices in an infant market*

(a) Access markup by entrant only

τ_1	0.5	0.5	0.5	0.5	0.5
τ_2	0.5	0.75	1	2	5
p_1	2	2.08	2.17	2.50	3.52
p_2	2	2	2	2	2
m_1	6000	5813	5628	4904	2904
m_2	4000	3907	3815	3457	2516
s_1	0.667	0.667	0.667	0.666	0.663
Π_1	213.33	203.37	193.49	154.80	47.93
Π_2	53.33	55.83	58.30	68.09	96.82
AR_2	0	4.98	9.91	29.19	82.90
CS	756.67	764.12	771.49	799.95	874.12
W	1023.33	1023.32	1023.28	1022.85	1018.87

(b) Access markup by both operators

τ_1	1.5	1.5	1.5	1.5	1.5
τ_2	0.75	1.5	1.75	2	3
p_1	2.08	2.33	2.42	2.50	2.83
p_2	2.67	2.67	2.67	2.67	2.67
m_1	6180	5629	5448	5270	4571
m_2	3541	3267	3177	3089	2749
s_1	0.667	0.667	0.667	0.667	0.666
Π_1	242.45	212.96	203.29	193.71	156.28
Π_2	45.98	53.33	55.76	58.17	67.22
AR_1	19.24	19.24	19.24	19.25	19.27
AR_2	4.97	19.61	20.58	29.15	47.71
CS	734.64	756.58	763.70	770.72	797.73
W	1023.07	1022.87	1022.75	1022.60	1021.73

Although the incumbent's per-minute price increases, all consumers receive higher net utilities if only the entrant charges an access markup. Thus, consumers gain from a higher access price τ_2 due to its positive effect on competition. Consumers who subscribe to the incumbent incur a higher per-minute price. However, their net utility still increases because of the reduction of the incumbent's subscription fee. More generally, Appendix 3.4 shows that net utility levels are increasing in the entrant's access price τ_2 on a large range of parameter values, given that the incumbent is subject to cost-based regulation.[28]

---

[28] The analysis in Appendix 3.4 relies on numerical evaluations and is adapted from Peitz (2001) which contains additional analytical results.

The second part of Table 3.8 demonstrates that allowing both operators to include markups in their access prices is, in terms of consumers surplus, welfare, and the entrant's profit level, inferior to an asymmetric access markup for the entrant only. Therefore, asymmetric access price regulation that allows a markup for the incumbent is not only less effective in stimulating competition but also, taking entry as given, negatively affects consumers.

In an infant market, a higher access price τ_2, while τ_1 is cost based, leads to a small loss in social welfare. The main reason is that the higher per-minute price creates a deadweight loss. Less important is that more switching costs are incurred by consumers, as the entrant slightly increases its market share.

> **Guideline 3.3**: Consider facilities-based entry. Suppose that operators compete in two-part tariffs. In an infant market, an access markup only for the entrant increases consumers surplus and the entrant's profits.

To summarize, asymmetric access price regulation that gives a higher access markup to the entrant strengthens the position of the entrant in terms of profits. This type of regulation is most effective if the incumbent's access price is cost based, and it results in a higher consumers surplus. The negative effect on social welfare is negligible compared to the effect on the entrant's profits and consumers surplus.

3.6   Linear pricing

3.6.1   Mature market

As we have seen in the analysis above, operators competing in two-part tariffs exercise market power through subscription fees and set per-minute prices equal to perceived marginal costs. It is interesting to compare this outcome with a situation of competition in linear prices, where the operators only charge per-minute prices p_1 and p_2 but no subscription fees. The case of linear pricing is the starting point in the existing literature on competition in telecommunications markets (see, for example, Laffont, Rey and Tirole, 1998a, on which the analysis below is based). As we will see, linear pricing gives rise to the possibility that the terminating access price is used to tacitly collude, which is a central result in the literature (see also Armstrong, 1998). We analyze linear pricing in more detail in Section 6.2.

By defining $m_1 = m_2 = 0$ in the previous set-up, one can see that linear pricing is a special case of competition in two-part tariffs. Therefore, we can use the notation of the previous model. For the sake of notational simplicity, we will eliminate subscription fees as arguments in various functions.

To make the analysis compatible with Laffont, Rey, and Tirole, we assume that $s_1^0 = s_2^0 = \frac{1}{2}$. Accordingly, the model does not depict competition between an incumbent and an entrant, but rather between two identical operators competing in a mature market.

An individual consumer's total net utility from using operator i's network to make phone calls can now be written as:

$$v_i[p_i] = u_i^0 + u[x[p_i]] - p_i x[p_i],$$

and realized market shares as:

$$s_i[p_1, p_2] = s_i^0 + \frac{v_i[p_i] - v_j[p_j]}{Z}.$$

Profits can be written as:

$$\begin{aligned}
\Pi_i[p_1, p_2] = &\, n \, s_i s_i x[p_i](p_i - c_1) \\
&+ n \, s_i s_j x[p_i](p_i - c_2 - \tau_j) \\
&+ n \, s_j s_i x[p_j](\tau_i - c_3) \\
&- n \, s_i f.
\end{aligned}$$

Restricting the analysis to reciprocal access pricing, profit functions can be simplified as follows:

$$\begin{aligned}
\Pi_i[p_1, p_2] = &\, n \, s_i \left((p_i - c_1)x[p_i] - f \right) \\
&+ n \, s_i s_j (\tau - c_3)(x[p_j] - x[p_i]).
\end{aligned}$$

Using the fact that $v_i'[p_i] = -x[p_i]$, it follows that:

$$\begin{aligned}
&\partial(\Pi_i[p_1, p_2]/n)/\partial p_i \\
&= -\frac{x[p_i]}{Z}\left((p_i - c_1)x[p_i] - f \right) + s_i(x'[p_i](p_i - c_1) + x[p_i]) \\
&\quad + \left(-\frac{x[p_i]}{Z}s_j + \frac{x[p_i]}{Z}s_i \right)(\tau - c_3)(x[p_j] - x[p_i]) \\
&\quad - s_i s_j (\tau - c_3)x'[p_i].
\end{aligned}$$

In a symmetric equilibrium, $s_1^* = s_2^* = \frac{1}{2}$ and $p^* \equiv p_1^* = p_2^*$. An operator's first-order condition can therefore be written as:

$$\begin{aligned}
&\frac{1}{2}(x'[p^*](p^* - c_1) + x[p^*]) - \frac{x[p^*]}{Z}((p^* - c_1)x[p^*] - f) \\
&\quad - \frac{1}{4}(\tau - c_3)x'[p^*] = 0.
\end{aligned}$$

Laffont, Rey, and Tirole show that if competition is not too intense (in our model, if Z is sufficiently large) and the reciprocal access price is sufficiently close to marginal costs, then a unique and symmetric equilibrium exists (recall that we need the same type of conditions if the operators compete in two-part tariffs; see Proposition 1).[29] The equilibrium is characterized by the first-order condition above.

An individual consumer's price elasticity of demand is defined as $\varepsilon[p] = x'[p]p/x[p]$. Using this definition, the first-order condition for profit maximization (see above) can be rewritten as a so-called Lerner index, that is, the ratio of the markup above marginal cost and the price:

$$\frac{p^* - c_1 - \frac{1}{2}(\tau - c_3)}{p^*} = -\frac{1}{\varepsilon[p^*]}\left(1 - \frac{2}{Z}((p^* - c_1)x[p^*] - f)\right).$$

(3.4)

Looking more closely at this formula, one can make the following important observation.

> **Proposition 3** Suppose that there exists a symmetric equilibrium. Then the equilibrium price p^* is increasing in the reciprocal access price τ. Consequently, the reciprocal access price can be used as an instrument of tacit collusion.

This result is a central result in Armstrong (1998) and Laffont, Rey, and Tirole (1998a). If operators first negotiate about the reciprocal access price, and next compete by choosing retail prices, they have incentives to choose the access price to maximize joint profits as far as the market can bear. A regulator can prevent the access price being used as a collusive device simply by imposing a sufficiently low access price.

Guideline 3.4: Consider facilities-based entry. Suppose that operators compete in linear prices and negotiate reciprocal access prices before setting retail prices. In a mature market, a reciprocal access price can be used as an instrument of tacit collusion.

Note that under linear pricing, consumers surplus and welfare can be increased (compared to their values under cost-based access prices) by setting a reciprocal access price τ below marginal costs c_3. Hence, in a mature market the

[29] As mentioned, existence of an equilibrium can only be shown under certain parameter restrictions. If operators do not agree on access prices but on access price rules that depend on retail prices, an equilibrium always exists for certain price rules, as shown by Doganoglu and Tauman (1996).

regulator can further improve upon the market outcome resulting from a cost-based access price. The reason is that market power in the retail market leads to markups which hurt consumers and are distortionary for welfare (they introduce a deadweight loss). By setting an access price below costs the regulator can reduce perceived marginal costs. This lower wholesale price leads to a lower retail price (although the *markup* above *perceived* marginal costs decreases in τ).

Laffont and Tirole (2000, Chapter 5) give several reasons why, in practice, access prices do not necessarily act as collusive devices. For instance, note that Proposition 3 critically depends on the existence of a symmetric equilibrium. Hence, if the lock-in effect is not too strong (in the model of Laffont, Rey, and Tirole, networks are sufficiently close substitutes), an equilibrium as characterized above does not exist and we cannot address this question.

Furthermore, perhaps more important, note that Proposition 3 depends on the assumption of linear pricing, whereas in telecommunications markets two-part tariffs are the norm. Recall that in a situation of two-part tariffs, per-minute prices are set at marginal cost levels so that collusion is completely absent. We want to emphasize, however, that the collusion result in the case of linear prices, and the non-collusion result in the case of two-part tariffs, are extremes. In reality, it is commonly observed that the incumbent's retail prices, in particular its subscription fee, are constrained by regulation. Operators may react to downward pressure on subscription fees by setting per-minute prices somewhat higher than marginal costs (see also Section 3.7). Hence one should not exclude access prices being used to collude, although the risk of collusion seems to be much smaller than in a situation where operators compete in linear prices (see also the discussion in Chapters 6 and 7).

3.6.2 *Access price regulation in an infant market*

We now leave the symmetric framework behind us to focus the situation where operator 1, the incumbent, initially has 100 percent market share, that is, $s_1^0 = 1$ and $s_2^0 = 0$. Table 3.9 depicts selected outcomes for different levels of a reciprocal access price.

These outcomes confirm the results of the previous subsection, in particular that both operators' profits as well as per-minute prices are increasing in the access price (and hence can be used as a collusive device). Moreover, a higher access price is more beneficial to the incumbent than to the entrant. This is due to the asymmetry in initial market shares. Because of this asymmetry, the entrant has relatively more off-net traffic and therefore its perceived marginal cost is pushed up to a larger extent. Notice also that consumers surplus and welfare are decreasing in the access price. This reflects the problem that prices above true marginal costs lead to a deadweight loss and thus reduce total surplus.

Table 3.9 *Reciprocal access prices with linear pricing*
in an infant market

τ	0.25	0.5	0.75	1.0	2.0
p_1	7.59	7.63	7.67	7.72	7.90
p_2	5.58	5.62	5.66	5.70	5.87
s_1	0.720	0.720	0.721	0.721	0.723
Π_1	133.97	135.60	137.23	138.87	145.38
Π_2	28.06	28.11	28.15	28.20	28.34
AR_1	−3.64	0	3.61	7.19	21.21
AR_2	−3.13	0	3.10	6.17	18.17
CS	803.92	801.21	798.49	795.76	784.70
W	965.94	964.92	963.88	962.83	958.43

3.7   Price cap regulation

3.7.1   Types of retail price caps

We now return to the standard case of competition in two-part tariffs and explore how a regulator can use retail price caps to constrain the incumbent's market power or to avoid price distortions. To do this, we analyze how price caps on the incumbent's retail prices affect entry and how they can be used to increase consumers surplus. We use the term *price cap* to refer to a price ceiling for the incumbent's prices. This price ceiling may be imposed on a single service or on a basket of services.[30]

Note that price caps on the incumbent's services may not only be useful to protect consumers' interests; they also provide strong incentives for the incumbent to reduce costs. For an overview of the incentive effects of price cap regulation, see Laffont and Tirole (2000). Here, we only look at price caps for the incumbent.

Two important types of price caps are:
- separate price caps on the subscription fee and the per-minute price (or, as special cases, on either one of them);
- a joint price cap on the per-minute price and the subscription fee together, according to some weighted average.

---

[30] According to the definition by Acton and Vogelsang (1989), price caps are defined by four properties: (i) price caps are a ceiling for prices to be charged by the regulated firm which may price below this ceiling; (ii) price ceilings are defined for baskets of services that are offered by the regulated firm and can be expressed as price indices for these baskets; (iii) these price indices are adjusted periodically by a preannounced adjustment factor that is exogenous to the regulated firm; and (iv) in longer intervals the indices can be revised. In our analysis, we take property (i) of the definition as the most important part. To satisfy property (ii), a basket may also contain a single service. In relation to properties (iii) and (iv), we abstract from periodical adjustments and revisions.

In the case of separate price caps, the regulator separately imposes maximum levels for the incumbent's per-minute price and subscription fee:

$$p_1 \leq \kappa,$$
$$m_1 \leq \mu.$$

For instance, the regulator can set the per-minute price below perceived marginal costs while simultaneously preventing a large markup in the subscription fee. This type of price cap may be very useful to address efficiency and distributive concerns, as it separates prices for connections and traffic.

Obviously, two special cases are to impose either a maximum subscription fee $m_1 \leq \mu$ or a maximum per-minute price $p_1 \leq \kappa$ (so that the other ceiling is not binding). We will see later why the regulator may wish to impose a ceiling on either one of these retail prices.

A joint price cap on the per-minute price and subscription fee can be considered as a price cap on total expenditures on a "basket" of services, consisting of a telephone connection and a certain number of call minutes. There are many possibilities to define the weights on the different services in the basket. We will consider the following, rather straightforward way:

$$\lambda p_1 + (1 - \lambda)m_1 \leq \kappa.$$

Thus, the regulator chooses cap κ, as well as a weight $\lambda \in [0, 1]$. Increasing λ while keeping cap κ constant, strengthens the downward pressure on the per-minute price but alleviates the pressure on the subscription fee. Similarly, the price cap can be made more stringent by reducing cap κ while keeping weight λ constant. Notice that for $\lambda = 0$ and $\lambda = 1$, one ends up in a separate price cap on either one of the prices.

In practice, weight λ and joint cap κ can be fixed by the regulator by considering a "representative" consumer.[31] For example, suppose that the representative consumer should be able to maintain a connection and make calls totaling 1200 call minutes for 60 euros. Then a consumer can consume this basket if $1200p_1 + m_1 \leq 6000$ (note that p_1 and m_1 are in euro cents), which can be rewritten as $\frac{1200}{1201}p_1 + \frac{1}{1201}m_1 \leq \frac{6000}{1201}$. Accordingly, $\lambda = \frac{1200}{1201}$, and $\kappa = \frac{6000}{1201} \approx 5$.

An alternative way to define a joint price cap is to design it such that prices guarantee a minimum level of net utility to consumers, that is:

$$u[x[p_1]] - x[p_1]p_1 - m_1 \geq \kappa,$$

---

[31] The UK regulator Oftel currently applies a retail price cap on a basket of services. "The current retail price control restricts annual increases in the average price of a group or 'basket' of services to the rate of inflation (RPI) minus 4.5 percent. The services controlled are connections, line rentals, local, national and international calls and operator assistance. Oftel calculates the relative weight of each service within the basket by looking at the expenditure patterns of the lowest 80 percent of residential customers by spend[ings]. This means that the control focuses price changes on services used largely by lower spending customers" (Oftel, 2001a, p. 3).

Table 3.10 Price cap on the incumbent's subscription fee in an infant market

μ	–	3500	2000	–	3500	2000
τ	0.5	0.5	0.5	1.5	1.5	1.5
p_1	2	4.1	5.52	2.33	4.19	5.66
p_2	2	2	2	2.67	2.69	2.70
m_1	6000	3500	2000	5629	3500	2000
m_2	4000	3864	3788	3267	3175	3125
s_1	0.667	0.689	0.702	0.667	0.686	0.699
Π_1	213.33	197.95	179.02	212.96	202.80	186.68
Π_2	53.33	46.31	42.61	53.33	46.49	42.19
CS	756.67	774.97	785.29	756.58	768.49	775.55
W	1023.33	1019.22	1006.92	1022.87	1017.78	1004.41

which, given our assumptions on the utility function, is equivalent to:

$$\frac{(p_1 - a)^2}{2b} - m_1 \geq \kappa.$$

Now the weights in the basket are implicitly defined by the condition on the net utility of an individual consumer. Notice that the relationship between the per-minute price and subscription fee is no longer linear. Also, the regulator needs to have information about demand parameters a and b in order to choose an appropriate level for κ.

3.7.2   Price cap on the subscription fee

In this subsection, we consider a separate price cap on the incumbent's subscription fee. Suppose that only the incumbent's subscription fee is subject to:

$$m_1 \leq \mu.$$

Table 3.10 depicts how the reciprocal access price combined with a price cap affects entry and competition.

One can observe from Table 3.10 that a more stringent price cap on the incumbent's subscription fee has the following consequences:

- It induces the incumbent to set its per-minute price above perceived marginal cost. In turn, the incumbent's customers make fewer phone calls. In general, the larger the difference between the per-minute price and the intrinsic cost of making a phone call (which is equal to $c_1 = 2$ in this case), the larger the distortion of the socially optimal number of calls. In other words, a price cap on the subscription fee leads to a deadweight loss.

- It reduces the entrant's subscription fee. In order to remain competitive, the entrant, to a certain extent, has to match the incumbent's reduction of the subscription.
- Both operators' profits are reduced, mainly as a result of the reduction of subscription fees. On the other side of the market, consumers benefit from lower retail prices so that consumers surplus increases.
- It reduces the entrant's market share (since the incumbent is forced to price more aggressively).
- It reduces welfare (because of the incumbent's distorted per-minute price).

These consequences happen irrespective of a markup in the reciprocal access price.

> **Guideline 3.5**: Consider facilities-based entry. Suppose that operators compete in two-part tariffs. A price cap on the incumbent's subscription fee can protect consumers from excessive prices. Disadvantages are that the incumbent's per-minute price is distorted and the entrant's profits are reduced.

3.7.3   Price cap on the per-minute price

Now consider the case that only the incumbent's per-minute price is subject to a price cap:

$$p_1 \leq \kappa.$$

In particular, suppose that the regulator wishes to avoid any distortions in calling behavior by forcing the incumbent to price calls at their true cost level, that is, $\kappa = c_1 = 2$. This price cap will be binding as soon as the incumbent has to pay an access markup for termination of calls on the entrant's network ($\tau_2 > 0.5$). Table 3.11 presents some selected outcomes.

For given access prices (with $\tau_2 > c_3$), one can observe the following consequences if the incumbent's per-minute price is subjected to a price cap equal to the *true* cost of making a call ($\kappa = 2$):

- The entrant, pricing at perceived marginal costs, sets essentially the same per-minute price independent of the price cap. The entrant receives more incoming calls because the incumbent is forced to set a lower per-minute price than in the absence of the price cap. Hence, it makes higher profits in the wholesale market.
- The incumbent increases its subscription fee, while the entrant decreases its subscription fee.
- The incumbent's profits decrease, but the entrant's profits increase. Consumers surplus increases.

Table 3.11 Price cap on the incumbent's per-minute price

κ	$-$	$-$	2	$-$	2
τ_1	0.5	1.0	1.0	0.5	0.5
τ_2	0.5	1.0	1.0	1.0	1.0
p_1	2.00	2.17	2.00	2.17	2.00
p_2	2.00	2.33	2.33	2.00	2.00
m_1	6000	5813	5998	5628	5813
m_2	4000	3629	3627	3815	3813
s_1	0.667	0.667	0.667	0.667	0.667
Π_1	213.33	213.24	213.09	193.49	193.33
Π_2	53.33	53.33	53.36	58.30	58.33
CS	756.67	756.64	756.82	771.49	771.67
W	1023.33	1023.22	1023.27	1023.28	1023.33

- Market shares are not affected in a substantial way.
- Welfare increases.

If the regulator imposes that the incumbent's access price is cost-based, that is, $\tau_1 = c_3$, then individually optimal per-minute prices are equal to $p_1^* = p_2^* = c_1$. This is true irrespective of the level of the entrant's access price τ_2. We will derive some comparative statics results related to an access markup for the entrant. Given our earlier assumptions, profit functions, which now only depend on m_1 and m_2, can be written as:

$$\Pi_1[p_1^*, p_2^*, m_1, m_2] = s_1 s_2 x[c_1](c_3 - \tau_2) + s_1(m_1 - f) \quad \text{and}$$
$$\Pi_2[p_1^*, p_2^*, m_1, m_2] = s_1 s_2 x[c_1](\tau_2 - c_3) + s_2(m_2 - f).$$

Supposing that $s_1^0 = 1$ and solving the system of first-order conditions yields:

$$m_1^* = f - \tfrac{1}{3}x[c_1](\tau_2 - c_3) + \tfrac{2}{3}Z \quad \text{and}$$
$$m_2^* = f - \tfrac{1}{3}x[c_2](\tau_2 - c_3) + \tfrac{1}{3}Z.$$

Given these prices, profit levels in equilibrium are equal to:

$$\Pi_1^* = \tfrac{4}{9}(Z - x[c_1](\tau_2 - c_3)),$$
$$\Pi_2^* = \tfrac{1}{9}(Z + x[c_1](\tau_2 - c_3)).$$

Now consider an increase in τ_2. Both the incumbent's and the entrant's subscription fee decrease. The entrant's profits increase, but the incumbent is worse off. Thus, a higher access markup for the entrant reduces the intensity of competition, but stimulates entry. Consumers benefit from reduced subscription fees.[32]

Guideline 3.6: Consider facilities-based entry. Suppose that operators compete in two-part tariffs and that only the entrant is allowed to set its access price above cost. A price cap on the incumbent's per-minute price can be used to enforce a cost-based per-minute price. Besides efficient retail prices, this results in an increase in the entrant's profits and consumers surplus, compared with a situation of cost-based access prices.

3.7.4   Separate price caps on per-minute price and subscription fee

By combining separate price caps on the per-minute price and the subscription fee:

$$p_1 \leq \kappa,$$

$$m_1 \leq \mu,$$

the regulator can avoid distortions in calling behavior and, at the same time, make sure that this does not lead to an increase of the incumbent's subscription fee.

Consider asymmetric access price regulation such that the incumbent is subject to cost-based access price regulation and the entrant can set an access markup ($\tau_2 = 1$). For example, by setting $\kappa = 2.0$ and $\mu = 5700$, consumers surplus increases to 779.31, and welfare increases to 1024.69, compared with 1023.28 in the case without price caps (see the fourth column of Table 3.11). Profit levels are $\Pi_1 = 190.00$ and $\Pi_2 = 55.37$. Comparing this outcome to the results under a price cap on only one or the other price, one can easily see that it may be very useful for the regulator to use separate price caps on both retail prices. Compared with cost-based access price regulation (without interference in the retail market), we observe that the above regulation essentially leads to a redistribution of surplus such that consumers and the entrant benefit (see second column of Table 3.6).

More generally, consider asymmetric access price regulation in combination with retail price regulation setting binding price caps $\kappa = c_1$ and μ. Hence, $p_1^* = c_1$ and $m_1^* = \mu$. An equilibrium is now found by maximizing the entrant's profit function $\Pi_2[c_1, c_2, \mu, m_2]$ with respect to m_2. Using the fact that

---

[32] One can show that these results also hold under the more general condition that the incumbent's initial market share is sufficiently large.

$s_2 = 1 - s_1^0 + (m_1 - m_2)/Z$ and solving the first-order condition yields:

$$m_2^* = \frac{\left(f + \mu + Z\left(1 - s_1^0\right)\right)Z + \left(2\mu + \left(1 - 2s_1^0\right)Z\right)(\tau_2 - c_3)x[c_1]}{2(Z + (\tau_2 - c_3)x[c_1])}.$$

How does the entrant's subscription fee in equilibrium react to an increase in access price τ_2? One can show that:

$$\frac{\partial m_2^*}{\partial \tau_2} = -\frac{Z\left(f - \mu + s_1^0 Z\right)x[c_1]}{2(Z + (\tau_2 - c_3)x[c_1])^2}.$$

Hence, the entrant's subscription fee is decreasing in τ_2 if and only if the price cap on the incumbent's subscription fee is not too large, in particular, if $\mu < f + s_1^0 Z$. For instance, in an infant market with $s_1^0 = 1$, this inequality is always satisfied (when the price cap is binding).

Furthermore, the entrant's market share in equilibrium equals:

$$s_2^* = \frac{\mu - f + \left(1 - s_1^0\right)Z + (\tau_2 - c_3)x[c_1]}{2(Z + (\tau_2 - c_3)x[c_1])},$$

and has partial derivative:

$$\frac{\partial s_2^*}{\partial \tau_2} = \frac{\left(f - \mu + s_1^0 Z\right)x[c_1]}{2(Z + (\tau_2 - c_3)x[c_1])^2} = -\frac{\partial m_2^*}{\partial \tau_2}.$$

Thus, consumers benefit from a higher access price for the entrant, τ_2, in the sense that the entrant's subscription fee decreases and its market share increases, if and only if $\mu < f + s_1^0 Z$, that is, the price cap on the incumbent's subscription fee is not too large. Also, one can directly observe that a more stringent price cap slows down the speed of entry, that is, $\partial s_2^*/\partial \mu > 0$.

3.7.5   Joint price caps

Suppose that the regulator imposes $\lambda p_1 + (1 - \lambda)m_1 \leq \kappa$. One can observe from Table 3.12 (where weight λ is varied while $\kappa = 5000$) that a more stringent price cap in the form of a low weight λ has the following consequences:

- A more stringent price cap induces the incumbent to set its per-minute price above perceived marginal cost.
- Both operators reduce their subscription fees. The reason is that a low weight λ corresponds to stronger pressure on m_1. The entrant is forced to go along with the incumbent.
- Both operators' profits are reduced. Consumers surplus increases.

We have observed these consequences also under a price cap on the subscription fee only. A common observation is that a lower value for λ intensifies price competition and therefore hurts both operators. An important difference,

Table 3.12 Joint price cap in an infant market

(a) Cost-based access

λ	≥ 0.17	0.15	0.10	0.005	0.001	0
τ	0.5	0.5	0.5	0.5	0.5	0.5
p_1	2	2.09	2.35	2.79	2.8	2.81
p_2	2	2	2	2	2	2
m_1	6000	5882	5555	5025	5005	5000
m_2	4000	3993	3974	3945	3944	3943
s_1	0.667	0.668	0.671	0.676	0.676	0.676
Π_1	213.33	212.95	211.74	209.26	209.16	209.13
Π_2	53.33	52.97	51.98	50.43	50.37	50.36
CS	756.67	757.58	760.08	764.05	764.20	764.24
W	1023.33	1023.50	1023.80	1023.74	1023.73	1023.72

(b) Reciprocal access markup

λ	≥ 0.12	0.11	0.10	0.005	0.001	0
τ	1.5	1.5	1.5	1.5	1.5	1.5
p_1	2.33	2.34	2.39	2.84	2.85	2.86
p_2	2.67	2.67	2.67	2.67	2.67	2.67
m_1	5629	5618	5555	5025	5005	5000
m_2	3267	3266	3263	3238	3237	3236
s_1	0.667	0.667	0.668	0.673	0.673	0.673
Π_1	212.96	212.94	212.80	211.26	211.19	211.17
Π_2	53.33	53.29	53.08	51.28	51.21	51.19
CS	756.58	756.65	757.04	760.24	760.35	760.38
W	1022.87	1022.88	1022.91	1022.77	1022.76	1022.75

however, is that by increasing weight λ the regulator can reduce the distortion of the incumbent's per-minute price, which increases welfare. On the other hand, this increases the entrant's market share, so that more switching costs are incurred by consumers. Arguably, the sum of these two countervailing effects is negligible, so that by choosing λ, while keeping κ constant, the regulator is actually making a roughly welfare-neutral trade-off between consumer surplus and producer surplus. Overall, the effects on market share and welfare are somewhat ambiguous.

3.7.6   Comparison between different versions of price cap regulation

We have seen that a price cap only on the incumbent's subscription fee leads to an increase in the incumbent's per-minute price, and hence distorts individual calling behavior of its customers. A joint price cap (based on a weighted average) reduces this distortion; this is better from a welfare point of view.

Because a joint price cap still leads to some distortion, it is better to combine separate price caps on the incumbent's subscription fee and per-minute price. This also opens up the possibility of putting a price cap on the per-minute price such that the incumbent cannot set its price above true marginal costs. Accordingly, the regulator can stimulate entry by allowing an access markup for the entrant, while avoiding a deadweight loss due to a distortion in calling behavior.

To summarize, retail price regulation can serve two aims: a distributive aim, namely to curb the incumbent's market power and increase consumer surplus; and an efficiency aim, namely to constrain behavior in the retail market so that interventions in the wholesale market do not lead to a welfare loss in the retail market. Increasing the entrant's profits may be motivated both by the distributive aim (so that consumers benefit in the medium to long term) and by the efficiency aim (to the extent that more competition is efficiency enhancing in the medium to long term). A retail price cap on the incumbent's subscription fee clearly cannot achieve this latter aim.

3.8   Summary

The results derived in this chapter were based on a relatively simple, one-period model of facilities-based competition with two competing operators. Although it is a stylized model, it is able to generate several important and robust insights. In the model, each operator has a long-distance backbone and a local access network with complete coverage. The only difference between the operators that we allow for is that the operators may have different initial market shares. In particular, in an infant market, the incumbent has an initial market share of 100 percent, which creates a large advantage because of consumer switching costs.

In the analysis, the operators' profit levels are based on traffic volumes of on-net, off-net, and incoming calls, and their associated traffic-dependent costs, as well as revenues from subscriptions and fixed costs of local connections. The operators maximize profits, and compete by choosing subscription fees and per-minute prices for a given regulatory regime. Regulation is characterized by the level of terminating access prices, and possibly also by price caps in the retail market.

The operators optimally choose per-minute prices equal to their perceived marginal costs, which is the average traffic-dependent cost resulting from on-net and off-net traffic initiated by its customers. They exercise any market power that they may have through their subscription fees. Note that, firstly, an operator's perceived marginal cost level is increasing in the access price it has to pay to deliver off-net calls to its rival's network. Secondly, the smaller the market share of an entrant which has to pay a terminating access price above cost, the larger its perceived marginal cost. The reason is that a large share of the calls made by its customers will be off-net calls.

Concerning terminating access prices, we obtained the following guidelines if the operators compete in two-part tariffs:

- In a mature market, the operators' profits do not depend on the level of the reciprocal access price. (Guideline 3.1)
- In an infant market, a reciprocal access markup reduces consumers surplus and the entrant's profits. In a mature market, it does not affect profits but again it reduces consumers surplus. Thus, reciprocal access prices should be cost-based. (Guideline 3.2)
- In an infant market, an access markup only for the entrant increases consumers surplus and the entrant's profits. (Guideline 3.3)

The nature of price competition crucially affects operators' possibilities to collude through the terminating access price. Whereas negotiated access prices under competition in two-part tariffs do not lead to tacit collusion, this possibility arises under linear prices:

- Suppose that operators compete in linear prices and negotiate reciprocal access prices before setting retail prices. In a mature market, a reciprocal access price can be used as an instrument of tacit collusion. (Guideline 3.4)

Suppose again that operators compete in two-part tariffs. The following guideline deals with retail price caps, that may be useful to restrict the incumbent's market power in an infant market. In particular:

- A price cap on the incumbent's subscription fee can protect consumers from excessive prices. However, such a price cap leads to a distortion in the incumbent's per-minute price, and also reduces the entrant's profits. (Guideline 3.5)

A price cap that pushes down the incumbent's subscription fee indirectly creates downward pressure on the entrant's subscription fee and profits. Accordingly, although price cap regulation can be useful to induce lower retail prices, it makes entry less attractive. On a more general level, price caps that are too low might prevent entrants from investing in local networks. It is therefore important to set the levels of price caps correctly, so that they do not make entry unattractive.

Finally, we formulated a guideline that applies to situations in which asymmetric access price regulation is combined with price caps on the incumbent's retail prices.

- Suppose that only the entrant is allowed to set its access price above cost. A price cap on the incumbent's per-minute price can be used to enforce a cost-based per-minute price. Besides efficient retail prices, this results in an increase in the entrant's profits and consumers surplus, compared with a situation of cost-based access prices. (Guideline 3.6)

Note that the guidelines obtained in this chapter are based on the assumption that there is facilities-based competition in an unsegmented market. In Chapters 5 to 8 we look at different competitive situations. We will see that some guidelines still apply, while others have to be adapted or do not apply at all. In the next chapter, we extend the model of facilities-based competition to a dynamic setting, allowing us to depict, in a more realistic way, the transformation from an infant market to a mature market.

APPENDIX 3.1: PROOF OF PROPOSITION 3.1

See also Laffont, Rey, and Tirole (1998a).

Part 1: Uniqueness of any equilibrium candidate
When both operators are active in equilibrium the system of first-order conditions has to be satisfied. Instead of using variables p_i and m_i, we use the transformation that the operators compete by choosing per-minute prices and consumers net surpluses $v_i = u_i^0 + u[x[p_i]] - x[p_i]p_i - m_i$. This transformation is useful because market shares directly depend on v_i. Without loss of generality we set market size n equal to 1. The corresponding profit functions are denoted by $\widetilde{\Pi}_i[p_1, p_2, v_1, v_2]$, and we define $v_i^g[p_i] \equiv u_i^0 + u[x[p_i]] - x[p_i]p_i$. Then, since $m_i = v_i^g[p_i] - v_i$:

$$\widetilde{\Pi}_i[p_1, p_2, v_1, v_2] = s_i \left((p_i - c_1)x[p_i] + v_i^g[p_i] - v_i - f_i \right)$$
$$+ s_i(1 - s_i)((\tau_i - c_3)x[p_j] - (\tau_j - c_3)x[p_i]).$$

We obtain the following partial derivative:

$$\frac{\partial \widetilde{\Pi}_i[p_i, p_j, v_i, v_j]}{\partial v_i} = \frac{1}{Z} \left((p_i - c_1)x[p_i] + v_i^g[p_i] - v_i - f_i \right) - s_i[v_i, v_j]$$
$$+ \frac{1}{Z}(1 - 2s_i[v_i, v_j])((\tau_i - c_3)x[p_j] - (\tau_j - c_3)x[p_i]).$$

As follows from the first-order condition $\partial \widetilde{\Pi}_i[p_i, p_j, v_i, v_j]/\partial p_i = 0$, the per-minute price is equal to perceived marginal costs in the best response of operator i, that is:

$$p_i[v_i, v_j] = c_1 + s_j[v_i, v_j](\tau - c_3).$$

Substituting the expressions for p_1 and p_2 in the first-order conditions implicitly defines pseudo reaction functions or optimal responses $v_i^* = r_i[v_j]$, taking into account the optimal per-minute prices. An equilibrium is defined by a fixed point of the reaction functions, that is, $v_1^* = r_1[v_2^*]$ and $v_2^* = r_2[v_1^*]$.

Using the implicit function theorem, the pseudo reaction $r_i[v_j]$ can be expressed as:

$$\frac{dr_i[v_j]}{dv_j} = \frac{\dfrac{\partial^2 \widetilde{\Pi}_i[p_i,p_j,v_i,v_j]}{\partial v_i \partial v_j} + \dfrac{\tau_j - c_3}{Z}\dfrac{\partial^2 \widetilde{\Pi}_i[p_i,p_j,v_i,v_j]}{\partial v_i \partial p_i} - \dfrac{\tau_i - c_3}{Z}\dfrac{\partial^2 \widetilde{\Pi}_i[p_i,p_j,v_i,v_j]}{\partial v_i \partial p_j}}{\dfrac{\partial^2 \widetilde{\Pi}_i[p_i,p_j,v_i,v_j]}{\partial v_i^2} - \dfrac{\tau_j - c_3}{Z}\dfrac{\partial^2 \widetilde{\Pi}_i[p_i,p_j,v_i,v_j]}{\partial v_i \partial p_i} + \dfrac{\tau_i - c_3}{Z}\dfrac{\partial^2 \widetilde{\Pi}_i[p_i,p_j,v_i,v_j]}{\partial v_i \partial p_j}}.$$

Market share functions can be written as:

$$s_i[v_i, v_j] = s_i^0 + \frac{v_i - v_j}{Z},$$

so that $\partial s_i[v_i, v_j]/\partial v_i = 1/Z$. We now calculate second-order derivatives:

$$\frac{\partial^2 \widetilde{\Pi}_i[p_i, p_j, v_i, v_j]}{\partial v_i^2} = \frac{1}{Z}\left(-2 - \frac{2}{Z}((\tau_i - c_3)x[p_j] - (\tau_j - c_3)x[p_i])\right),$$

$$\frac{\partial^2 \widetilde{\Pi}_i[p_i, p_j, v_i, v_j]}{\partial v_i \partial v_j} = -\frac{\partial^2 \widetilde{\Pi}_i[p_i, p_j, v_i, v_j]}{\partial v_i^2} - \frac{1}{Z}.$$

Hence, if τ_1 and τ_2 are sufficiently close to c_3 then $dr_i[v_j]/dv_j \approx \frac{1}{2}$. Finally, note that $\partial^2 \widetilde{\Pi}_i[p_i, p_j, v_i, v_j]/\partial v_i \partial p_i$ and $\partial^2 \widetilde{\Pi}_i[p_i, p_j, v_i, v_j]/\partial v_i \partial p_j$ vanish as Z turns to infinity so that one also has $dr_i[v_j]/dv_j \approx \frac{1}{2}$ for Z sufficiently large.

Summarizing, when τ_1, τ_2 are close to c_3 or Z is relatively large, the slope of the pseudo reaction satisfies:

$$0 < \frac{dr_i[v_j]}{dv_j} < 1.$$

Since increasing reaction functions with a slope less than 1 can intersect at most once, there exists at most one equilibrium.

Part 2: Existence of an equilibrium
Operator i maximizes profits Π_i for given prices p_j and m_j. Again, profit functions are transformed to depend on variables p_i and v_i and market size is set equal to 1. For any given v_i operator i chooses p_i optimally so as to maximize profits.

We substitute optimal per-minute prices as depending on v_1 and v_2 into the profit function, which is then denoted by $\widehat{\Pi}_i[v_1, v_2]$ and ask whether an equilibrium exists in the game where each firm chooses v_i and adjusts p_i optimally. Such an equilibrium is also an equilibrium in the original game in which each operator i chooses p_i and m_i. A sufficient condition for existence is that profits $\widehat{\Pi}_i$ are concave in v_i. Note that profits from on-net and off-net calls add up to zero because per-minute prices are equal to perceived marginal costs. Profits can be written as:

$$\widehat{\Pi}_i[v_1, v_2] = s_i\left((p_i - c_1)x[p_i] + v_i^g[p_i] - v_i - f_i\right)$$
$$+ s_i(1 - s_i)((\tau_i - c_3)x[p_j] - (\tau_j - c_3)x[p_i])$$
$$= \left(s_i^0 + \frac{v_i - v_j}{Z}\right) \cdot$$
$$\left(v_i^g\left[c_1 + \left(1 - s_i^0 + \frac{v_j - v_i}{Z}\right)(\tau_j - c_3)\right] - v_i - f_i\right)$$
$$+ \left(s_i^0 + \frac{v_i - v_j}{Z}\right)\left(1 - s_i^0 + \frac{v_j - v_i}{Z}\right)(\tau_i - c_3)x[p_j].$$

Note that $(v_i^g)'[p] = -x[p]$. The first-order derivative is:

$$\frac{\partial\widehat{\Pi}_i[v_1, v_2]}{\partial v_i} = \frac{1}{Z}\left(v_i^g\left[c_1 + \left(1 - s_i^0 + \frac{v_j - v_i}{Z}\right)(\tau_j - c_3)\right] - v_i - f_i\right.$$
$$+ \left(1 - s_i^0 + \frac{v_j - v_i}{Z}\right)(\tau_i - c_3)x[p_j]\right)$$
$$+ \left(s_i^0 + \frac{v_i - v_j}{Z}\right) \cdot$$
$$\left(\frac{\tau_j - c_3}{Z}x\left[c_1 + \left(1 - s_i^0 + \frac{v_j - v_i}{Z}\right)(\tau_j - c_3)\right]\right.$$
$$\left.- 1 - \frac{\tau_i - c_3}{Z}x[p_j]\right),$$

while the second-order derivative can be written as:

$$\frac{\partial^2\widehat{\Pi}_i[v_1, v_2]}{\partial v_i^2}$$
$$= \frac{2}{Z}\left(\frac{\tau_j - c_3}{Z}x\left[c_1 + \left(1 - s_i^0 + \frac{v_j - v_i}{Z}\right)(\tau_j - c_3)\right]\right.$$
$$\left.- 1 - \frac{(\tau_i - c_3)}{Z}x[p_j]\right) + \left(s_i^0 + \frac{v_i - v_j}{Z}\right) \cdot$$
$$\left(-\left(\frac{\tau_j - c_3}{Z}\right)^2 x'\left[c_1 + \left(1 - s_i^0 + \frac{v_j - v_i}{Z}\right)(\tau_j - c_3)\right]\right)$$
$$= \frac{1}{Z^2}\left(- 2Z + 2((\tau_j - c_3)x[p_i] - (\tau_i - c_3)x[p_j])\right.$$
$$\left.- (\tau_j - c_3)^2\left(s_i^0 + \frac{v_i - v_j}{Z}\right)x'[p_i]\right).$$

Clearly, for τ_j close to c_3 (and $\tau_i \geq c_3 - \varepsilon$, ε small) or for Z sufficiently large this second-order derivative becomes negative. This implies that $\widehat{\Pi}_i[v_1, v_2]$ is concave in v_i. $\square$

Part 3: Deviation profits

In our numerical examples (see Tables 3.6 and 3.8), we claimed that we indeed have found equilibria by solving the system of first-order conditions. We will now address this issue.

In equilibrium, each consumer receives some net utility v_i^*. One way to check that we have found an equilibrium is to consider deviations in net utilities using profit functions $\widehat{\Pi}_i[\cdot, v_j^*]$. Equilibrium existence becomes more problematic for a larger access markup. We therefore provide plots for our scenarios with reciprocal and non-reciprocal access markups where this markup is 4.5 euro cents. We only document the situation an infant market, that is, the entrant has an initial market share of zero. Figures 3.1 to 3.4 give the incumbent's and the entrant's profits on the range of net utilities such that market share is between zero and one. As one can see, profits are single-peaked and our solution to the first-order conditions is a global maximizer.

APPENDIX 3.2: NEWTON'S METHOD

We shortly explain the general idea behind Newton's method and then describe how it is applied to finding a Nash equilibrium in our model. For details on Newton's method and other algorithms which might be used alternatively see Judd (1998, p. 103).

Newton's method gives a solution $x^* \in \mathfrak{R}^n$ to the problem $f[x] = 0$. In our application of Newton's method, this corresponds to a system of first-order conditions. To run an algorithm using Newton's method, one has to give a starting value x^0 and a stopping rule for the algorithm to end: to end the

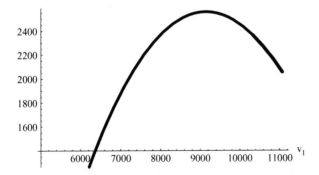

Figure 3.1   Incumbent's deviation profits under reciprocal access prices $\tau = 5$

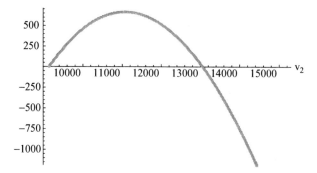

Figure 3.2   Entrant's deviation profits under reciprocal access prices $\tau = 5$

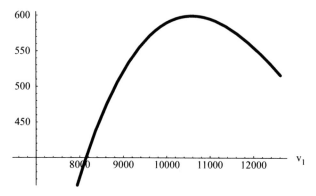

Figure 3.3   Incumbent's deviation profits under non-reciprocal access prices $\tau_1 = 0.5$, $\tau_2 = 5$

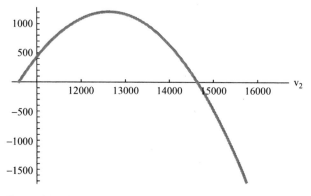

Figure 3.4   Entrant's deviation profits under non-reciprocal access prices $\tau_1 = 0.5$, $\tau_2 = 5$

algorithm a number of maximal iterations K is given; to decide whether the algorithm has converged, one gives an accuracy goal δ for f, such that the solution to the algorithm x^k satisfies $||f[x^k]|| < \delta$ where x^k is the kth iteration of the algorithm. The FindRoot algorithm by *Mathematica* (see Wolfram, 1996), which will be applied, can be described as follows:

> *Initialization* Choose starting value x^0, accuracy goal δ, dampening factor d, and a number of maximal iterations K. Set $k = 0$.
>
> *Step 1* Increase k by 1; determine the step size s^{k-1} according to Newton's method.
>
> *Step 2* Determine new value as $x^k \equiv x^{k-1} + d\,s^{k-1}$.
>
> *Step 3* Check whether the stopping rule is satisfied: go to step 4 if $k = K$ or $||f[x^k]|| < \delta$; return to step 1 otherwise.
>
> *Step 4* If $||f[x^k]|| < \delta$ report "success," otherwise report "failure."

To explain the basic idea behind Newton's method we start with the one-dimensional problem to find a solution $x^* \in \Re^1$ to $f[x] = 0$. In this case, the step size is $s^k = f[x^k]/f'[x^k]$. Clearly, as $f[x^k]$ becomes smaller so does the step size. This makes it possible to converge on a solution.

In the multidimensional setting we are interested in, one has to evaluate a vector $f[x^k] = (f_1[x^k], \ldots, f_n[x^k])$ where $x^k = (x_1^k, \ldots, x_n^k)$ is also an n-dimensional vector. In addition, the matrix of partial derivatives has to be evaluated at x^k. This matrix is denoted by:

$$G[x] = \left(\frac{\partial f_i[x]}{\partial x_j}\right)^n_{i,j=1}.$$

The step size s^k, which is an n-dimensional vector, is then found as a solution to $G[x^k]s^k = -f[x^k]^T$. Under a regularity condition, G can be inverted which gives the step size in each direction. Hence, according to steps 1 and 2, one obtains $x^k \equiv x^{k-1} - dG[x^k]^{-1}f[x^k]^T$.

The iterative process stops if the iterative process gives values of f sufficiently close to 0. A drawback of this FindRoot algorithm is that although the value of f is close to 0, the point x^k at which the algorithm stops may be far away from the unknown x^*. This happens if f is rather insensitive to changes in x at x^k. In order to avoid such a possibility, one should also make a convergence test of the sort that the algorithm only stops if $||x^k - x^{k-1}|| < \varepsilon(1 + ||x^{k-1}||)$, where ε is a stopping parameter. This means that the step size has become very small.

To rule out the drawback of the stopping rule, one can check that $G[x^k]^{-1} f[x^k]^T$ is small when the algorithm stops at x^k. In the simulations in this chapter, we also used an algorithm with this additional check. Since we did not encounter any problems in applying the FindRoot algorithm we decided to restrict ourselves to documenting only those programs which make use of the FindRoot algorithm without further checks.

In our problem of finding a solution to a system of first-order conditions, we work with four-dimensional vectors so that the inversion of the matrix G is rapidly accomplished.[33] We have $x = (p_1, m_1, p_2, m_2)$ as well as $f_1 = \partial\Pi_1/\partial p_1$, $f_2 = \partial\Pi_1/\partial m_1$, $f_3 = \partial\Pi_2/\partial p_2$, and $f_4 = \partial\Pi_2/\partial m_2$.

Mathematica uses the predefined value for the dampening factor $d = 1$, an accuracy goal is predefined as ten digits less the machine precision of the computer (in our case, the latter is sixteen digits). The maximal number of iterations is predefined with fifteen. We did not change these predefined values.

Note that Newton's method only converges on a subset of the set of all possible starting values of the algorithm. Alternatively, using a globally converging algorithm, for instance based on Herings and Peeters (2001), one can guarantee that a solution is always found (see also Watson, 1979).[34]

APPENDIX 3.3: ALTERNATIVE FORMULATION – ASYMMETRIC, DIFFERENTIATED NETWORKS

A different formulation with horizontally differentiated networks leads to the same expressions for market shares and can therefore be used equivalently for the positive analysis. Suppose consumers have ideal points of the network specifications. They are assumed to be uniformly distributed on the $[0, 1]$-interval. Operator 1 is located at $l_1 = 0$, and operator 2 at $l_2 = 1$. Consumer $z \in [0, 1]$ incurs a disutility $-\theta|l_i - z|$, which is linear in the distance between consumer location and the location of the operator. Here, the parameter θ expresses the substitutability between networks: if $\theta = 0$, networks are perfect substitutes; the larger θ the more differentiated networks are. This is the Hotelling specification that has been used by Armstrong (1998) and Laffont, Rey, and Tirole (1998a) on two-way access.

To extend this description of the consumer side, assume that, in addition, there exists a fixed utility for each network that depends linearly on market share. This market share might be realized or initial market share. We consider initial market share, denoted by s_i^0. Formally, denote the fixed utility for an operator serving the whole market by u^1. Then the fixed utility for operator i is of the form $s_i^0 u^1$. Conditional indirect utility of consumer at $z = l_i$ can then be written as:

$$\tilde{v}_i[p_i, m_i] = u_i^0 + s_i^0 u^1 + u[x[p_i]] - p_i x[p_i] - m_i$$

Consumer z subscribes to network i if $v_i[p_i, m_i] - \theta|l_i - z| > v_j[p_j, m_j] - \theta|l_j - z|$. If $u^1 = \theta$, aggregate consumer behavior coincides with the one

---

[33] We also could have solved the maximization problem of $\hat{\Pi}_i$ as defined in Appendix 3.1, so that we would need to consider a system of only two equations. We did not follow this path to find a solution because Π_i can be used directly and can easily be adapted to modifications of the model.

[34] Note also that we were not concerned with minimizing computation time.

derived from the model with switching costs for $Z = 2\theta$. (Note that consumer surplus and welfare do not coincide across the models.)

One justification for a fixed utility that depends linearly on market share is that a larger market share may translate into better services: it may be more convenient to maintain a subscription to a network with a larger market share, for instance because "hotlines" are busy less often (number of inquiries at any point in time can be predicted more accurately for a large operator), service personnel is more readily available, or a service center is in the proximity of the physical location of the consumer. Another justification for a fixed utility that depends linearly on market share is that a larger market share may translate into a better reputation for reliability from the viewpoint of a consumer, more prestige among fellow users, or just the feeling to be "safe" in the big crowd. Similar justifications can be made for an incumbency advantage or disadvantage (see Chapter 4). Asymmetries that are due to differences in fixed utility are explored in detail in de Bijl and Peitz (2001a).

APPENDIX 3.4: NET UTILITIES UNDER ASYMMETRIC ACCESS PRICE
REGULATION

Suppose that the incumbent is subject to cost-based regulation while the entrant is allowed to charge an access markup $\tau_2 \geq c_3$. First consider the entrant's profits while taking into account that the entrant sets its per-minute price equal to true marginal costs c_1. For this we use profits function $\hat{\Pi}_2$, which was defined in Appendix 3.1. Using the notation of Appendix 3.1, marginal profits are:

$$\frac{\partial \hat{\Pi}_2}{\partial v_2} = \frac{1}{Z} \left(v_2^g[c_1] - v_2 - f_2 + \left(1 - s_2^0 + \frac{v_1 - v_2}{Z}\right)(\tau_2 - c_3)x[p_1]\right)$$
$$+ \left(s_2^0 + \frac{v_2 - v_1}{Z}\right)\left(-1 - \frac{\tau_2 - c_3}{Z}x[p_1]\right).$$

We can easily calculate the cross derivative:

$$\frac{\partial^2 \hat{\Pi}_2}{\partial v_2 \partial v_1} = \frac{1}{Z} + \frac{2(\tau_2 - c_3)}{Z}x[p_1] > 0,$$

which implies that the entrant's best response is upward sloping. One also obtains that an increase in the access price τ_2 moves the best response outward as long as the entrant's consumer base remains smaller than the incumbent's consumer base (this implicitly puts a bound on the access markup). This holds because:

$$\frac{\partial^2 \hat{\Pi}_2}{\partial v_2 \partial \tau_2} = (s_1 - s_2)\frac{x[p_1]}{Z^2} > 0 \quad \text{for} \quad s_1 > s_2.$$

Secondly, consider the incumbent's profits. Marginal profits are:

$$
\frac{\partial \hat{\Pi}_1}{\partial v_1} = \frac{1}{Z} \left(v_1^g \left[c_1 + \left(1 - s_1^0 + \frac{v_2 - v_1}{Z} \right) (\tau_2 - c_3) \right] - v_1 - f_1 \right.
$$
$$
+ \left(s_1^0 + \frac{v_1 - v_2}{Z} \right) \left(\frac{\tau_2 - c_3}{Z} x \left[c_1 + \left(1 - s_1^0 + \frac{v_2 - v_1}{Z} \right) \right. \right.
$$
$$
\left. \left. \times (\tau_2 - c_3) \right] - 1 \right).
$$

On a large set of parameter values one obtains that the cross-derivative is positive: $\partial^2 \hat{\Pi}_1 / \partial v_1 \partial v_2 > 0$ is implied by:

$$
Z > 2(\tau_2 - c_3) x[c_1] + (\tau_2 - c_3)^2 \max_{p \in [c_1, c_1 + \tau_2]} |x'[p]|.
$$

Under our parameter constellation, this inequality is equivalent to $\tau_2 < 2.99$. We also obtain on a large set of parameter values that an increase in the entrant's access markup shifts the incumbent's best response outward: $\partial^2 \hat{\Pi}_1 / \partial v_1 \partial \tau_2 > 0$ is implied by:

$$
(s_1 - s_2) x[c_2 + \tau_2] > s_1 s_2 (\tau_2 - c_3) \max_{p \in [c_1, c_1 + \tau_2]} |x'[p]|.
$$

Under our parameter constellation, we find that as long as $s_1 \geq \frac{2}{3}$ the inequality holds for $\tau_2 \leq 11.3$. Reducing s_1 to 0.65 (compare Table 3.8), the inequality holds for $\tau_2 \leq 10.7$.

Summarizing, the upperbound on τ_2 is large so that the result that net utilities are increasing in the entrant's access markup holds for large deviations from cost-based regulation.

4 Facilities-based entry in a non-segmented market

4.1 Introduction

The previous chapter presented the basic model and results based on analysis and simulation in a static context. This chapter introduces dynamics into the model. Operators compete during several periods, which allows us to analyze a telecommunications market from its infancy to its maturity. In this chapter, we look at facilities-based entry (the entrant has a network consisting of a long-distance backbone and a customer access network).

The model used to analyze facilities-based entry is a repeated version of the basic model of Chapter 3. Operator 2 represents, for example:

- an entrant that has built a customer access network similar to the incumbent's network;
- a cable operator that has upgraded its cable network to a two-way communications network;
- an entrant that uses new technology to build a customer access network that is quite different from the incumbent's network, but enables it to deliver similar services (e.g. wireless local loop).

In reality, these types of entrants may have different cost structures. We assume here, as a starting point, that operator 2's network is similar to the incumbent's, and therefore it incurs identical connection-dependent and traffic-dependent costs. Also, we would expect that costs change over time and that, more importantly, there exists uncertainty with respect to future costs. By keeping costs constant over time, we greatly simplify the regulator's problem if it intends to set price caps.

Part of our analysis considers retail price regulation so that the incumbent is subject to a price cap. In this chapter, we consider the following cases of retail price regulation: (i) the regulator imposes a price cap on the incumbent's subscription fee; (ii) the regulator imposes a price cap on the incumbent's per-minute price; or (iii) the regulator imposes both price caps (which are both binding). In this last case, the incumbent's retail prices are fully regulated. The regulatory instruments are summarized in Table 4.1.

Table 4.1 *Regulatory instruments under*
facilities-based competition

Instrument	Description
τ_1	Terminating access price charged by operator 1
τ_2	Terminating access price charged by operator 2
μ	Retail price cap on the incumbent's subscription fee
κ	Retail price cap on the incumbent's per-minute price

In Section 4.2 we present a multi-period extension of the basic model of Chapter 3. It contains a brief explanation about model parameters and regulatory instruments. Facilities-based competition is investigated in the remaining sections. Cost-based access price regulation, discussed in Section 4.3, serves as a point of reference. Sections 4.4 and 4.5 explore the role of reciprocal and asymmetric terminating access prices, respectively. Section 4.6 explores the role of price caps on subscription fees and per-minute prices. Section 4.7 contains an analysis of parameter and model variations. Section 4.8 contains a summary of the chapter.

4.2   Incorporating market dynamics

4.2.1   Motivation

To start with, we explain how we adapt the benchmark model to incorporate market dynamics. Put simply, the one-period model is repeated during a certain number of periods, while in each period initial market shares are updated. This is done by redefining the "new" initial market shares as the realized market shares of the previous period. In this multi-period model, we "repair" the observed outcomes of the basic model in which the entrant gained market share at an unrealistically high speed. The reason for gaining market share at a high speed was that the asymmetry between incumbent and entrant was rather small. A stronger asymmetry results, in particular, from initially bigger fixed utility differences for consumers who decide between the incumbent's and the entrant's network. Such a fixed utility may be related to the experience in the market, approximated by the number of periods the entrant is active, or to market share (see Chapter 3; see also de Bijl and Peitz, 2001a). Here, we add the first formulation. Results on the evolution of prices and market shares would be similar under the second formulation, although effects on consumers surplus and welfare differ somewhat, as explained in Subsection 4.7.2.

The length of a single period in the model can be thought of as the minimum amount of time that operators need in order to adjust their prices. In reality in the market for fixed telephony, it may take about two months for a regulated operator to adapt its prices (one month to get approval from the regulator, and one month to implement the price change).[1] Therefore, it seems reasonable to think of a single period as two months.

We simulate the game with a time horizon of fifteen periods. Because of the considerations above, this corresponds to a time period of (roughly) 2.5 years. We will see in our simulations that within this time frame, the entrant is able to catch up with the incumbent, given that any long-run fixed utility differences between the operators have faded out over the time horizon. Hence, our simulations capture a market from infancy to maturity. In the first periods after entry has taken place, the market will be called an infant market; in particular, this is the case in period 1. In later periods the market matures. When the market is in a situation that initial and realized market share coincide the market is said to be mature.

4.2.2   Repeated short-run profit maximization

To keep the analysis and simulations tractable, we assume that in each period the operators maximize their profits, and consumers maximize utility, of that period only.[2] To do so, we make the following two assumptions: (i) consumers ignore the future lock-in effect of their current decision; (ii) firms ignore the effect of current market share on future profits. Accordingly, market participants are short-sighted in their pricing and consumption decisions.

We believe that the second assumption, in particular, is restrictive; in a fully-fledged model one would incorporate firms maximizing the sum of per-period profits, allowing one to investigate, for instance, the fast build-up of market share at the expense of short-run profits. Nevertheless, the assumption that operators are "myopic" can be motivated by realistic concerns. For instance, investors may implement compensation schemes for managers that result in fast recovery of investments. In addition, a quick turnover of personnel at sales and marketing departments (where pricing decisions are taken) may make it difficult to implement long-term pricing strategies. To the extent that the main asymmetry between incumbent and entrant is the initial lack of a track record of the latter, our qualitative results tend to be independent of the time horizon that operators use in their pricing decisions (see Section 4.7; see also de Bijl and Peitz, 2001a).

---

[1] We maintain the assumption that operators set prices simultaneously. In early periods, in which only the incumbent needs regulatory approval of its retail prices, a Stackelberg model of price competition, in which the incumbent is the first mover and the entrant is the second mover, is an interesting alternative to the model considered here.

[2] The hypothesis that firms' pricing decisions can be modeled as a (one-shot) strategic game has also been made in some of the empirical industrial organization literature, see for instance Berry, Levinsohn, and Pakes (1995).

If one accepts the assumption of short-sighted pricing decisions, one might still argue that our model is not very useful for understanding investment decisions, which are usually driven by medium- to long-term considerations. Nevertheless, the assumptions of a short horizon for pricing decisions and a longer one for investment decisions are only at odds if one views operators as single decision-making units, or if there are no agency problems between investors and managers. In our view, it is acceptable to separate the investment and pricing decisions. This implies that: (i) when making long-run investment decisions, operators take into account how these decisions affect the path of prices that come from short-term profit maximization; and (ii) when making short-term pricing decisions, they take investment decisions as given.[3]

The dynamics in our model are generated by changes of the market asymmetry over time. These changes are partly endogenous and partly exogenous. The endogenous part is due to the change of market share, the exogenous part is due to changes of the consumers' fixed utility generated by the entrant's network.

Consider the endogenous change (in the following subsection we consider the exogenous change). Recall that, in our model, the initial division of the market strongly affects market outcomes. At the beginning of the game, initial market shares are given by the incumbent serving the whole market, that is, $s_1^0 = 1$ and $s_2^0 = 0$. Let s_i^t denote operator i's market share realized in period $t = 1, 2, \ldots$ At the start of each period $t = 1, 2, 3, \ldots$, initial market shares are the realized market shares of the previous period s_i^{t-1}. Initial market shares are updated by defining the "new" initial share as s_i^{t-1} in each period t and for these updated values a new equilibrium is determined.

For the evolution of market shares, we have to consider the realization of the effective switching cost for a customer of type z who previously subscribed to network i. Recall that we assumed that a high initial market share leads to, on average, high switching costs, and that switching costs are distributed uniformly. Furthermore, we assume that consumer types are uncorrelated over time, so that in each period t switching costs for customers of operator i are uniformly distributed on the interval $[0, Zs_i^{t-1}]$.[4]

---

[3] Formally speaking, we split each operator into two players, one player making investment decisions and the other player making pricing decisions.

[4] Klemperer (1987) distinguishes between switching costs as consumer characteristics which are preserved over time and those which are not. The latter are straightforward to work with whereas the former lead to non-existence problems of equilibrium, because for a range of prices, no consumer switches from the incumbent to the entrant. In the latter case, the most loyal customers stay with the incumbent's network; since loyalty is preserved over time, the entrant is more vulnerable because its customers are an easier target. This means that in a model with several entrants, the incumbent could lean back after a while, as all the competition for customers is among the entrants. With our assumptions of switching costs, we exclude such a persistent disadvantage for entrants.

4.2.3   Evolution of the fixed utility levels of a connection

The reader may recall from Chapter 3 (see, for example, Section 3.3) that in
the benchmark model the incumbent's realized market share in equilibrium is
roughly equal to 0.67 for many parameter cases. This phenomenon is due to the
particular way firms compete in the market and due to the fact that in the model,
the entrant could offer the same utility level at the same cost as the incumbent.
Consequently, under price competition the entrant builds up market share pretty
fast. Actually, the operators can be thought of as being "excessively symmetric,"
while, in reality, entrants typically increase quality levels and range of services
over time. In this chapter and the following one (and partly in Chapter 6), we
will preclude this rather extreme result by assuming that, in an infant market,
the fixed utility of a connection at the entrant's network is lower than at the
incumbent's network, and that it increases over time. To do so, we assume that
the potential fixed utility is:

$$u^0 \equiv u_1^0 = u_2^0,$$

and make the actual traffic-independent utility level for the entrant u_2^t dependent
on the period t. As a simple, linear specification we take:

$$u_2^t = u^0 \min\{(t-1), k\}/k,$$

where k is the number of periods needed by an entrant to fully build a "track
record" of quality. After k periods, the entrant has caught up with the incumbent
and operators are symmetric apart from possible differences in their installed
consumer base. In all our simulations, we set k equal to twelve, which corresponds to two years for the entrant to fully build up a track record of quality.
Conditional indirect utility becomes:

$$v_i[p_i, m_i] = u_i^t + u[x[p_i]] - x[p_i]p_i - m_i. \tag{4.1}$$

We refer to this version as the "track record version". Although the updating
of traffic-independent utility may look a bit artificial at first sight, one can
interpret it in several meaningful ways:
- Utility level u_i^t may capture the utility derived from services additional to
  basic telephony (e.g. wake-up calls, information services, voice mail), which
  are of a public good nature for the subscribers of one network. Initially, the
  entrant offers only a limited number of additional services. Over time, it is
  able to introduce more, resulting in an increase of u_2^t. Investments are needed
  to develop such services. The accumulated investment is modeled here as
  proportional to the number of periods in the market (alternatively, it can be

modeled as proportional to the installed consumer base; see Section 4.7.2., see also de Bijl and Peitz, 2001a).[5]

- Utility level u_i^t may capture the utility derived from the quality of service (e.g. accuracy of helpdesk, assistance with problems). As the entrant serves its customers longer, it gains experience in serving these customers. Alternatively, if telephony is a good experience and consumers are risk averse, an operator may gain a reputation for having a reliable network (remember the saying: "Nobody ever got fired for hiring AT&T.").
- Utility level u_i^t may capture the utility derived from the quality of infrastructure (e.g. quality of local connections, sound quality of voice traffic, capacity of switches). Entrants may be quick to roll out networks to offer voice telephony and gain market share, but initially their networks may not satisfy the same quality standards as the incumbent's network. Over time, they improve the quality of their infrastructure.

Let us remark that our assumption on the updating of traffic-dependent utilities allows us to preclude the initial big jump of the entrant's market share observed in the previous chapter. More importantly, this is realized without affecting the qualitative insights of the model. Hence, one can also view this assumption purely as a method of smoothing, carried out to generate a more natural evolution of the market, which can be helpful for presentation and interpretation of the results.

To summarize, we look at telecommunications markets which start with two asymmetries favoring the incumbent:

- switching costs depend on installed consumer base, which the entrant initially lacks;
- the utility from a subscription to the entrant depends on a track record of quality, which the entrant initially lacks.

Either of these two asymmetries on its own would generate some market dynamics. We have chosen to present simulations which incorporate these two asymmetries together (see also Section 4.7.2). The modification of the simulation model is explained in Appendix 4.1.

4.3   Cost-based access price regulation

If terminating access prices are equal to traffic-dependent costs, the operators set per-minute prices equal to true marginal costs and do not make profits on incoming calls. Effectively, the operators compete only in subscription fees. The incumbent initially sets a significantly higher subscription fee than the entrant.

---

[5] If the disadvantage of the entrant vanishes hyperbolically, in our simulations the shape of the evolution of fixed utility is very much the same as the one resulting from using installed consumer base.

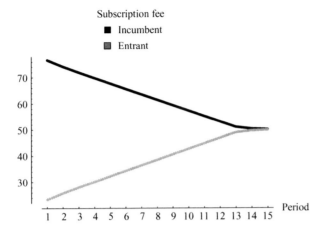

Figure 4.1   Subscription fees under cost-based regulation

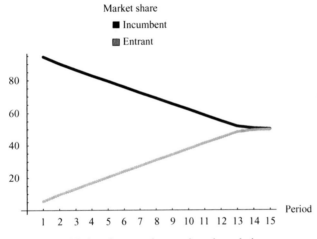

Figure 4.2   Market shares under cost-based regulation

This price differential decreases over time: the incumbent becomes more aggressive as its market share deteriorates, whereas the entrant becomes softer as it gains market share (Figures 4.1 and 4.2). Consequently, the incumbent's profits are decreasing over time, whereas the entrant's profits are increasing. Both profit levels are approaching each other as time goes by and the market matures (Figure 4.3). The kink which can be observed in the time path of the variables in period 13 is due to the fact that by then the entrant has fully built up its track record of quality.

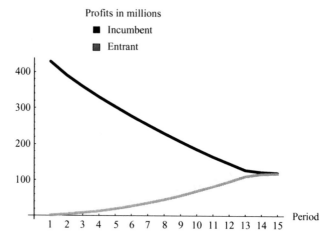

Figure 4.3   Profits under cost-based regulation

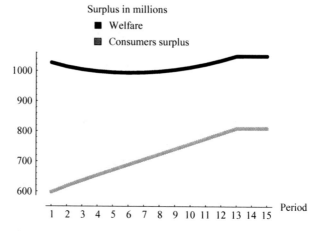

Figure 4.4   Welfare under cost-based regulation

Let us turn to Figure 4.4. As the market matures, competition becomes more intense so that producer surplus is falling. Consumers benefit from more competition. Consumers surplus also changes over time due to:

1. consumers suffering a utility loss when switching operators;
2. the change of fixed utility for consumers switching from the incumbent to the entrant as long as the latter has not fully built up its track record;
3. the change of fixed utility for consumers who are subscribed to the entrant while the entrant is building up its track record.

Since operators compete in subscription fees and usage-based prices are equal to marginal costs, the level of prices does not directly affect welfare. Welfare depends only on the effects 1 to 3 above. If the entrant is gaining market share faster, then the effect of 1 is negative, the effect of 2 is also negative, and the effect of 3 is positive. This explains that welfare is non-constant. As can be seen from the simulation, the negative effects initially dominate and, as the market matures, are dominated by the positive effect (see Figure 4.4).

4.4   Reciprocal terminating access price

The most basic questions in a situation of facilities-based competition concern the level of access prices. These questions include how high they should be, whether they should be reciprocal (i.e., symmetric), whether they should be regulated, and if yes, how. We will first address the level of reciprocal terminating access prices.

Note that the access price of one operator increases the other operator's perceived marginal cost; raising the rival's costs may seem a successful strategy but it is a priori not clear whether this is in the interest of operators, especially if access prices are not set unilaterally but rather through negotiating a reciprocal access price. As we have shown in Chapter 3, operators of equal sizes and with equal market shares do not have an incentive to deviate from reciprocal, cost-based access prices. Because this is efficient from a welfare point of view, regulation may not be needed apart from obliging operators to negotiate the level of the reciprocal access prices; the regulator then only has to step in if negotiation breaks down (see, however, below).

As the market matures, in our simulations[6] a "small" reciprocal access markup does not give rise to big changes in market outcomes compared with a cost-based access price. Profit levels and producers surplus are hardly affected. The main change is distorted per-minute prices, so that consumers surplus and welfare are slightly reduced.

The picture changes if we analyze the whole evolution of the market. Consider an increase in the reciprocal access price above marginal costs. We make the following observations: initially the entrant's market share is slightly reduced. There is a small, positive effect on consumers surplus. Both operators' profits, and therefore also producers surplus, are reduced.

The consequences for welfare, consumers surplus, and the entrant's profits are now analyzed in detail. Notice that from a welfare point of view, the best that can be done (ignoring the social cost of buying from the initially less valuable entrant and of switching) is to set access prices equal to marginal costs. In this case, the operators do not make profits in the wholesale market; they exercise

---

[6] The simulation output is available on the Cambridge University Press Web site, http://uk. cambridge.org/resources/0521808375

market power through subscription fees only. Hence, efficient prices are attained because the demand for subscription is price inelastic.

Higher access prices are transmitted via traffic-dependent costs into per-minute prices, and thus lead to a deadweight loss. Nevertheless, the existence of terminating access revenues makes price competition more intense; even the entrant, in spite of its higher perceived marginal costs, becomes a tougher competitor. The reason is that if an operator reduces its subscription fee to attract a consumer, it also attracts calls from the other network to that consumer. Because of this effect, a marginal consumer is especially valuable for an operator with a small market share. This explains that, in an infant market, we do observe a downward pressure on subscription fees which overcompensates the higher per-minute price that is equal to perceived marginal costs.

In an infant market, consumers benefit from intensified competition; we have checked that consumers obtain higher net utilities under a reciprocal access markup. Therefore, consumers surplus increases in an infant market. With regard to consumers surplus, note that lower switching costs are incurred, because fewer consumers switch and consumers obtain on average a higher fixed utility (because fewer consumers subscribe to the entrant). In our simulations, consumers surplus is maximized over time if reciprocal access prices are relatively large initially, but tend towards cost levels as the entrant gains market share.

In an infant market, the entrant faces a disadvantage: its perceived marginal costs are much higher than those of the incumbent. In fact, the entrant's profits are lower under a reciprocal access markup than under cost-based regulation of the wholesale prices.[7] Hence, the profit neutrality result does not hold in an infant market. In later periods, the effect of access prices on operators' profits vanishes so that the profit neutrality result holds in a mature market (as has been shown in Section 3.3).

Because the entrant initially obtains a smaller market share than under cost-based regulation, the negative effect of a reciprocal access markup on the entrant's profits is propagated into the next period. Therefore, in an infant market, a reciprocal access price above marginal costs slows down the speed and reduces the attractiveness of entry; however, in our simulations this effect was negligible.

> **Guideline 4.1:** Consider facilities-based entry. In an infant market, a reciprocal access markup increases consumers surplus,[8] but it reduces the entrant's market share and profits. In a mature market, it does not affect profits and market shares, but it introduces a deadweight loss in welfare and hence a reduction of consumers surplus. (Adaptation of Guideline 3.2)

---

[7] Since the entrant is at a stronger disadvantage than in the model of Chapter 3, the effect on the entrant's profits is no longer negligible.

[8] This is in contrast to Guideline 3.2 and is explained by the much stronger asymmetry between incumbent and entrant in the present setup (because of the initial lack of the entrant's track record).

Since neither of the operators makes higher profits from a reciprocal access markup, one may conclude that such a situation will not be observed under a wide range of rules according to which the reciprocal access price is set by the operators. For instance, the regulator may allow the incumbent to set a reciprocal access price; this would lead to a cost-based access price.

While it is true that in our model both operators lose from a reciprocal access markup this does not mean that *ex ante* the incumbent cannot gain from such a markup. In particular, if it is known that operators will face a reciprocal access markup (for instance, by including certain fixed costs in a so-called cost-based access price) entry may be deterred. This is clearly in the interest of the incumbent and shows that the regulator has to be careful not to make the reciprocal access prices a commitment device for the incumbent.

4.5   Asymmetric terminating access prices

Dropping the reciprocity requirement with regard to terminating access prices gives the regulator two instruments instead of one in the wholesale market: the regulator sets possibly different access prices for the two operators. It is now possible to give an advantage to the entrant by allowing it a higher access markup. Asymmetric access price regulation is in accordance with the rules set in the European Union (see Subsection 2.2.1). For example, in the Netherlands, the regulator Opta has approved a positive access markup by the entrant, while the incumbent is forced to grant access at cost-based prices.[9]

Consider the effects of an increase in the entrant's terminating access price, while the incumbent's terminating access price is cost based. Again, we view access prices equal to marginal costs as the point of reference.

An increase in the entrant's terminating access price leads to an increase in the incumbent's level of traffic-dependent costs. Therefore, the incumbent increases its per-minute price above true marginal costs and its customers' demand for call minutes decreases. Since, for given market shares, the cost of access increases for the incumbent, it has an incentive to compete more fiercely by reducing its subscription fee. At the same time, increasing its market share is more valuable for the entrant because it also generates profits from terminating access. Thus, both operators price more aggressively.[10] In the simulation reported here, the entrant initially even prices below costs, namely its per-minute price is equal to marginal costs and its subscription fee is below the cost per line (which in the example is 20 euros, compare Figure 4.5). This means that initially the

---

[9] In 1999, the incumbent KPN demanded reciprocity of access prices. It claimed that the entrant Enertel should set cost-oriented prices for access, as KPN was forced to do so. Opta rejected this following European regulation that operators with significant market power have to base access prices on costs, whereas operators without significant market power are only required to set "reasonable" access prices. See Opta (1999).

[10] To make this a complete argument, it has to be checked that operators offer strategic complements.

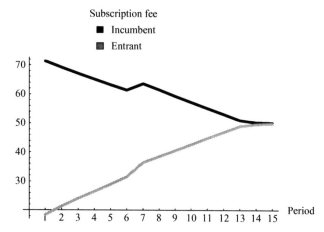

Figure 4.5   Subscription fees under asymmetric access prices (first six periods)

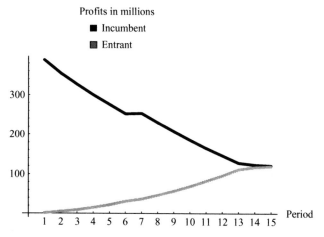

Figure 4.6   Profits under asymmetric access prices (six periods)

entrant makes losses in its retail activities; it only makes profits in its wholesale activities.

More generally, in an infant market an increase in the entrant's terminating access price leads to an increase in the entrant's profits while its market share remains more or less unaffected. This profit increase arises from incoming traffic. The incumbent's profits are reduced. The evolution of profits under non-reciprocal access prices for the first six periods are depicted in Figure 4.6. In an infant market, consumers benefit from this more competitive situation.

An access markup only for the entrant has a strong positive effect on consumers surplus and a strong negative effect on producers surplus. The effect on welfare is negligible in our simulations. To understand this, first observe that, in equilibrium, market shares hardly change so that effects via switching costs and fixed utility levels can be ignored (these effects were explained in Section 4.3). Secondly, welfare is also reduced if per-minute prices deviate from true costs. Because of the asymmetric access markup, the incumbent's perceived marginal costs differ from true marginal costs which, in effect, reduces welfare. However, as the entrant's market share is initially small, perceived marginal costs remain relatively close to true marginal costs, and the welfare effect is small.

Suppose asymmetric access prices are not phased out. As the market matures, the entrant's market share slightly increases and its profits increase substantially, compared to a situation with cost-based access prices. The incumbent's profits are reduced. Moreover, the incumbent's profit reduction roughly equals the entrant's profit increase. In the long run, when the operators are equally large in terms of market share, asymmetric access prices lead to asymmetric profit levels without substantial effects on producers surplus, consumers surplus, and welfare (consumers surplus and welfare are reduced).

Consumers surplus is maximized over time if the entrant's access price is relatively large initially and tends towards its underlying cost level as the entrant gains market share. Access regulation of this type, although it only slightly increases the speed at which the entrant gains market share, is an attractive regulatory policy because it initially skims the incumbent's profits, while increasing the entrant's profits and consumers surplus.

Guideline 4.2: Consider facilities-based entry. In an infant market, an asymmetric access markup only for the entrant increases consumers surplus and the entrant's profits (Reformulation of Guideline 3.3). In a more mature market, it distorts competition (because of a non-level playing field) and it reduces consumers surplus.

Consequently, it is desirable:
- in an infant market: to regulate the incumbent's access price at a level equal to marginal cost and allow the entrant to charge an access markup;
- in a mature market: to regulate both operators' access prices at levels equal to marginal costs.

What is the optimal length of time during which the entrant should be allowed to charge an access markup? To answer this question, one has to assess the trade-off between the beneficial effects on the entrant's profits and the (modest) reduction in social welfare due mainly to a price distortion. An assessment of this trade-off is outside the scope of the model since it depends on the weights the regulator puts on different goals. If the regulator aims at making facilities-based entry attractive, then the optimal length of time will be relatively long, constrained by welfare concerns.

Summarizing, in an infant market, the regulator can use asymmetric regulation of terminating access prices to:

- make facilities-based entry more attractive for the entrant and increase consumers surplus;
- reduce the incumbent's monopoly rents.

In later periods, when competition has matured, we do not see any rationale to deviate from cost-based regulation. Possibly, if reciprocal access prices are freely negotiated between operators, regulation is not needed because operators may settle at cost-based access prices (they are indifferent with respect to the reciprocal access price so that we cannot be sure that they will negotiate cost-based access). Since the outcome of the negotiation depends on the particular model, regulation of the wholesale prices may be necessary even in the long run.

4.6   Retail price caps

4.6.1   Retail price caps and competition

We will focus on retail price caps that are binding for a limited number of initial periods only. Indeed, when the market matures, retail price control should no longer be necessary to prevent the exploitation of market power by the incumbent, and to guarantee reasonable prices for consumers. In an infant market, however, the former monopolist enjoys a very strong and comfortable position which allows it to charge consumers prices which are possibly far beyond those typically needed to recover fixed costs. Therefore, price cap regulation may be desirable in the early stages of competition.[11]

We only consider retail price regulation of the incumbent. Since entry results in more competition and consumers have to be convinced to switch to the entrant, a price cap on the entrant would be rather unusual, possibly eliminating investment incentives at an earlier stage. Also, since the entrant typically has to price more aggressively than the incumbent, a price cap which is binding for the incumbent (i.e., actually holds its prices down) will, in many cases, not be binding for the entrant.

---

[11] This judgement corresponds to regulatory practice. For instance, the UK regulator Oftel states that "retail price controls should be used only where competition is ineffective and is likely to remain that way. In a competitive market, competition would act as a pricing constraint on all players in that market. Price controls would not therefore be necessary. However, price controls may be appropriate if there is insufficient competition to provide a competitive constraint on prices" (Oftel, 2001a).

As in Chapter 3, consider a basket of services that contains the incumbent's connection and a number of call minutes. The regulator imposes a joint retail price cap or separate price caps on the incumbent's per-minute price and subscription fee. We will look at two extreme cases: first, a price cap on the subscription fee; second, a price cap on the per-minute price.

Recall from Chapter 3 that a binding price cap on the subscription fee introduces welfare-reducing distortions on per-minute prices. Hence, if the welfare effect due to this distortion is small, it is necessarily also small in the case of a joint retail price cap.

While a price cap on subscription is motivated by distributive concerns, a price cap on the per-minute price is based on efficiency considerations in our setup. In particular, if true and perceived marginal costs differ, a price cap on the per-minute price can reduce the deadweight loss caused by a price above true marginal costs.

4.6.2   Reciprocal access price and retail price caps

In this subsection, we consider a price cap on subscription fees under reciprocal access prices. We compare the situation with a binding price cap with the situation without. As long as the incumbent's price cap is binding, the incumbent prices more aggressively than in its absence. This results in lower subscription fees combined with higher per-minute prices charged by the incumbent and lower subscription fees by the entrant, as can be seen from Figures 4.7 and 4.8. Hence, both operators suffer from the price cap, while the entrant gains

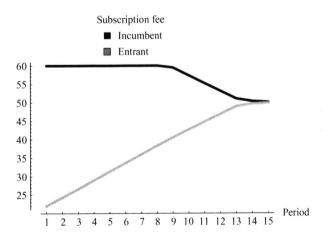

Figure 4.7   Subscription fees under price cap regulation of the incumbent's subscription fee

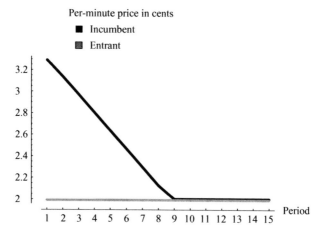

Figure 4.8   Per-minute prices under price cap regulation of the incumbent's subscription fee

market share much more slowly. Therefore, price cap regulation makes entry slower and less attractive, and investment incentives are reduced. On the other hand, price cap regulation can boost consumers surplus in the early stages of competition, when the entrant is still too small to discipline the incumbent. In the light of these results, price cap regulation should be carefully applied in an infant market because the regulator faces a trade-off between the entrant's profits and consumers surplus.

Two additional aspects of subscription fee regulation deserve attention. Firstly, since the entrant gains market share more slowly under a binding price cap on the incumbent's subscription fee, a regulated subscription fee remains longer binding than without such regulation, because the incumbent can more easily exert market power for a longer time if the entrant grows more slowly. As a consequence, the market matures more slowly, which conflicts with the particular regulatory aim of stimulating competition.

Secondly, there is also a trade-off between consumers surplus in an infant market and consumers surplus as the market matures. This can be explained as follows: suppose the price cap is binding in eight periods. Then, in period 9, the entrant's installed consumer base is smaller under regulation of the incumbent's subscription fee than it would be without. This implies that, in period 9, competition will be less intense in the presence of this type of retail price regulation that in its absence. Hence, although subscription fee regulation makes competition more intense in early periods, it does the opposite in the periods when the price cap is no longer binding. This result holds independent of the type of access price regulation that is applied (kept fixed while comparing different price cap regimes). Therefore, this trade-off is also present under asymmetric access price regulation, which is analyzed in the next subsection.

In the long term, a price cap that is not too stringent will no longer bind. Over time, the entrant is able to recover from its initially lower market share. Given that the entrant remains active in the market, there is no harm in the long run. A price cap reduces both operators' aggregate (over time) profit levels. There is a positive effect on consumers surplus and possibly welfare. Welfare increases due to lower aggregate switching costs and fixed utilities (for a discussion of these effects, see Section 4.3). Depending on the parameter constellation, the overall effect on welfare can equally well be negative because a binding subscription fee implies that the incumbent chooses its per-minute price at a higher level above true marginal costs.

We have seen above that a price cap on subscription fee makes the incumbent more aggressive in early periods, thus leading to an increase in consumers surplus in those periods. Such a price cap has a number of negative consequences:
- the entrant makes lower profits, reducing its incentives to enter and to invest;
- the speed at which the entrant gains market share is reduced;
- consumers surplus can be lower in later periods;
- the price cap leads to retail markup of the per-minute price, which generates a deadweight loss.

To summarize, we formulate the following guideline; this is a reformulation of Guideline 3.5 in Subsection 3.7.2:

> **Guideline 4.3**: Consider facilities-based entry. In an infant market, when the entrant is too small to exert substantial competitive pressure, a price cap on the incumbent's subscription fee increases consumers surplus. However, it reduces the entrant's profits, and hence its incentives to enter. (Reformulation of Guideline 3.5)

Note that this guideline was derived under reciprocal access regulation. In the following subsection, we check that it also applies if access prices are non-reciprocal.

4.6.3 Asymmetric access prices and a price cap on subscription fee

Despite its drawbacks, subscription fee regulation (by using a price cap) has its appeal for a regulator, since it is an effective means of reducing prices in the short term. This holds in particular if it is applied together with asymmetric access price regulation, as will be demonstrated in this subsection. Simulations show that asymmetric access and retail price regulation can safely be combined. In particular, the negative effect of a price cap on the entrant's profits, which

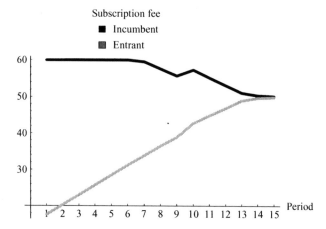

Figure 4.9   Subscription fees under asymmetric access regulation (nine periods) and price cap regulation of the incumbent's subscription fee

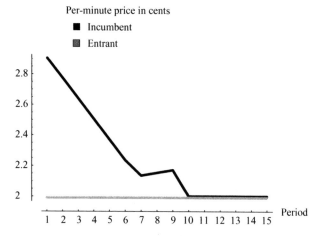

Figure 4.10   Per-minute prices under asymmetric access regulation (nine periods) and price cap regulation of the incumbent's subscription fee

was encountered in the previous subsection, can be diminished by allowing the entrant to charge an access markup. Accordingly, by raising its revenues from incoming traffic, the negative effect on the entrant's profits of more intense competition in the retail market is diminished.

Applying asymmetric access price regulation, for instance, for nine periods gives the entrant an advantage which is reflected in the pricing behavior of both operators. In our simulation (see Figures 4.9 and 4.10), the price cap is binding for the incumbent for six periods. Consequently, the incumbent's per-minute price decreases over time. The subsequent rise until period 9 reflects the increasing perceived marginal costs as the entrant gains market share. As the asymmetric access prices are replaced by cost-based access prices, the incumbent charges a higher subscription fee. For our parameter constellation, the entrant's profits are strictly larger than in a situation with cost-based access pricing (with the same price cap), because of revenues from incoming calls.

Relating our simulation outcomes to the policy guideline in the previous subsection, we remark that the role of retail price regulation does not depend on the level and symmetry of access prices.

4.6.4   Asymmetric access price regulation and a price cap on the per-minute price

As already pointed out in Chapter 3, efficiency concerns may lead a regulator to impose a price cap on the incumbent's per-minute price. A price cap on the per-minute price is possibly welfare enhancing for two reasons:
• perceived marginal costs are not equal to true marginal costs;
• one or both operators set per-minute prices above perceived marginal costs.

This means in particular that the regulator may want to intervene because other interventions (in the wholesale or the retail market) have led to welfare-reducing distortions. Firstly, we have seen that perceived marginal costs do not equal true marginal costs if there exists an access markup.[12] Secondly, we have seen that the incumbent's per-minute price is above perceived marginal costs if the incumbent is subject to a binding price cap on its subscription fee. To start with, we discuss the effects of a price cap on the incumbent's per-minute price in the presence of an access price markup.[13] Next, we consider, in addition, a price cap on subscription fee so that the second welfare-reducing distortion is present.

We will first discuss the case in which the operators set per-minute prices equal to perceived marginal costs, while the incumbent faces a price above marginal costs for terminating traffic on the entrant's network. We already know from the previous subsection that in an infant market, this type of access price regulation stimulates competition and increases the entrant's profits as well as consumers surplus (compared to cost-based regulation). If the regulator now imposes a price cap on the incumbent's per-minute price equal to true marginal cost, the incumbent has to deviate from its individually optimal two-part tariff. Clearly, it will increase its subscription fee to compensate for the loss in profits for off-net calls. The deviation makes the incumbent a less aggressive competitor: an additional consumer is less attractive because of the

---

[12] We do not consider an access price below marginal costs. In this case, the regulator has to set a price floor on per-minute price to achieve per-minute price equaling true marginal costs.

[13] For more details, see also Section 3.7.

loss from off-net traffic. Because of the strategic complementarity relationship, the entrant also prices less aggressively under this regulatory policy in the retail market. Obviously, the entrant's profits increase. Simulations demonstrate that the competitive effect may be so strong that the incumbent's profits also increase.

Apart from the entrant's profits, the regulator is interested in welfare and consumers surplus. Regulation of the per-minute price can eliminate any difference between per-minute price and true marginal costs with the effect of improving welfare. As we have seen, both operators price less aggressively, so do consumers lose? This is not necessarily the case: simulations demonstrate that consumers surplus can increase. This means that the welfare gain from preventing a per-minute price above true marginal costs is split between entrant, incumbent, and consumers. In other words, given an asymmetric access price markup, regulating the per-minute price at the true marginal cost level is a Pareto improvement (i.e., it is beneficial to all parties). We summarize these observations in the following guideline (compare also Subsection 3.7.3).

> **Guideline 4.4**: Consider facilities-based entry. Suppose that there is an asymmetric access markup for the entrant only. In an infant market, a price cap on the incumbent's per-minute price (pushing it down to marginal costs) leads to efficient retail prices, relaxes the intensity of competition, and hence makes entry more attractive. (Reformulation of Guideline 3.6)

We will now briefly discuss the case where the incumbent is already subject to retail price regulation: it faces a binding price cap on its subscription fee. Without a price cap on the per-minute price, as we have seen, the incumbent optimally sets its per-minute price above perceived marginal costs. Hence, under cost-based or reciprocal access price regulation (with a positive access markup), the per-minute price would be above true marginal costs if it was not regulated. The regulator can therefore also put a ceiling on the per-minute price so that it effectively fixes both prices of the incumbent. The entrant simply chooses its best response to the incumbent's regulated retail prices. Clearly, a lower price cap on the per-minute price implies that the incumbent's two-part tariff is more aggressive, so that the entrant makes lower profits.

Furthermore, there is a qualitative difference between the consequences of a retail price cap on the per-minute price depending on the presence or absence of a binding price cap on the subscription fee. If a binding price cap on the subscription fee is already in place, cost-based retail price regulation of the incumbent's per-minute price increases consumers surplus but reduces the entrant's profits.

4.7   Discussion of parameter and model modifications

4.7.1   Asymmetries between incumbent and entrant

In an infant market, existing asymmetries may be more or less pronounced than in our specification and additional asymmetries may exist that we have not considered yet. Here, we address the consequences of such asymmetries.

Switching cost parameter   Recall that parameter Z is a measure of the amount of market power that the operators have, comparable to a parameter of horizontal differentiation. It can be interpreted as the stickiness of market shares. Therefore, an increase in Z softens price competition, resulting in higher profits. More precisely, an increase of switching cost parameter Z:

• does not affect per-minute prices;
• increases both operators' subscription fees;
• increases both operators' profits.

Stronger asymmetries in fixed utilities   If the difference in fixed utility between incumbent and entrant is increased, then the entrant starts in a worse condition. Its market share and profits will therefore be lower. The incumbent gains from this increase by enjoying more market power in the early stages of competition.

Asymmetric traffic-dependent costs   Suppose that the entrant is more efficient in terms of marginal (that is, traffic-dependent) costs than the incumbent, while the reciprocal terminating access price is equal to the incumbent's marginal cost of access. Compared with the situation with symmetric operators at the efficiency level of the incumbent:

• the entrant charges a lower per-minute price, since its average marginal cost is lower;
• the incumbent's per-minute price is not affected;
• both operators set lower subscription fees;
• the incumbent's profits decrease;
• the entrant's profits and speed of entry increase (measured by the growth of market share in early periods);
• consumers surplus increases, while producers surplus is reduced.

Asymmetric connection-dependent costs   Suppose that the entrant is more efficient in terms of traffic-independent but connection-dependent costs than the incumbent. Compared with the situation with symmetric operators:

• per-minute prices are not affected;
• both operators set lower subscription fees;

- the incumbent's profits decrease;
- the entrant's profits and speed of entry increase (measured by the growth of market share in early periods);
- consumers surplus increases, while producers surplus is reduced.

Overall, a more efficient entrant stirs up competition in subscription fees, and increases consumers surplus.

4.7.2   Installed consumer base and fixed utility

In this chapter, we have reported results from the model in which the entrant initially lacks a track record. As an alternative, we also performed simulations in the case where the actual traffic-independent utility u_i^t of both operators depends on the market share of the previous period, that is, the installed consumer base. We refer to this version as the "market share version." In this case, the incumbent's quality parameter decreases as the market matures. With respect to the alternative interpretation as asymmetric, differentiated networks (see Appendix 3.3), this version implies that the asymmetry between the two networks is more pronounced.[14]

In the market share version, both operators' fixed utility levels change over time as they gain or lose market share respectively. This can be expressed as $u_i^t = s_i^{t-1} u^0, i = 1, 2$. Financing the provision of services may be tied to installed consumer base, in which case the incumbent might be forced to reduce the range or quality of services offered as it loses market share. Also, the specification may reflect the fact that consumers learn from others' past experience about which services are available and how they can be used: a larger installed consumer base makes it more likely that they can obtain this knowledge without effort.

Both the track record version and the market share version introduce asymmetries between the fixed utilities of the two networks. However, there are two important differences between the two versions:

- In the track record version, fixed utilities change exogenously, that is independently of past (and present) actions of the operators. In the market share version, fixed utilities change endogenously, that is, prices in period $t - 1$ determine initial market shares in period t, and fixed utilities depend on these market shares.
- In the track record version, a small market share of the entrant while it builds up its track record is beneficial for consumers surplus and welfare. In the long run, fixed utilities do not imply any advantage of monopoly over oligopoly. In the market share version, networks display network externalities. At any

---

[14] Formally, $u^0 + u^1 > Z$. This specification strengthens the network externality (with a lag of one period); in terms of consumers surplus and welfare this stronger network externality would favor a monopoly compared to an oligopoly. In a more general version, one can take the full history of market shares into account.

point in time, fixed utilities imply an advantage of monopoly over oligopoly in terms of consumers surplus and welfare.

Simulation results in the market share version closely resemble the ones derived in the track record version, with the exception that some conclusions concerning the evolution of consumers surplus and welfare have to be modified (see also footnote 14 above).

An additional way to make the incumbent's utility depend on time or market share arises from the hypothesis that the incumbent, a former state-owned monopolist, initially experiences difficulty in adapting to a liberalized environment. Its personnel may not have a clear notion of customers' preferences, and a reorganization may be needed to help them cope with the discipline of the market. One can imagine that this process of restructuring, because of limited span of attention of management and personnel, degrades the incumbent's quality of service. Accordingly, while the incumbent loses market share, its perceived quality level is negatively affected, and it becomes relatively less attractive in the eyes of consumers.

4.7.3   The entrant as a maximizer of market share in early periods

In reality, one may observe that an entrant chooses not to maximize profits in the early periods, but rather to capture as much market share as possible, by choosing prices close to (or below) costs. The purpose of gaining market share quickly is to arrive faster at a situation in which the "standard" level of duopoly profits are realized, that is, the relatively large profits level that an operator enjoys if the market is shared equally. If the entrant's time horizon is long enough, and the incumbent plays its best-response strategy in each period, such a "strategy" may be superior to maximizing per-period profits.

Notice that it is uncertain how the incumbent would react in reality. The incumbent may react aggressively by choosing prices below the myopic profit-maximizing levels as well. Also, the market share maximization strategy is risky in the sense that future expected profits may never be realized. For example, if more (unexpected) entry occurs, future profit levels will be much lower, and the initial losses may not be recovered. Therefore, following the myopic profit-maximization strategy may be a good bet after all.

Summarizing, if the entrant initially maximizes market share, one needs to make an assumption about the incumbent's reaction to such a strategy, and it must be plausible that the entrant will indeed be able to recoup its initial losses by a comfortable duopoly position in the medium and long term.

4.7.4   Operators as intertemporal maximizers

Forward-looking operators should take into account the fact that current market share affects the switching behavior of consumers in the future and is therefore relevant for future profits. We have postulated that operators ignore this effect. Obviously, if firms are only interested in current profits any effects on future profits are irrelevant. In an interior equilibrium in period t the equations $\partial \Pi_i^t / \partial p_i^t = 0$ and $\partial \Pi_i^t / \partial m_i^t = 0$ are satisfied.[15]

If operators are forward-looking they maximize the discounted sum of profits $\psi_i[p_i^t, p_j^t, m_i^t, m_j^t; s_i^{t-1}] \equiv \sum_{s=t}^{\infty} \delta^{s-t} \Pi_i[p_i^s, p_j^s, m_i^s, m_j^s; s_i^{s-1}]$. Future profits in periods $t+1, t+2, \ldots$ depend on current prices through the market share in period t. We can rewrite $\psi_i[p_1^t, p_2^t, m_1^t, m_2^t; s_i^{t-1}] = \Pi_i[p_1^t, p_2^t, m_1^t, m_2^t; s_i^{t-1}] + \delta \psi_i[p_1^{t+1}, p_2^{t+1}, m_1^{t+1}, m_2^{t+1}; s_i^t]$. In an interior solution with forward-looking operators, the following first-order conditions of profit functions have to be satisfied:

$$
\underbrace{\frac{\partial \Pi_i[p_1^t, p_2^t, m_1^t, m_2^t; s_i^{t-1}]}{\partial p_i^t}}_{+/-} + \delta \underbrace{\frac{\partial \psi_i[p_1^{t+1}, p_2^{t+1}, m_1^{t+1}, m_2^{t+1}; s_i^t]}{\partial s_i^t}}_{+} \underbrace{\frac{\partial s_i^t}{\partial p_i^t}}_{-} = 0,
$$

$$
\tag{4.2}
$$

$$
\underbrace{\frac{\partial \Pi_i[p_1^t, p_2^t, m_1^t, m_2^t; s_i^{t-1}]}{\partial m_i^t}}_{+/-} + \delta \underbrace{\frac{\partial \psi_i[p_1^{t+1}, p_2^{t+1}, m_1^{t+1}, m_2^{t+1}; s_i^t]}{\partial s_i^t}}_{+} \underbrace{\frac{\partial s_i^t}{\partial m_i^t}}_{-} = 0.
$$

$$
\tag{4.3}
$$

As indicated in the equations a higher present market share is unambiguously positive for future profits. This implies that one must have $\partial \Pi_i^t / \partial p_i^t > 0$ and $\partial \Pi_i^t / \partial m_i^t > 0$ in an interior equilibrium with forward-looking operators.

Intuition suggests that operators price more aggressively than under myopic decision making because market share is valuable for the future. This intuition is correct if operator i's more aggressive pricing that is due to an inclusion of future profits is not outweighed by the cumulative reactions of the two operators to this more aggressive two-part tariff. This holds, for instance, if access prices are close to the corresponding marginal costs (see Appendix 4.2 for a formal analysis). If this intuition is correct, a regulator which presumes that operators act myopically in their pricing decisions underestimates consumers surplus if operators are, to some extent, forward-looking.

While consumers benefit from one or both operators taking future profits into account, an entrant finds it more difficult to achieve a certain level of profits in a market in which both operators are forward-looking than in one in which they are myopic.

---

[15] This subsection is adopted from de Bijl and Peitz (2001a).

With forward-looking operators, asymmetric access price regulation improves the profits of the entrant and thus stimulates competition; this is the same qualitative result as in Section 4.5. Since a higher symmetric discount factor reduces the entrant's profits (at least around $\delta = 0$), asymmetric access price regulation seems even more appropriate in the case where the regulator expects operators to be likely to include future profits in their current pricing strategies.

4.8 Summary

The duopoly model of facilities-based competition, presented and analyzed in Chapter 3, was extended to a repeated setting in this chapter. This allowed us to depict, in a more realistic way, the transformation process of an infant market into a mature market. In each period, the operators maximize their profits based on their market shares in the previous period. Market shares change gradually because there are consumer switching costs, and also because the entrant has to build up a track record before its reputation and quality level are at the same level as the incumbent's.

We formulated several guidelines on terminating access prices, and how they can be optimally regulated in different phases of the market. Note that, in an infant market, the advantage of the incumbent over the entrant is twofold: the incumbent starts with a large customer base; and customers enjoy a larger fixed utility level when subscribed to the incumbent (since the entrant lacks a track record). Although a reciprocal access markup may seem fair at first sight, it increases the entrant's perceived marginal cost above the incumbent's perceived marginal costs, due to the entrant's small market share. On the other hand, asymmetric access prices can give the entrant an advantage. They can be useful for stimulating competition in an infant market (as we have also seen in Chapter 3):

- In an infant market, a reciprocal access markup increases consumers surplus, but it reduces the entrant's market share and profits. In a mature market, it does not affect profits and market shares, but it introduces a deadweight loss in welfare and hence a reduction of consumers surplus. (Guideline 4.1)
- In an infant market, an asymmetric access markup only for the entrant increases consumers surplus and the entrant's profits. In a more mature market, it distorts competition (because of a non-level playing field) and it reduces consumers surplus. (Guideline 4.2)

It does not seem likely that free negotiation of access prices between a dominant incumbent and a small entrant will result in optimal access prices. Consequently, regulation of access prices will typically be needed. Because optimal access prices change over time, it is important that the regulator announces the price path at an early stage and credibly commits to it.

With regard to retail prices, the following guidelines were obtained:
- In an infant market, when the entrant is too small to exert substantial competitive pressure, a price cap on the incumbent's subscription fee increases consumers surplus. However, it reduces the entrant's profits, and hence its incentives to enter. (Guideline 4.3)
- Suppose that there is an asymmetric access markup for the entrant only. In an infant market, a price cap on the incumbent's per-minute price (pushing it down to marginal costs) leads to efficient retail prices, relaxes the intensity of competition, and hence makes entry more attractive. (Guideline 4.4)

Hence, subjecting the incumbent to price cap regulation may be useful in an infant market, although the entrant's short-term prospects deteriorate. Therefore, price cap regulation should be only temporary, and operators should be able to form expectations about the length of time that it will apply. Early announcement by the regulator, combined with credible commitment, is vital. Moreover, combined with asymmetric access price regulation, a price cap is an effective tool for controlling the incumbent's market power in an infant market. It can achieve the entrant's profits in the market being at least as high as under cost-based regulation, while consumers surplus is increased.

As in the previous chapter, we note that the guidelines obtained here are based on the assumption that there is facilities-based competition in an unsegmented market. Some of these guidelines may not apply, or simply are not relevant, in other entry situations. Other ways to enter the market may arise if the incumbent's local loop is unbundled, or if the incumbent sells originating access to entrants. These entry modes are explored in the next chapter.

APPENDIX 4.1: MODEL ADAPTATION

Compared to the one-period model in Chapter 3, the model introduces a fixed-utility asymmetry between incumbent and entrant as explained in Section 4.2. Starting values in each period t are given by realized market shares in period $t - 1$. Otherwise, the model is identical to the one-period model in Chapter 3.

Simulations   Numerical simulations are carried out with the parameter constellations in Chapter 3. The access markup in our simulations is chosen to be equal to 0.5 euro cents.

APPENDIX 4.2: INTERTEMPORAL MAXIMIZATION AND MONOTONE COMPARATIVE STATICS

The intuition that operators price more aggressively than under myopic decision making, because market share is valuable for the future, can be shown to be correct in the neighborhood of cost-based regulation around $\delta = 0$. To make the argument, we check for two sets of properties. Firstly, equations (4.2) and

(4.3) (in Subsection 4.7.4) translate into:

$$\frac{\partial^2 \psi_i \left[p_1^t, p_2^t, m_1^t, m_2^t; s_i^{t-1} \right]}{\partial p_i^t \partial \delta} < 0,$$

$$\frac{\partial^2 \psi_i \left[p_1^t, p_2^t, m_1^t, m_2^t; s_i^{t-1} \right]}{\partial m_i^t \partial \delta} < 0.$$

Secondly, under cost-based regulation operators set per-minute prices equal to true marginal costs along their best responses so that we only have to consider subscription fees as strategic variables. Similar to Section 3.5.1, it can be shown that:

$$\left. \frac{\partial^2 \Pi_i \left[p_1^t, p_2^t, m_1^t, m_2^t; s_i^{t-1} \right]}{\partial m_i^t \partial m_j^t} \right|_{p_1^t = p_1^{t*}, p_2^t = p_2^{t*}, m_1^t = m_1^{t*}, m_2^t = m_2^{t*}} > 0.$$

Hence, under cost-based regulation networks are strategic complements in a neighborhood around an equilibrium, given $\delta = 0$.[16] This property also holds in a neighborhood around $\delta = 0$. (For this, note that profits functions are thrice continuously differentiable.) By these two sets of properties, one obtains monotone comparative statics in δ under regulation that is close to cost-based regulation for a discount factor close to 0.[17] We find that m_1^t and m_2^t are decreasing in δ for δ close to 0, formally $dm_i^{t*}(\delta)/d\delta < 0$. Consequently, if operators take future profits into account, competition is more intense and consumers benefit.

---

[16] The relationship between the two networks is one of strategic complementarity if incremental profits increase when the competitor increases the value of its strategic variable. This implies that best responses are upward sloping, a property that holds in many price competition models in which products are not perfect substitutes.

[17] The (local) monotone comparative statics property follows from the theory of supermodular games (see Milgrom and Roberts, 1990; Vives, 1990). In our model, the corresponding properties are satisfied on a product of intervals which has the (locally unique) equilibrium in its interior.

5 Non-facilities-based entry in a non-segmented market

5.1 Introduction

Whereas the previous chapter explored facilities-based entry, in this chapter we examine two alternative modes of entry, namely:

1. local-loop-unbundling-based entry: the entrant has a network consisting of a long-distance backbone, and leases local lines from the incumbent;
2. carrier-select-based entry: the entrant has a network consisting of a long-distance backbone, and serves end users through originating access to the incumbent's customer access network.

Taken together with facilities-based entry analyzed in the previous chapter, these three modes of entry represent the range of levels of investment required for entry in the market, going from entry that requires the largest investments in the local loop, to an entry mode that is relatively easy. Correspondingly, we speak of facilities-based competition (FBC), local-loop-unbundling-based competition (LLU), and carrier-select-based competition (CSC). Thus, instead of the duplication of the local loop under FBC, there can be unbundled or resale-based access to the local loop. In each case, the regulatory instruments that apply in that situation will be analyzed. Note that FBC is a situation of two-way access, whereas CSC is a situation of one-way access. Concerning the subscription of consumers, LLU is also a situation of one-way access (with regard to unbundled access to the local loop) but, for given consumer subscriptions, it is a situation of two-way access (with regard to terminating access to end users). The regulatory burden is larger in the case of LLU and CSC than in the case of FBC. Hence, although the duplication of the local loop leads to higher sunk costs, which in itself reduces welfare, such investment may be socially beneficial when accounting for the social costs of more invasive regulation under CSC and LLU. The regulator, analyzing the desirability of different entry modes, can influence investment incentives through regulation. By comparing the three situations, conclusions on entrants' incentives to invest in a network can be drawn, depending on the different regulatory variables.

Table 5.1 summarizes the important characteristics of the three different modes of entry. In all these entry modes the entrant has at least a long-distance

Table 5.1 *Modes of entry*

	Facilities-based competition	Unbundling-based competition	Carrier-select-based competition
Elements of entrant's network	• backbone • customer access network	• backbone	• backbone
Entrant's access to end users	• direct access (consumers can subscribe) • terminating access (off-net calls)	• direct access (consumers can subscribe) • terminating access (off-net calls)	• indirect access (consumers cannot subscribe) • terminating access (all calls) • originating access (carrier select)
Relevant wholesale prices	• terminating access prices	• terminating access prices • line rental	• incumbent's terminating and originating access prices
Other relevent details			• possibility of capacity shortage of carrier-select service

network at its disposal. For example, a carrier-select entrant (usually) only has a long-distance backbone. In reality, though, this need not even be the case, as entrants may lease lines from the incumbent.[1] The table does not depict entry by entrants which do not own any infrastructure at all but offer communications services through resale only. The existence of pure resellers may seem odd at first sight, but resellers can make profits from arbitrage opportunities between substantial wholesale discounts and large retail markups, or from targeting a market niche and offering specialized services (see Laffont and Tirole, 2000). As long as entrants lease long-distance capacity from the incumbent, the analysis still applies, although it ignores regulation or negotiations between operators about the terms of these agreements.

Section 5.2 investigates LLU. It explores the role of the lease price of the incumbent's local line, and retail price regulation. The third entry situation, CSC, is the subject of Section 5.3. The section starts with an analysis of retail price regulation, and regulation of originating and terminating access prices. Next, it explores capacity shortages of the carrier-select service, and the way they interact with price caps. Section 5.4 discusses the incentives for network investment. The last section contains a summary of the chapter.

---

[1] An example of an operator that is active with minimal network investment is Tele2, active in, among other countries, the Netherlands. Tele2 leases lines from KPN and thus, to a large extent, operates as a pure reseller.

Table 5.2 *Regulatory instruments under LLU*

Instrument	Description
τ_1	Terminating access price charged by operator 1
τ_2	Terminating access price charged by operator 2
μ	Retail price cap on the incumbent's subscription fee
l	Lease price of local line (line rental)

5.2   Local loop unbundling

Under local loop unbundling (LLU), an entrant gains access to the local line through the main distribution frame (see Chapter 2), sometimes also denoted by "copper loop rental." This type of access is often considered as the most relevant type of access to stimulate competition. Under main distribution frame access, a connection to a customer of the incumbent, which consists of a local line (the connection to the customer up to and including the main distribution frame) and a linecard (part of the local switch), is unbundled. Hence, an entrant can "plug in" by creating a link from its switch to the incumbent's main distribution frame, allowing for access to the transmission medium in the local loop. The entrant gets access to the incumbent's "raw copper," but still has to provide a transmission system. Therefore, the entrant incurs a traffic-independent cost, in addition to the line rental it has to pay to the incumbent.

LLU makes it possible for the entrant to operate its own transmission system to provide access, and to take over the incumbent's subscriber. Appendix 5.1 contains a description of the details of the model of LLU.

The central question in a situation of LLU is the level of the lease price of the incumbent's local line. Table 5.2 lists the regulatory instruments which we consider.

5.2.1   Cost-based regulation

Cost-based regulation under LLU means that access prices are equal to marginal costs and the lease price is equal to the fixed cost of the local line. Retail prices then are the same as under FBC. Consequently, neither market shares nor profits gross of fixed costs are affected. European legislation requires that the price for unbundled access be based on costs.[2] Compared to FBC, society saves on the duplication of the local loop which is reflected in a higher producers surplus net of fixed costs.

---

[2] See European Parliament and Council (2000); see also European Commission (2000a).

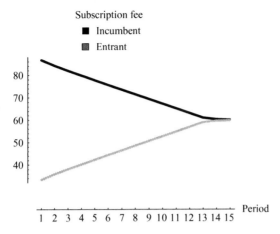

Figure 5.1   Subscription fees with lease price above costs

5.2.2   *Lease price of the incumbent's local line*

The higher the lease price of the incumbent's local line is, the larger is the traffic-independent cost of a connection incurred by the entrant. The entrant faces a higher traffic-independent cost (due to the higher lease price), but is able to pass this cost increase on to end users. Both operators' subscription fees increase by the same amount as the lease price. This is depicted in Figure 5.1 (for a lease price markup of 10 euros), which can be compared with Figure 4.1. As long as no price caps are effective, per-minute prices are equal to perceived marginal costs, which are not affected by the fixed cost of connections.

An increase in the lease price of the incumbent's local line has the following consequences:

• the incumbent's profits increase;
• the entrant's market share and profits are not affected;
• consumers surplus is reduced, while welfare remains constant.

The crucial observation is that a line rental markup reduces the intensity of competition in the retail market. A markup leads to a *transfer from consumers to the incumbent operator*. Similarly, a lease price of the local line below cost makes competition more intense: it is, effectively, a transfer from the incumbent to consumers, which is neutral for the entrant.

A persisting lease price above costs creates a long-term asymmetry between incumbent and entrant. In particular, profits of incumbent and entrant do not converge; see Figure 5.2.

The conclusion for policy is straightforward. If feasible, setting the lease price below the local line's fixed cost is the best for consumers, because it is transmitted one-to-one into lower subscription fees. Nevertheless, it may not

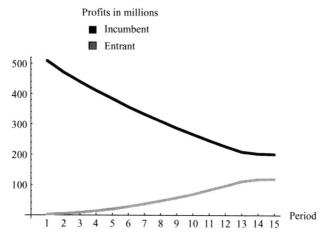

Figure 5.2   Profits with lease price above costs

be possible or desirable to force the incumbent to supply at a price below cost. It may not be possible because it has been politically agreed that the incumbent should be able to recover its connection-dependent costs through the lease price. It may not be desirable because it may lead to underinvestments in maintenance and upgrading of the local loop. To maximize consumers surplus under this constraint, it is best for consumers surplus to set the line rental equal to the traffic-independent cost of the local line.

> **Guideline 5.1:** Consider unbundling-based entry. In an infant and a mature market, a cost-based lease price allows the incumbent to recover its connection-dependent costs. Under the constraint that the lease price has to recover these costs, a cost-based lease price maximizes consumers surplus. A lease price below costs can (temporarily) be used to increase consumers surplus (at the cost of the incumbent's profits).

5.2.3   Asymmetric access price regulation

In a situation of LLU, the main effects of access price regulation are similar to those in a situation with facilities-based entry (see Section 4.5). Nevertheless, we will see that there is an additional benefit of asymmetric regulation of access prices. The negative effect on consumers surplus of a line rental markup encountered in the previous subsection can be compensated for by allowing the entrant to charge an access markup in the early stages of competition.

5.2.4   Price cap on the subscription fee

As we already know from Section 4.6, consumers surplus can be increased by subjecting the incumbent's retail prices to price cap regulation. In a situation of LLU, the main effects are similar to those described in a situation with facilities-based entry. Nevertheless, the level of the price cap on the incumbent's subscription fee may need to be adjusted to account for the competition-reducing effect of a line rental markup.

If there is a line rental markup, then a price cap on the incumbent's subscription fee reduces the markup's harm to consumers. As with facilities-based entry, both operators' profits decrease, so that price cap regulation should be applied with care.

Given that the incumbent is subject to a certain price cap regime, an increase of the lease price of the local line has the following consequences:[3]
- the incumbent's profits and market share increase;
- the entrant's profits and market share decrease;
- consumers surplus decreases (although not as much as in the case without price cap regulation), and welfare also decreases.

Hence, if the incumbent's retail prices are also regulated, the policy implication is straightforward. To maximize consumers surplus, it is optimal to set the line rental equal to (or even below) the fixed cost of the local line. Hence, the guideline that the lease price of the incumbent's local line should be cost based in the long run also holds if the incumbent's subscription fee is constrained by a price cap.

5.2.5   Combined access and retail price regulation of the incumbent

To illustrate how regulatory instruments can be applied together in a sensible manner, we consider the following combination of regulatory instruments:
- the lease price of the incumbent's local line is initially below cost for several periods, and equal to cost later on;
- only the entrant is allowed to charge an access markup, but only in the early stages of competition;
- the incumbent's subscription fee is subject to a price cap, which is binding in an infant market.

A low lease price increases consumers surplus at the expense of the incumbent's profits. The access mark-up tips competition in favor of the entrant, limiting the detrimental effect for the entrant of intensified competition due to the price cap. In our simulation, the asymmetric access prices apply for nine periods and the low lease price for six periods. The price cap on the subscription fee turns out to be binding for the incumbent for four periods. This is reflected

---

[3] Our simulation outcomes show this. They are available on the Cambridge University Press Web site, http://uk.cambridge.org/resources/0521808375.

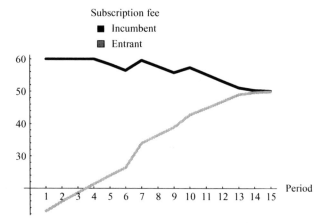

Figure 5.3   Subscription fees under combined regulation

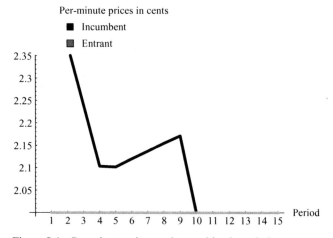

Figure 5.4   Per-minute prices under combined regulation

by subscription fees and per-minute prices (see Figures 5.3 and 5.4). The incumbent's profits reflect the loosening of the regulatory policy as time passes (see Figure 5.5). In particular, the lease price below cost regulation expires after period 6 and the higher access price of the entrant after period 9.

In this environment, the entrant gains market share more slowly in the first three periods. This is good for welfare because of the strong low fixed utility of the entrant's network in initial periods.[4] As Table 5.3 shows, a regulator which

---

[4] Note that this result depends on time-dependent fixed utility. It would not hold if the fixed utility was time independent (but linear in market share).

Table 5.3 *Cost-based versus combined regulation*

	Cost-based regulation	Combined regulation
Consumers surplus (period 1)	597.4	684.9
Consumers surplus (periods 1–15)	10790.0	11281.5
Entrant's profits (periods 1–15)	810.0	827.4
Social welfare (periods 1–15)	15249.0	15256.9

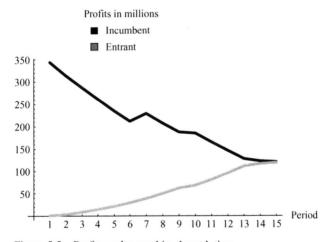

Figure 5.5   Profits under combined regulation

aims at high consumers surplus, welfare, and entrant's profits can improve on cost-based access price regulation by using the combined regulatory policy.

5.3   Carrier-select-based competition

Suppose that the entrant only has a long-distance backbone but no customer access network. In such a situation, an alternative to direct access to end users through an unbundled local loop is indirect access. The most common form of indirect access is originating access to end users: consumers select an alternative carrier by dialing a (usually four-digit) prefix before entering the phone number of the person they want to call. This situation is known as "carrier-select- based" competition (CSC).[5] In contrast to FBC and LLU, which consider two-way access, CSC is a situation of one-way access where the incumbent remains the bottleneck owner. Without access at a sufficiently low access price, entry is not worthwhile under CSC.

The model of competition between a facilities-based incumbent and a carrier-select-based entrant is described in Appendix 5.2. An important detail of the model concerns retail prices. Since the entrant's customers keep their subscription to the incumbent, the entrant only charges a per-minute price p_2. The incumbent, as before, charges prices m_1 and p_1.

5.3.1   The incumbent's market power

Carrier select, and more general situations of one-way access, may give rise to "price squeezes" (see Oftel, 2000f). In general, if a vertically integrated incumbent is dominant in the wholesale market and supplies key inputs (originating and terminating access) to an entrant in the retail market, the incumbent may be tempted to abuse its dominant position. In particular, the incumbent could increase the entrant's cost of access or reduce its per-minute price in the retail market (or do both). The effect would be to reduce, or even eliminate, the entrant's profit margin. If the regulator cannot perfectly observe the incumbent's cost levels, the incumbent may try to hide such a price squeeze by allocating to its wholesale activities costs that are actually incurred as a result of its retail activities. Accordingly, in practice the risk of a price squeeze is closely linked to information asymmetries, which are not present in our model. This provides a strong argument in favor of access price regulation and a careful evaluation of cost data provided by the incumbent.

A consumer who selects the entrant to carry their calls keeps their subscription to the incumbent operator. Moreover, they continue to enjoy the connection-dependent utility of the incumbent's network. Because all consumers, including those that use the carrier-select service, subscribe to the incumbent, its subscription fee must be regulated.

> **Guideline 5.2:** Consider carrier-select-based entry. To protect consumers from excessive prices, the incumbent's subscription fee has to be regulated.

---

[5] The analysis also applies to "carrier-preselect," which means that consumers have to enter the prefix code only once, instead of each time they want to make a call. It can be argued that carrier-preselect helps to create a level playing field in that it eliminates the systematic disadvantage of an entrant under carrier-select that consumers always have to dial more numbers. Translated into our model, this means that carrier-preselect is likely to increase the fixed utility of the entrant compared to carrier-select.

Table 5.4 *Regulatory instruments under CSC*

Instrument	Description
τ_1	Terminating access price charged by operator 1
δ_1	Originating access price charged by operator 1
μ	Retail price cap on the incumbent's subscription fee
κ	Retail price cap on the incumbent's per-minute price

Without regulation, the incumbent would set its subscription fee at the monopoly level. In our simulations, we set the regulated subscription fee at its cost level; for our qualitative results, it is important that the regulated subscription fee is lower than the subscription fee that would result if the incumbent was not constrained in its pricing behavior.

Table 5.4 contains the possible regulatory variables in the case of CSC. It includes the possibility of putting a price cap on the incumbent's per-minute price. Such a (binding) price cap may be desirable if the incumbent enjoys excessive markups in the retail price in the absence of such regulation.

5.3.2   Cost-based originating and terminating access prices

From closer inspection of the operators' profit structure (see also Appendix 5.2), it is clear that it is the sum of the incumbent's originating and terminating access prices, $\delta_1 + \tau_1$, that affects the outcomes, and not the individual access prices δ_1 and τ_1. The reason is that for any call made by a customer of the entrant, both access prices must be paid to the incumbent by the entrant. We can therefore focus on the "total access markup" charged by the incumbent, which is the sum of the originating and terminating access markups $(\delta_1 - c_{13}) + (\tau_1 - c_{13})$. This access markup is zero if regulation is cost based.

Following Guideline 5.2, the incumbent's subscription fee has to be regulated because there is no competition for subscription. Restricted in its pricing, the incumbent exerts its market power through its per-minute price. Hence, the incumbent's per-minute price is necessarily distorted away from marginal costs.

Since the entrant can only make profits from setting its per-minute price above marginal costs, the entrant's per-minute price will also always be distorted away from costs so that both per-minute prices are distorted even under cost-based regulation (in contrast to FBC and LLU). Consequently, since there are consumer switching costs, both operators enjoy some market power, so that per-minute prices above perceived marginal costs can be sustained in equilibrium. In order to build up a subscriber base to its carrier-select service, the entrant

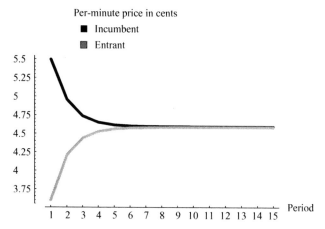

Figure 5.6   Per-minute prices under cost-based regulation

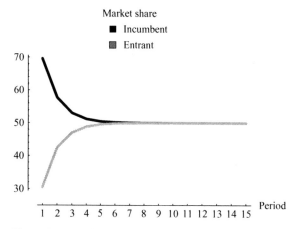

Figure 5.7   Market shares under cost-based regulation

must initially price more aggressively than in later periods; the reverse holds for the incumbent (see Figure 5.6).

If the price cap on the subscription fee is equal to the connection-dependent but traffic-independent cost, and access prices are cost based, the entrant does not suffer any long-run disadvantage. Its profits will catch up with the incumbent's profits as it gains a subscriber base over time (see Figures 5.7 and 5.8). To the extent that CSC limits the asymmetry between operators, an entrant can easily gain market share under cost-based regulation so that the incumbent's retail price is pushed away from the monopoly price towards the duopoly price.

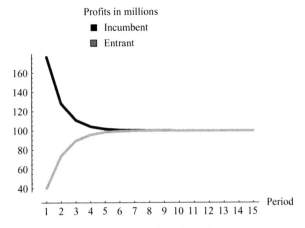

Figure 5.8   Profits under cost-based regulation

Compared to the FBC and LLU modes of entry, the entrant gains market share very rapidly in our simulations under CSC. This is due to the fact that under CSC, there is no need for the entrant to build up a track record of quality. This allows it to attract consumers much more easily.

Note that in our simulations, we keep the level of switching costs constant across modes of entry. In reality, they are likely to be lower under CSC than under FBC or LLU. Lower switching costs would put more pressure on prices than in the simulations reported here.[6]

5.3.3   Access markup

In the case of CSC, the effects of access markups are different from its effects in situations of FBC or LLU. The reason is that an operator which only offers carrier-select services, but does not own or lease local lines to have direct access to consumers, has to pay the incumbent for access but does not receive any access revenues itself. Because of this asymmetry, the entrant suffers from high access prices.

An access markup creates an asymmetry between incumbent and entrant which does not vanish in the long term. Namely, an increase of the total access markup increases the entrant's traffic-dependent cost. Hence, from the

---

[6] In the extreme case that switching costs (and differences between operator due to product differentiation arising from bundled services) are absent, both operators are Bertrand competitors. In this case, cost-based terminating and originating access would achieve non-distorted per-minute prices. In the case of cost differences between operators, per-minute price equals $2c_{13} + \max\{c_{14}, c_{24}\}$, where c_{i4} is the marginal cost of the backbone (for more details, see Subsection 2.3.2).

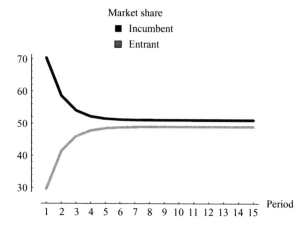

Figure 5.9   Market shares with an access markup

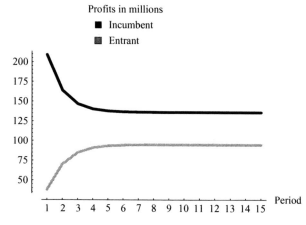

Figure 5.10   Profits with an access markup

incumbent's viewpoint, an access markup *raises the rival's cost*, and thus softens price competition in the retail market. In particular, a higher access markup has the following consequences:

• the incumbent's market share and profits increase;
• the entrant's market share and profits decrease;
• consumers surplus and welfare decrease.

The effects of access markups on market shares and profits are depicted in Figures 5.9 and 5.10. In order to maximize welfare and consumers surplus (under the constraint that the access price covers the incumbent's marginal costs in the wholesale market), there should not be any access markup, that is, the originating and the terminating access price should be set equal to marginal costs.

> **Guideline 5.3**: Consider carrier select-based entry. In an infant and a mature market, cost-based originating and terminating access prices maximize consumers surplus and welfare.

It is implicit in the guideline above that the regulator is able to clearly distinguish between the incumbent's upstream and downstream costs, so that only the traffic-dependent cost of local connections is taken into account. If this is not the case, the risk of a price squeeze becomes larger (see the discussion in the introduction of this section). Moreover, this guideline may need to be modified if there exist alternative modes of entry and regulatory policy is aimed at establishing effective competition in the long term (see Section 5.4).

5.3.4 *Price cap on the incumbent's per-minute price*

Initially, the incumbent enjoys a strong market position because the entrant has to build up a consumer base. A price cap on its per-minute price can be used to limit the incumbent in exercising market power for some initial periods. For the price cap to become non-binding after some periods, it has to be set above the duopoly price.

Surprisingly, in some periods when the price cap is still binding the incumbent may enjoy higher profits than in the absence of the price cap. This can be understood as follows: since the incumbent is forced to be aggressive, the entrant gains a subscriber base more slowly. In some periods, the positive effect on the incumbent's profits due to a larger installed base may overcompensate the negative effect due to more aggressive pricing.

The direct gains in consumers surplus that result from a price cap on the incumbent's per-minute price can be substantial. Unambiguously, the entrant suffers from a price cap. Therefore, the regulator must take into account the fact that a price cap increases the risk of a price squeeze, which would be harmful for consumers in the longer term, given that it may reduce entrants' profits and induce them to exit the market.

5.3.5 *Price cap and access markup*

If there is a positive total access markup (i.e., in the originating or the terminating access price charged by the incumbent), then price cap regulation of the incumbent's per-minute price can alleviate the problem of a reduced intensity

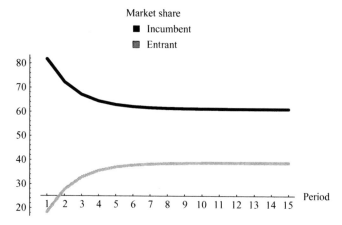

Figure 5.11   Market shares with price cap and access markup

of competition. In particular, the regulator can use such a price cap to prevent retail prices being raised by the operators, or even to restore retail prices to the level that would prevail if there was no access markup. Nevertheless, such a policy may have undesirable side effects, as discussed below.

Consider a price cap set at the level of the long-run competitive level if the total access markup equals zero. Compared to the situation without a price cap but with a positive access markup, we observe that:

- the incumbent's profits are lower in an infant market, but higher in a mature market;
- the entrant's profits decrease;
- the entrant's market share decreases;
- consumers surplus and welfare increase.

The evolution of market shares and profits is depicted in Figures 5.11 and 5.12. Notice that the price cap alleviates the harm of an access markup to consumers and social surplus. Side effects are that the speed of entry is reduced, that the entrant remains smaller in the long term, and that the entrant's profits are substantially reduced. Note also the positive effect on the incumbent's profits in the long term. The reason is that the price cap reduces the entrant's long-term market share. Hence, as the incumbent loses less market share in the long term if it is subject to a price cap, its net revenues from on-net calls increase.

The implication for policy is straightforward. A price cap on the incumbent's per-minute price may prevent an access markup softening competition in the retail market, but it seriously harms the entrant and the development of competition (recall also our earlier remarks on the risk of a price squeeze). It is

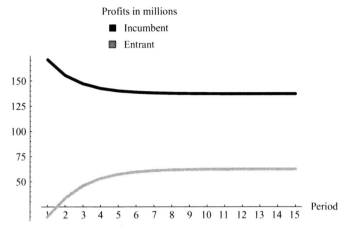

Figure 5.12   Profits with price cap and access markup

therefore better to prevent an access markup in the first place, than to try to repair its detrimental effect on consumers surplus with a price cap.

5.3.6   Capacity shortage of carrier-select service

Often an incumbent operator has limited capacity in its relevant switches or points of interconnection to provide originating access to carrier-select operators.[7] To take this into account, let us assume that there is a small probability, which is exogenous and denoted by α, that a consumer who tries to make a call through carrier-select experiences the capacity shortage. If that happens then, although the called party is not busy, the consumer gets the busy tone and a connection is not established. We suppose that they then use their regular subscription to the incumbent to make the desired phone call. Note that if α is exogenous, an additional call through carrier-select does not increase the probability that other consumers cannot establish a connection. Assuming that α is exogenous reduces the complexity of the analysis while still delivering useful insights.[8]

---

[7] Capacity shortages are especially relevant in the light of the substantial growth in Internet traffic; see, for example, Oftel (2000e).

[8] If the probability that a consumer does not get a connection through carrier-select, α, is endogenous (that is, the entrant buys a fixed capacity) and if consumers experience a disutility from not establishing the connection, then: (i) a per-minute price of the entrant equal to true marginal costs is not equal to the true marginal *social* cost because the social cost that stems from the negative externality on other consumers that use carrier-select is not included; and (ii) the true marginal social cost depends on the total number of calls made through carrier-select.

A consumer who selects the entrant to carry their call but does not get a connection, can at no cost switch back to the incumbent: they just have to dial again, but this time without the carrier-select prefix. In reality, however, a consumer who does not get the quality they expect from the carrier-select service, may get irritated. If they are not aware of the fact that it is the incumbent's limited interconnect capacity that caused the problem, there may even be a negative repercussion on the entrant's reputation. We have not incorporated the possibility of consumers' dissatisfaction in the model. It will turn out, however, that the policy conclusions would only be strengthened by incorporating consumers' dissatisfaction.

How does limited capacity for originating access influence competition? Compared to the case $\alpha = 0$, a capacity shortage of the carrier-select service (i.e., an increase in α) turns out to have the following consequences, which are independent of the level of the incumbent's access prices:
- both operators' profits increase;
- consumers surplus and welfare decrease.

To illustrate this, profits for the case $\alpha = 0.10$, while access prices are cost based, are depicted in Figure 5.13. For comparison, we note that without a capacity shortage, long-run profits would be around 100 for each operator. The reason that the incumbent, as well as the entrant, benefits from a capacity shortage is that it softens price competition. The entrant faces a softer competitor and can therefore increase its per-minute price. In turn, the price pressure faced by the incumbent is reduced. The situation is similar to a duopolistic market in which one of the firms is a passive shareholder of a competitor, so that lost sales hurt less because part of the profits of the competitor belong to this firm.

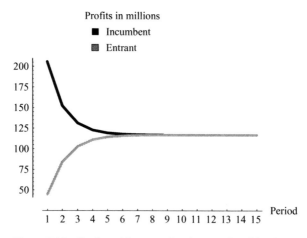

Figure 5.13   Profits with a capacity shortage faced by the entrant

> **Guideline 5.4:** Consider carrier-select-based entry. A capacity shortage in the carrier-select service (in the incumbent's point of interconnection) softens price competition so that consumers surplus is reduced. It also slows down the growth of the entrant's market share.

5.3.7   Capacity shortage and price cap

Can a price cap on the incumbent's per-minute price alleviate the harm of a capacity shortage to consumers and social surplus? Suppose that there is no access markup, and consider a price cap set at, say, the incumbent's per-minute price that would result in the long run if there is no capacity shortage and no price cap on per-minute price. Compared with the situation without a price cap, simulations show that:

- both operators' profits decrease;
- the entrant's market share decreases;
- consumers surplus and welfare increase.

Accordingly, the price cap alleviates the harm of a capacity shortage to consumers and social surplus. A side effect is that the speed of entry is reduced, and the entrant remains smaller in the long term. This happens because the price cap is so severe that it is below the incumbent's unrestricted long-run per-minute price under a capacity shortage. Market shares and profits in our simulations are depicted in Figures 5.14 and 5.15.

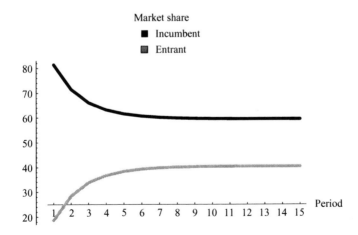

Figure 5.14   Market shares with a capacity shortage and price cap

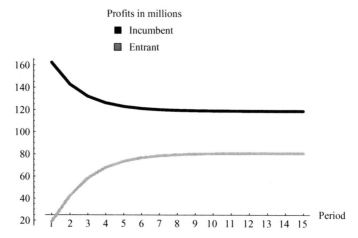

Figure 5.15   Profits with a capacity shortage and price cap

It may also be interesting to compare the situation without a capacity shortage and without a price cap with the situation with a capacity problem and price cap regulation. The main observation is that the incumbent benefits from a capacity shortage and that the entrant is worse off (in terms of profits and market share). Recall from Subsection 5.3.6 that without a price cap, the entrant also benefits from a capacity shortage. Thus, without such a price cap, *both* operators may have an incentive to maintain the capacity shortage, so that the industry itself will not hurry to take care of the capacity problem. If such a price cap is in place, then at least the carrier-select operator will try to exert pressure on the incumbent or the regulator to take action.

The overall conclusion from this and the previous subsections for policy is that to maximize consumers surplus and welfare, the regulator should force the incumbent to provide sufficient capacity for access to its network. In this subsection we have seen that as long as there is still a capacity problem, a price cap on the incumbent's per-minute price can prevent consumers surplus being reduced.

> **Guideline 5.5:** Consider carrier-select-based entry. Given that there is a capacity shortage in the carrier-select service (in the incumbent's point of interconnection), a price cap on the incumbent's per-minute price helps to prevent the softening of price competition that is due to the capacity shortage. However, a price cap reduces the entrant's profits, and hence its incentives to enter.

Above, we only addressed the problem of a capacity shortage in the incumbent's network that affects the carrier-select entrant in need of originating access. If there were more general capacity shortages, for instance directly affecting both operators, the problem would be of a different nature.[9]

5.3.8 Pure resale

In the entry modes analyzed above, the entrant has its own backbone at its disposal. Alternatively, as pointed out in Section 5.1, the entrant may sign a lease contract that allows it to use part of the total capacity of the incumbent's backbone during a certain period. It then effectively acts as a pure reseller. To the extent that the associated fees that are paid by the entrant are fixed, the earlier results of this section apply if the entrant gains access to the local loop through resale. Accordingly, the results of Section 5.2 apply if the local loop is unbundled.

In this subsection, we take a short look at pure resale, that is, a reseller offers local or long-distance telephony by buying retail services at wholesale prices and selling them on to end users.[10]

Although contracts to lease long-distance capacity constitute fixed costs, to the extent that additional capacity can be purchased by the reseller such contracts influence retail pricing. In this case, a reseller pays a usage-based fee for the use of the incumbent's backbone.

A pure reseller requires access to all parts of the incumbent's network, namely to the incumbent's customer access network (terminating and originating access) as well as to the incumbent's backbone. If the use of the incumbent's long-distance network for other purposes than network interconnection and call termination is not regulated, then the incumbent will only sell wholesale capacity if it is in its own interest. There may be several reasons why this may be the case. Firstly, the incumbent may have spare capacity in its backbone, and insufficient marketing resources to generate sufficient traffic to fill up its capacity. Secondly, entrants may contribute to overall market growth, because they pursue aggressive marketing campaigns, develop new services, and therefore trigger consumers to use more services. Thirdly, since the incumbent is typically not allowed to price discriminate, selling wholesale capacity to an

---

[9] We do not consider such a problem here. In that case, each call leads to a negative externality on all other consumers. Per-minute prices should then reflect this disutility imposed on other consumers, so that socially optimal per-minute prices would be above true marginal costs c_1.

[10] In the United States, regulatory policy intends to encourage competition through resale. According to the US Telecommunications Act of 1996, "local exchange carriers have the duty not to prohibit, and not to impose unreasonable or discriminatory conditions or limitations on, the resale of its telecommunications services." *Incumbent* local exchange carriers have, in addition, the duty "to offer for resale at wholesale rates any tele-communications service that the carrier provides at retail to subscribers who are not telecommunications carriers."

entrant which then targets a specific segment may implicitly enable the incumbent to implement a targeted strategy. This may be in the interest of both the incumbent and the entrant, at least as long as the entrant does not compete with the incumbent head-on. Actually, these three reasons may also be relevant in cases where backbone capacity is sold to entrants on a different basis than per minute.

Under pure resale we can treat the incumbent's network as a single essential facility. Under two-part tariffs, the incumbent sets its per-minute price equal to its costs c_{11} if it is not restricted in the choice of its subscription fee. Abstracting from costs such as billing which may be incurred by the reseller, the incumbent is then indifferent between carrying the call out itself and offering a call minute wholesale to the reseller at price c_{11}. To the extent that the reseller but not the incumbent can bundle additional services or target particular consumers, resale is beneficial to all market participants. The incumbent's retail per-minute price is equal to marginal costs; in the retail market it exerts its market power through the subscription fee. Given an access charge equal to marginal costs, the entrant will set its retail price above cost if its service is an imperfect substitute to the incumbent's service.

Suppose the incumbent is free to choose the wholesale price. Then it will set it above marginal costs which leads to lower profits for the entrant and lower consumers surplus.

To stimulate resale-based competition, the regulator may want to intervene in the wholesale market by imposing rules on access to the local loop and to the backbone. The analysis is then in line with the earlier analysis of carrier-select-based competition except that access to the backbone also has to be regulated.

5.4   Investing in infrastructure

5.4.1   Comparing different entry modes

Comparing different entry modes entails an evaluation of their relative attractiveness in terms of profit levels, while taking into account the necessary investments (see also Chapter 9). The attractiveness of a particular entry mode is typically influenced by regulation. In order to draw conclusions about the entrant's incentives to roll out a customer access network, we will compare the results, especially how well the entrant is doing in terms of aggregate profits over time, in the situations of:

• facilities-based competition (FBC) (Chapter 4);
• local-loop unbundling-based competition (LLU) (Section 5.2);
• carrier-select-based competition (CSC) (Section 5.3).

Recall that in the previous sections, implications for policy and regulation were valid given the entry situation. Nevertheless, if one compares the three entry situations in order to assess the possibilities for stimulating a specific type of entry, the implications for policy and regulation may be different.

The entrant's aggregate profits during the periods in which the operators compete, net of any fixed cost of investment associated with a particular entry strategy, give an indication of the entrant's incentives to choose that strategy and incur the associated investment cost. Reasonable values of these investment costs should reflect that the fixed cost of FBC entry is much larger than the entry cost under LLU, which is in turn larger than the entry cost of a carrier-select operator. Since it is difficult to calibrate the costs of investment for our models, we have not attached specific values to these cost levels. Instead, the relative attractiveness of an entrant's investment choices will be discussed in a qualitative manner.

Within the framework of the models, it is in principle possible to obtain any outcome by conditional regulation. For example, if a regulator favors FBC over LLU, it can impose a tight price cap regime conditional on LLU entry taking place, while allowing higher prices under FBC entry. In reality, though, there is a large variety of entrants, so that FBC, LLU, and CSC take place simultaneously. Therefore, conditional regulation may neither be feasible nor desirable. In the comparisons of different entry modes below, we will take this practical restriction into account.

5.4.2   *Facilities-based versus unbundling-based entry*

Terminating access prices play the same role in FBC as in LLU. We therefore abstain from discussing access price regulation as an instrument for influencing entry choices. Because, in the case of LLU, an increase in the lease price of the local line results in an increase in both the incumbent's and the entrant's subscription fee, we focus on the role of the lease price in combination with the possibility of a price cap on the incumbent's subscription fee.

Firstly, suppose that the lease price of the incumbent's local line is equal or close to its fixed cost. Ignoring the investment cost of building a customer access network, the entrant would be indifferent between FBC and LLU. Hence, the large investment cost that is needed to roll out a customer access network tilts the balance towards LLU.

Next, suppose that the lease price of the incumbent's local line includes a markup. If, in a situation of LLU, the incumbent's subscription fee is not subject to a price cap, an entrant can pass on the markup on the lease price to consumers by increasing its subscription fee. Therefore, again the large investment cost that is needed to roll out a customer access network tilts the balance towards LLU.

The picture may change if the incumbent's subscription fee is subject to a price cap. Now, in a situation of LLU, an entrant may not be able to pass on a markup in the lease price of the local line to consumers. Accordingly, a lease price above cost in combination with a price cap regime makes building a customer access network relatively more attractive for the entrant, compared to leasing local lines from the incumbent.

In a situation of LLU, the simulations indicate that a lease price above cost, in combination with price cap regulation, decrease an entrant's profits to only a limited extent. Thus, according to the models, it seems unlikely that regulation of the lease price and price cap regulation are very effective if one wants to give an entrant incentives for network investment, and to create a bias towards FBC.

In our model, we assumed that LLU does not restrict the entrant in terms of quality or services offered, compared to the incumbent. Therefore, given proper policy and regulation, it does not matter for consumers surplus whether FBC or LLU occurs. In reality, though, technological restriction imposed by the particular way in which local loops are unbundled, may hamper an entrant wishing to offer innovative services over the network, and therefore may provide incentives for rolling out its own customer access network. In market segments in which the duplication of the local loop seems desirable the regulator can impose a "sunset" clause with the effect that the lease price will no longer be cost based after a certain number of periods.[11] Hence, the entrant can directly access consumers and has to pay only a lease price equal to costs for a certain number of periods, during which it can start rolling out its own customer access network.

The argument in favor of FBC becomes stronger if the entrant has lower costs than the incumbent had in building up a customer access network, or if the quality improvement is significant compared to LLU. If the entrant can offer higher quality customer access, a commitment to a lease price above costs may increase the incentive for the entrant to choose FBC. The reason is that it creates an additional source of profits for the entrant (because of the possibilities of leasing local lines to the incumbent or other competitors).

5.4.3   Carrier-select-based entry versus entry with direct access to the local loop

Access prices play a different role in CSC than in FBC and LLU. The reason is that in CSC only the incumbent charges an access price, while an entrant depends on the incumbent's local loop to have access to end users. This dependency implies that terminating access prices above cost hurt a carrier-select entrant more than they hurt an entrant that owns or leases a customer access network.

---

[11] For example, the Dutch regulator Opta uses such a sunset clause in the regulation of tariffs for unbundled access to KPN's local loop; a review is however possible (see Opta, 2001).

Consequently, a lenient policy on terminating access prices creates a bias away from CSC.

Another obvious way to make either building or leasing local lines more attractive for the entrant compared to offering carrier-select services, is to have a high originating access price. Also, a price cap on the incumbent's per-minute price, while keeping capacity shortages of carrier-select intact, creates a bias away from CSC.

If there are no capacity shortages, then CSC may, in the short term, result in a larger consumers surplus than FBC or LLU. Hence, it is beneficial for consumers to stimulate CSC in the short term. Under CSC, a heavy-handed regulatory policy seems necessary. This implies regulatory costs and possibly efficiency losses. In order to reduce or even to abandon regulatory interventions in the long term without damaging competition, it may be desirable that entrants get direct access to end users, by FBC or LLU. In this case, policy should discourage CSC relative to FBC or LLU in the longer term. This suggests that an attractive regulatory environment for CSC should be provided with a sunset clause.

5.5   Summary

Whereas Chapters 3 and 4 explored facilities-based competition, this chapter looked at alternative entry modes, based on local loop unbundling and carrier-select. Since these entry modes give rise to different access issues, additional wholesale prices were introduced, with new implications for regulation.

Firstly, consider unbundling-based entry. Note that an entrant leasing the incumbent's local connections is able to offer the same type of subscriptions to consumers as the incumbent does. Consequently, the entrant not only needs terminating access to the incumbent, but also vice versa. Hence, with regard to terminating access prices, the situation is similar to facilities-based competition (see Chapters 3 and 4 for regulatory guidelines on terminating access prices). Accordingly, the main regulatory variable that has not been addressed in previous chapters is the lease price of the incumbent's local loop. In fact, the incumbent's local connections to end users are an essential facility if an entrant wants unbundled access. Allowing the incumbent to include a markup in the line rental is beneficial only for the incumbent, while market shares are not affected and consumers surplus is reduced. Therefore:

- In an infant and a mature market, a cost-based lease price allows the incumbent to recover its connection-dependent costs. Under the constraint that the lease price has to recover these costs, a cost-based lease price maximizes consumers surplus. A lease price below costs can (temporarily) be used to increase consumers surplus, although at the cost of the incumbent's profits. (Guideline 5.1)

Price cap regulation has the same qualitative effects as in the case of facilities-based competition. If there is a lease price markup, however, a given price cap regime is more stringent compared to facilities-based entry. Moreover, price cap regulation can, to some extent, reduce the detrimental effect on consumers surplus of an increase of the lease price.

Secondly, consider carrier-select-based entry. Now the entrant cannot offer subscriptions to consumers as the incumbent does. Consumers who choose to make calls through the entrant's backbone have to keep their subscription to the incumbent. The entrant is able to offer telephony to its customers only if it has originating and terminating access to the incumbent's subscribers. However, the incumbent does not need to buy any input from the entrant, even with regard to calls terminating to the entrant's customers (since they still subscribe to the incumbent). Because of the strong asymmetries between an incumbent and a carrier-select entrant, not only originating and terminating access prices but also the incumbent's subscription fee need regulatory attention:

- To protect consumers from excessive prices, the incumbent's subscription fee has to be regulated. (Guideline 5.2)
- In an infant and a mature market, cost-based originating and terminating access prices maximize consumers surplus and welfare. (Guideline 5.3)

In some countries, carrier-select operators have had experience of the incumbent having insufficient capacity for interconnection with its competitors. The first guideline below demonstrates that, somewhat surprisingly, this might be in the interest not only of the incumbent, but also of entrants. The second guideline suggests a possible short-term remedy, which can be applied as long as the incumbent's capacity has not yet been expanded.

- A capacity shortage in the carrier-select service softens price competition so that consumers surplus is reduced. It also slows down the growth of the entrant's market share. (Guideline 5.4)
- Given that there is a capacity shortage in the carrier-select service, a price cap on the incumbent's per-minute price helps to prevent the softening of price competition that is due to the capacity shortage. However, a price cap reduces the entrant's profits, and hence its incentives to enter. (Guideline 5.5)

Thus, although a capacity shortage of the carrier-select service slows down the growth of the entrant's market share, it reduces the entrant's profits only if the incumbent's per-minute price is subject to a price cap. Furthermore, the incumbent has strong incentives to maintain the capacity shortage. Taking into account that consumers will experience dissatisfaction from failed connections, capacity shortages should be minimized.

Note that the guidelines obtained in this chapter are based on the assumption that either there is local-loop unbundling, or there is carrier-select-based competition. That is, they take a particular type of entry as given, and do not address the entrant's choice for a particular entry mode. Also, both entry situations were explored in an unsegmented market. They need not apply in different settings, such as a segmented market with targeted or mixed entry (see Chapter 8).

By comparing facilities-based competition, local loop unbundling, and carrier-select-based competition, one can assess the relative attractiveness of each entry mode. The long-term goal of reducing the active role of the regulator may be a reason to favor facilities-based competition and local loop unbundling over carrier-select-based competition, or even to prefer facilities-based competition over unbundling of the local loop (in the longer term). Although facilities-based competition involves a duplication of network investments, it creates a level playing field between incumbent and entrants in the absence of regulatory intervention.

Temporary biases towards certain types of entry can be introduced by using sunset clauses. To create a bias towards facilities-based entry and away from local loop unbundling, the regulator can set the lease price of the local loop above costs (in combination with a binding cap on subscription fee), at least when entrants with unbundled access have gained substantial market share and confidence to start rolling out their own networks. It may, however, be desirable to avoid lease price markups immediately after liberalization, when the purpose is to stimulate any type of competition. Furthermore, note that access prices above marginal costs hurt a carrier-select entrant (which does not collect any access revenues) more than entrants that build or lease local networks. Therefore, a commitment to eliminate cost-based originating access at some point in time may be a means to stimulate carrier-select entrants to invest in networks. Note that such a policy does not have to interfere with regulation of terminating access prices (of the type discussed in Chapters 3 and 4).

In this and the preceding chapters, most attention was paid to competition in two-part tariffs. The next chapter considers alternative modes of price competition.

APPENDIX 5.1: LOCAL LOOP UNBUNDLING

Operator 2 only has a long-distance backbone. To have access to end users, it can lease operator 1's local line at a monthly rental l, while incurring a fixed cost for a linecard. A connection in the incumbent's customer access network comprises the local line and the line card. The associated fixed costs satisfy:

$$f_1 = f_1^{\text{local-line}} + f_1^{\text{linecard}}.$$

If operator 2 rents a local line from the incumbent, a wire is diverted from the incumbent's local switch to a plant provided by operator 2, instead of to operator 1's main distribution frame. Hence operator 2 incurs a fixed cost f_2^{linecard}.

The lease price of operator 1's local line is denoted by L. Operator 1's traffic-independent revenues become:

$$n\, s_1(m_1 - f_1) + n\, s_2\left(l - f_1^{\text{local-line}}\right),$$

while operator 2's traffic-independent revenues become:

$$n\, s_2\left(m_2 - l - f_2^{\text{linecard}}\right).$$

The remaining parts of the profit function coincide with those for facilities-based competition (see Chapter 3).

Simulations   The only additional parameter specification which is needed is the split of the fixed costs f_1 into its two parts. We chose $f_1^{\text{local-line}} = 1000$ and $f_1^{\text{linecard}} = f_2^{\text{linecard}} = 1000$. All other parameter values are as in Chapter 3.

APPENDIX 5.2: CARRIER-SELECT-BASED COMPETITION

Operator 2 only has a long-distance backbone. To have access to end users, it uses originating access via a carrier-select service. Operator 1's originating access price is denoted by δ_1. Operator 2's traffic-dependent cost of its backbone is denoted by c_{24}.

Consumers who select operator 2's network to carry their calls, keep their subscription to the incumbent. Therefore, they can continue to enjoy the fixed utility of having a connection to operator 1's network u_1^0.

Furthermore, we assume that a consumer who wants to use carrier-select has to register with the operator that offers it. Hence, it is reasonable to assume that a consumer switching cost is incurred by anyone who tries to use the carrier-select service (even if they experience capacity overload and use the incumbent's network).

Note   In order to avoid problems of equilibrium existence, we also assume (somewhat less convincingly) that consumers experience (on average) significant consumer switching costs when switching from the entrant back to the incumbent, that is, when no longer using the carrier-select service. This assumption is more convincing in the case of carrier-preselect. Also, according to the alternative interpretation of asymmetric, differentiated networks (see Appendix 3.3) our specification appears to be more reasonable. Clearly, if the utility that depends on market share is independent of access to or from the local loop, it is appropriate to maintain utility level u_i^1.

Limited capacity   Suppose that there is a small probability α that a consumer who tries to make a call through carrier-select, does not get a connection although the called party is not busy. Also, suppose that whenever this happens, they use their regular subscription to the incumbent's network to establish a connection. Further, assume that in this case their demand for call minutes is according to $x[p_1]$.

A consumer who decides to use the carrier-select service obtains expected one-period net benefits $(1 - \alpha)v_2[p_2, m_1] + \alpha v_1[p_1, m_1]$. They base their decision to switch on this expected utility level for the next period. After their decision to register for the carrier-select service, they are able to use it successfully with probability α. Accordingly, market shares of subscribers satisfy:

$$\tilde{s}_1^t = s_1^{t-1} + \frac{1}{Z}(1 - \alpha)(v_1 - v_2),$$

$$\tilde{s}_2^t = s_2^{t-1} + \frac{1}{Z}(1 - \alpha)(v_2 - v_1).$$

These market shares have to be corrected by the share α of consumers who are subscribed to the entrant's network but who, on average, make calls through the incumbent's network. For simplicity, we assume that individual demand for call minutes is a linear combination of the individual demands for the two different networks, i.e., $\alpha x[p_1] + (1 - \alpha)x[p_2]$. Corrected market shares (in terms of consumers) are:

$$s_1^t = s_1^{t-1} + \frac{1}{Z}(1 - \alpha)(v_1 - v_2) + \alpha\left(s_2^{t-1} + \frac{1}{Z}(1 - \alpha)(v_2 - v_1)\right),$$

$$s_2^t = (1 - \alpha)\left(s_2^{t-1} + \frac{1}{Z}(1 - \alpha)(v_2 - v_1)\right).$$

Profit functions can be written as:

$$\Pi_1^t[p_1^t, p_2^t, m_1^t] = ns_1^t x[p_1^t](p_1^t - c_{11}) + ns_2^t x[p_2^t](\delta_1 + \tau_1 - 2c_{13})$$
$$+ n(m_1^t - f_1),$$

$$\Pi_2^t[p_1^t, p_2^t, m_1^t] = ns_2^t x[p_2^t](p_2 - \delta_1 - \tau_1 - c_{24}).$$

Consumers surplus become:

$$CS = ns_1^t v_1[p_1, m_1] + ns_2^t v_2[p_2, m_2]$$
$$- \frac{n}{2Z}((1 - \alpha)(v_2[p_2, m_2] - v_1[p_1, m_1]))^2.$$

Note Under limited capacity, one may want to introduce into the model an additional asymmetry which puts the entrant at a disadvantage: the positive probability that a consumer has to redial because of the entrant's overload implies a disutility for the consumer. By including this type of disutility in the model, the entrant's profits would suffer and the incumbent's profits would gain.

6 Entry in a non-segmented market: alternative pricing strategies

6.1 Introduction

This chapter explores alternative pricing strategies. In particular, we consider linear prices (operators do not charge subscription fees), flat fees (operators do not charge per-minute prices), and termination-based price discrimination (operators charge different per-minute prices for on-net and off-net calls).

Under competition in linear prices, operators can only make profits from traffic-dependent consumer expenditures, so linear pricing is more distortionary than two-part tariffs. The reason is that, with two-part tariffs, per-minute prices in equilibrium are set equal to perceived marginal costs, while this is not the case with linear prices.

Under two-part tariffs, operators exercise market power fully through subscription fees. When they cannot do this, they will set their per-minute prices above perceived marginal costs. In the extreme case, they can exercise their market power only through per-minute prices. Therefore, the analysis of linear pricing is an important complement to our analysis of two-part tariffs.

We focus our analysis of linear pricing on reciprocal and asymmetric access price regulation. In particular, we show that, in an infant market, asymmetric access price regulation is superior to cost-based access price regulation in terms of the entrant's profits, consumers surplus, and welfare. We also analyze the competitive effects of lease price regulation under local loop unbundling.

If operators compete on flat rates, then traffic-dependent costs have to be recovered solely from subscription fees. We will observe that, from a social point of view, competition in flat fees performs worse than competition in two-part tariffs. Nevertheless, it is interesting to know more about its implications.

Termination-based price discrimination implies that a consumer may pay a different price for an on-net call than for an off-net call. This pricing mode is relevant because the marginal cost of delivering on-net calls is usually different from the cost of off-net call termination. Such a cost difference may be mainly due to differences in access prices; think, in particular, of interconnection of fixed and mobile operators. Interestingly, we will see that operators try to negotiate an access price below marginal costs in a mature market. We show the beneficial effects of asymmetric access price regulation that allows the entrant to charge an access markup. Also, we discuss non-balanced calling patterns, which are likely to emerge under termination-based price discrimination.

The rest of this chapter is organized as follows. Section 6.2 focuses on linear prices. Section 6.3 considers competition in flat fees. Termination-based price discrimination (operators compete in two-part tariffs) is investigated in Section 6.4. Finally, Section 6.5 summarizes our findings.

6.2   Linear pricing

In this section we take up again the topic of linear pricing (see also Section 3.6). Hence, each operator i sets a single retail price p_i per call minute. The first lesson we learned in Chapter 3 was that in a symmetric setting, in which neither incumbent nor entrant has an advantage, the access price can be used to support collusive prices. This suggests that, even in a mature market, access price regulation is necessary (and freely negotiated access prices have to be ruled out). The second lesson is that in an asymmetric setting, a higher reciprocal access markup tends to favor mainly the incumbent in both relative and absolute terms.

Using the same framework as in Section 3.6, we will take a closer look at equilibrium prices and at the evolution of the market. We analyze in detail asymmetric access price regulation. Also, in addition to facilities-based entry, we consider local-loop-unbundling-based entry (LLU). Under LLU, lease price regulation affects per-minute prices in the market.

Linear pricing is easily implemented in the simulation programs for two-part tariffs by setting subscription fees at zero. We slightly modify our parameter configuration. As in Chapters 4 and 5, the entrant has to build up a track record over time.[1]

6.2.1   Cost-based and reciprocal access price regulation

Under cost-based access price regulation, both operators' perceived marginal costs are equal to the true marginal costs of call termination. In contrast to two-part tariffs where operators can raise revenues without creating a deadweight loss, under linear pricing operators can only make profits by setting their per-minute price above marginal costs.

Suppose that access prices are cost-based. It is interesting to consider the trajectories of equilibrium prices (see Figure 6.1). We observe that the incumbent's per-minute price decreases over time. This reflects that its initially strong

---

[1] We reduce the initial difference in fixed utility levels of the incumbent and the entrant to 25 euros instead of 50 euros. The reason is that under linear pricing it is more difficult for the entrant to gain market share (because higher per-minute prices lead to a deadweight loss). With an initial utility difference of 50, the entrant would not be active in the first period and not be able to establish a track record of quality.

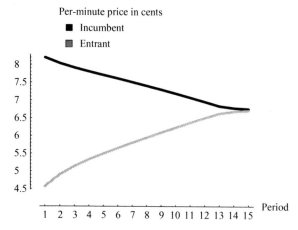

Figure 6.1   Prices under cost-based regulation

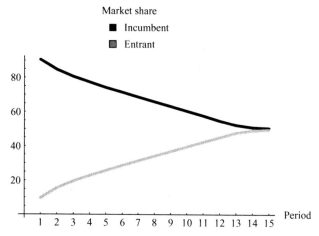

Figure 6.2   Market shares under cost-based regulation

position in the market deteriorates, as the entrant gradually gains market share and builds up a track record of quality. Correspondingly, the entrant is able to increase its per-minute price over time.

Similar to the price trajectories, the incumbent's market share decreases and the entrant's market share increases over time (see Figure 6.2). Consequently, we obtain the pattern of profits over time that we already know from the model with two-part tariffs: the incumbent's profits decrease, whereas the entrant's profits increase (see Figure 6.3).

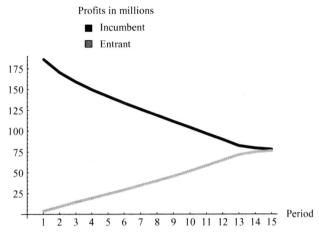

Figure 6.3   Profits under cost-based regulation

Similar patterns of price, market share, and profit trajectories are obtained if reciprocal access prices are above the marginal cost of call termination. An increase in the reciprocal access price leads to higher equilibrium prices that follow a pattern similar to the one observed in Figure 6.1 (see Tables 6.1 and 6.2). Owing to profits from incoming calls, both operators have an incentive to compete more aggressively. However, higher perceived marginal costs have an upward effect on per-minute prices. Overall, an access markup inflates per-minute prices in equilibrium.[2] Hence there exists the possibility to support a collusive outcome by agreeing on a reciprocal access price above cost. That is, if access prices are negotiated among operators rather than regulated the danger of tacit collusion arises (see also Chapter 3).

Note that initially a higher reciprocal access price is strongly felt by the entrant on its cost side, for almost all of its customers' calls terminate on the incumbent's network. The difficulty in gaining market share explains why the entrant is not competing more aggressively in initial periods. As a consequence, the entrant gains market share more slowly when the symmetric access price is above costs than when it is equal to the marginal cost of the local loop.

---

[2] Compare for instance long-run prices under a moderate, reciprocal access markup with prices under cost-based regulation. Perceived marginal costs are 2.25 compared with 2 euro cents. Equilibrium prices increase by only around 0.05 euro cents.

   The access markup multiplier, that is, the factor by which a higher access price translates into higher prices, is in early periods larger than in later periods. Intuitively, this is so because in early periods the entrant is rather tame and its higher perceived marginal costs generate a less competitive outcome.

Table 6.1 *Incumbent's prices under symmetric access price regulation*

τ_1, τ_2	0.5	1.0	2.0
p_1^1	8.20	8.32	8.56
p_1^2	8.04	8.15	8.38
p_1^3	7.91	8.02	8.24
p_1^{15}	6.76	6.83	6.97

Table 6.2 *Entrant's prices under symmetric access price regulation*

τ_1, τ_2	0.5	1.0	2.0
p_2^1	4.58	4.69	4.91
p_2^2	4.92	5.01	5.20
p_2^3	5.15	5.23	5.40
p_2^{15}	6.72	6.79	6.93

Table 6.3 *Incumbent's profits under symmetric access price regulation*

τ_1, τ_2	0.5	1.0	2.0
Π_1^1	185.8	190.2	198.7
Π_1^2	170.0	174.5	183.5
Π_1^3	158.8	163.2	172.0
$\sum_{t=1}^{15} \Pi_1^t$	1826.9	1871.6	1961.5

We have observed in the specification of Chapter 3 that both operators benefit from an increase in the access price above marginal costs. The simulations in Chapter 3 demonstrated that the entrant gains little compared to the incumbent, in both absolute and relative terms. The model in this chapter is more asymmetric in the sense that it takes time for the entrant to build up its track record, and to compete with the incumbent on equal terms. The resulting non-level playing field means that the incumbent strongly benefits from a reciprocal access markup (see Table 6.3), whereas such a regime is undesirable from the entrant's viewpoint (see Table 6.4). Hence, an access markup not only leads to higher prices and

Table 6.4 *Entrant's profits under symmetric access price regulation*

τ_1, τ_2	0.5	1.0	2.0
Π_2^1	3.75	3.51	3.01
Π_2^2	9.26	8.85	7.97
Π_2^3	14.41	14.00	13.06
$\sum_{t=1}^{15} \Pi_2^t$	619.47	624.83	634.52

thus a larger deadweight loss and lower consumers surplus, it also reduces the incentives for the entrant to enter the market, at least from a short-term perspective. This makes a reciprocal access markup undesirable in an infant market.[3]

The main message of the analysis above not only applies to situations of linear pricing, but, more generally, to situations in which operators (e.g. those competing on two-part tariffs) exert at least some market power through their per-minute prices. Hence, we have the following guideline.

> **Guideline 6.1:** Consider facilities-based entry. Suppose that operators exert market power through per-minute prices. In an infant and a mature market, a reciprocal access markup reduces consumers surplus. In an infant market, it also reduces the entrant's profits.

6.2.2   Asymmetric access price regulation

Suppose that the incumbent is subject to cost-based regulation of the access price while, initially, the entrant is allowed to charge an access markup. With reciprocal access prices, we saw that a higher access price leads to higher retail prices of both firms. We will see that if access prices are asymmetric, an increase of the entrant's access prices leads to the opposite outcome, that is, lower retail prices. Furthermore, asymmetric access price regulation under competition in linear prices can lead to higher welfare than cost-based regulation; this was not the case for competition in two-part tariffs.

---

[3] To the extent that the ECPR favors a positive access markup, this rule can be seen as counter-productive to the aim of promoting competition and enhancing consumer surplus and welfare. For a discussion of the ECPR in the context of linear pricing, see Laffont, Rey, and Tirole (1998a).

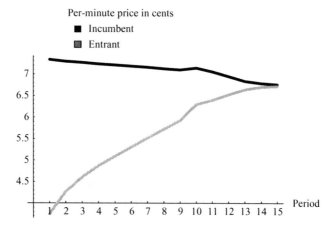

Figure 6.4   Prices under asymmetric access price regulation

Consider equilibrium prices in period 1.[4] In the simulations reported here, we consider three access price regimes and obtain equilibrium retail prices in each regime. In the case of cost-based regulation ($\tau_1 = \tau_2 = 0.5$), equilibrium prices are $p_1^{1*} = 8.20$ and $p_2^{1*} = 4.58$. If the entrant's access markup is moderate ($\tau_2 = 1$), then in equilibrium we have $p_1^{1*} = 7.91$ and $p_2^{1*} = 4.29$. Finally, a relatively large markup ($\tau_2 = 2$) results in equilibrium prices $p_1^{1*} = 7.34$ and $p_2^{1*} = 3.75$. Hence, a larger access markup leads to lower equilibrium prices of both operators. Appendix 6.2, part 1, shows formally that this observation is a general result.

It is interesting to take a closer look at equilibrium prices over time. See Figure 6.4 for the case in which $\tau_2 = 2$ for the first nine periods. As can be seen in the figure, the incumbent's price is relatively flat during these nine periods. This is due to two countervailing effects which almost hold the balance. Firstly, the relative advantage of the incumbent in terms of its track record vanishes over time, making competition more intense; owing to this effect there is a downward pressure on the incumbent's price. Secondly, the entrant gains market shares so that the perceived marginal cost of the incumbent is increasing over time; owing to this effect the incumbent's price has a tendency to rise.

Tables 6.5 and 6.6 compare equilibrium prices for the cases $\tau_2 = 1$ and $\tau_2 = 2$ in periods 1, 2, 3, and 9. The effect of the access price on retail prices is followed by changes of installed customer bases, starting in period 2. These changes tend to increase the entrant's price and decrease the incumbent's price as access price

---

[4] Only first period prices are directly comparable across different constellations of the regulatory variables, because only in the first period do the same initial conditions hold.

Table 6.5 *Incumbent's prices under asymmetric access price regulation*

τ_1	0.5	0.5	0.5
τ_2	0.5	1.0	2.0
p_1^1	8.20	7.91	7.34
p_1^2	8.04	7.78	7.30
p_1^3	7.91	7.68	7.26
p_1^9	7.30	7.22	7.10

Table 6.6 *Entrant's prices under asymmetric access price regulation*

τ_1	0.5	0.5	0.5
τ_2	0.5	1.0	2.0
p_2^1	4.58	4.29	3.75
p_2^2	4.92	4.69	4.27
p_2^3	5.15	4.96	4.61
p_2^9	6.10	6.03	5.92

regulation is more asymmetric. Both operators compete more fiercely, resulting in a more competitive situation in early periods. Once the entrant has gained sufficient strength in terms of market share and track record, asymmetric access price regulation is replaced by cost-based regulation.[5]

See Tables 6.7 and 6.8 for simulation results for the evolution of profits under different regulatory regimes. The profit difference between incumbent and entrant is quite small compared to the case of cost-based regulation. This explains in Figure 6.5 the jumps in the trajectories of the operators' profits after period 9, the period after which access is priced at marginal costs. One would perhaps think that lower retail prices generally translate into lower profits. Here this holds prominently for the incumbent, because its position is weakened by the entrant's access markup. However, it does not hold for the entrant; its profits

---

[5] If asymmetric access price regulation remained in place the entrant would eventually gain more than half of the market and $\partial^2 \Pi_i / \partial p_i \partial \tau_2 > 0$, so that the monotone comparative statics would be reversed in sign (see Appendix 6.2). In such a case, an increase in the access markup would lead to higher prices in the long term.

Table 6.7 *Incumbent's profits under*
asymmetric access price regulation

τ_1	0.5	0.5	0.5
τ_2	0.5	1.0	2.0
Π_1^1	185.8	173.3	145.5
Π_1^2	170.0	156.5	128.3
Π_1^3	158.8	145.3	117.7
$\sum_{t=1}^{15} \Pi_1^t$	1826.9	1712.03	1481.4

Table 6.8 *Entrant's profits under*
asymmetric access price regulation

τ_1	0.5	0.5	0.5
τ_2	0.5	1.0	2.0
Π_2^1	3.75	5.04	8.09
Π_2^2	9.26	11.97	18.22
Π_2^3	14.41	18.11	26.43
$\sum_{t=1}^{15} \Pi_2^t$	619.47	664.01	760.84

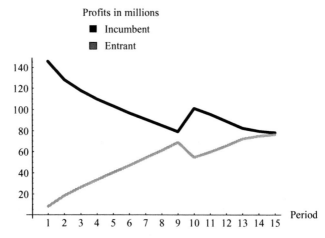

Figure 6.5   Profits under asymmetric access price regulation

Table 6.9 *Consumers surplus under asymmetric access price regulation*

| τ_1 | 0.5 | 0.5 | 0.5 |
τ_2	0.5	1.0	2.0
CS^1	550.4	568.2	604.5
CS^2	561.3	577.4	608.4
CS^3	568.7	583.0	609.7
$\sum_{t=1}^{15} CS^t$	9014.9	9118.1	9305.4

Table 6.10 *Welfare under asymmetric access price regulation*

| τ_1 | 0.5 | 0.5 | 0.5 |
τ_2	0.5	1.0	2.0
W^1	740.0	746.5	758.1
W^2	740.6	745.9	754.9
W^3	741.9	746.4	753.9
$\sum_{t=1}^{15} W^t$	11461.3	11494.2	11547.6

increase in spite of its deteriorated retail markup. Thus, asymmetric access price regulation creates an advantage for the entrant that leads to a gain in market share and, more importantly, to profits from incoming calls. If the access markup is high enough, the entrant may even make losses in the retail market during the first periods, attributing traffic-independent costs of connection to retailing. Entry is profitable because, due to the access markup, the entrant's wholesale activity generates profits.

Consumers gain from asymmetric access price regulation, as Table 6.9 shows. Also, welfare increases (see Table 6.10). This is in spite of a higher market share for the less "efficient" operator, which is the entrant (recall that the lack of a track record makes the entrant the less attractive operator in terms of fixed utility).

Guideline 6.2: Consider facilities-based entry. Suppose that operators exert market power through per-minute prices. In an infant market, an asymmetric access markup only for the entrant increases consumers surplus and the entrant's profits. (Similar to Guideline 4.2)

At first sight, Guideline 6.2 above stands in contrast to Guideline 6.1 in the previous subsection. However, the two guidelines complement each other. In the early periods of competition, a non-reciprocal access price may be very useful, whereas a reciprocal access markup is typically harmful in both early periods and a mature market.

In the model with two-part tariffs, we have also seen that entrant and consumers gain under certain forms of asymmetric regulation as compared to cost-based regulation. There we have seen that welfare does not increase when favoring the entrant. The explanation was that per-minute prices are equal to their efficient level under cost-based regulation. A deviation leads to a deadweight loss. In addition, an increase of the entrant's market share raises the social costs of switching, and the social costs of lower utilities stemming from more consumers subscribing to a network with a lower fixed utility. While the latter observation still holds under linear pricing, prices are never set at their socially efficient level. As we have seen, prices actually fall as the entrant charges an access markup. This fall in prices implies a smaller deadweight loss. It makes asymmetric regulation desirable in an infant market even if regulatory policy is solely based on maximizing welfare (see Table 6.10). Clearly, the access markup for the entrant should only be in place as long as the entrant is at a disadvantage compared to the incumbent.

6.2.3   Price cap regulation

In previous chapters, we saw that a binding price cap limits the possibility of the incumbent initially extracting substantial profits from its dominant position in the market. Price cap regulation under linear pricing means that the incumbent is subject to a price cap on its per-minute price. Hence, a binding price cap necessarily reduces the deadweight loss which is due to prices above marginal costs for the entrant.

Clearly, with a price cap, competition will be tougher, leading to lower retail prices. This necessarily holds under cost-based access price regulation, because networks are strategic complements so that the entrant's best response is upward sloping. We find in our simulations that with both reciprocal and asymmetric markups the entrant's best response is upward sloping in the incumbent's retail price. Therefore, typically the entrant's price is lower under a binding price cap on the incumbent's price. This effect is unambiguously positive for consumers surplus. It is always positive for welfare as long as the price cap is above true marginal costs.

It is important to realize that a price cap may hinder the build-up of the entrant's market share. Nevertheless, this effect may be positive for welfare. As in the case of two-part tariffs, we would argue that interfering with retail

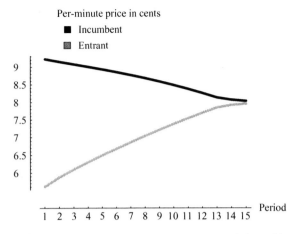

Figure 6.6   LLU: per-minute prices under regulation with cost-based access and lease price markup

price setting may be desirable in the early stages of competition in which the behavior of the incumbent remains largely unchecked by the entrant.

Note that it may be risky for a regulator to use retail price caps. A regulator that cannot perfectly forecast profit levels of the operators faces the risk that, under a binding price cap of the incumbent, an entrant does not find entry attractive because it cannot recover its fixed costs.[6] This shows that retail price caps can be too intrusive because tough price caps, which are controlling the behavior of the incumbent, never become obsolete. In the absence of price cap regulation, competition would have eventually limited the market power of the incumbent.

6.2.4   Linear prices and local loop unbundling

To conclude the discussion on linear pricing, we briefly go into the case of entry based on local-loop unbundling. We are particularly interested in the interplay of access prices and the lease price of the incumbent's local loop. We start with reciprocal access prices.

Recall from Section 5.2 that, with two-part tariffs, any lease price markup (or subsidy) directly translates into subscription fees, and not into per-minute prices, as these are not used to exert market power. In this section, although we explore linear pricing, we are more broadly interested in situations in which operators do exert market power through per-minute prices.

---

[6] An access markup for the entrant may alleviate this problem to some extent.

With linear pricing, a lease price markup leads to higher retail prices and a lower market share for the entrant.[7] Consequently, higher prices result in lower traffic-dependent utility levels. Figure 6.6 depicts the evolution of equilibrium prices with a lease price markup while access prices are equal to costs (compare this to Figure 6.1, which depicts the evolution of prices under a cost-based lease price). Simulations show that a markup in the lease price affects both operators: they charge higher prices and their customers get lower indirect utility from making calls. However, the reduction of the indirect utility from calling is larger for the entrant's customers. This implies that the entrant gains market share more slowly under a lease price markup.

We remark that this also holds when access price regulation is not cost-based. In Appendix 6.2, part 2, we report prices and the entrant's market share across different regulatory regimes. We distinguish four cases: (i) cost-based access and cost-based unbundling; (ii) cost-based access and lease price markup; (iii) reciprocal access markup and cost-based unbundling; and (iv) reciprocal access markup and lease price markup.

In these simulations, we observe that the changes in entrant's profits and market shares are substantial. Under two-part tariffs, we did not observe a reduction of the entrant's market share. As argued above, the substantial reduction of the entrant's market under linear pricing is explained by the distortionary effect of per-minute prices.

It is important to observe that a lease price markup affects welfare. Firstly note that, for given market shares, higher retail prices reduce welfare because of the associated deadweight loss. Introducing a lease price markup strongly decreases welfare if the individual demand for call minutes is rather inelastic. Secondly, note that the entrant sets a lower price than the incumbent and its market share decreases because of the markup in the lease price. Hence, some consumers who would switch to the entrant in the case of no markup, no longer switch. This leads to a deadweight loss. Consequently, because the entrant loses market share when the lease price is increased, the aggregate deadweight loss is unambiguously negative. Hence, operating through traffic-dependent utilities, the effect of a higher lease price markup on welfare is negative. Nevertheless, operating through traffic-independent utility, the effect on welfare is positive: as the entrant gains fewer consumers, aggregate switching costs are lower and more consumers enjoy the better track record of the incumbent. Clearly, the difference in track record fades out after a while and consumers stop switching between networks as the market matures, so that eventually a

---

[7] The reason is that a higher lease price moves the best response of the entrant upward because marginal profits are higher $(\partial^2 \Pi_2^t / \partial p_2^t \partial l = -n \partial s_2^t / \partial p_2^t > 0)$. It also moves the incumbent's best response upward because it receives the lease price markup for each consumer that is lost to the entrant $(\partial^2 \Pi_1^t / \partial p_1^t \partial l = n \partial s_2^t / \partial p_1^t > 0)$.

Local monotone comparative statics similar to the lemma in Appendix 6.2 are obtained; here we obtain $\mathrm{d}p_i^t[l]/\mathrm{d}l > 0$.

lease price markup necessarily reduces welfare. In our simulations the effect operating through traffic-dependent utility is in all periods stronger than the effect operating through traffic-independent utility. Hence, an increase of the lease price above costs reduces welfare.

> **Guideline 6.3**: Consider LLU-based entry. Suppose that operators exert market power through per-minute prices. A lease price markup relaxes competition. In an infant and a mature market, a cost-based lease price allows the incumbent to recover its connection-dependent costs. Supposing that the lease price has to recover these costs, a cost-based lease price maximizes consumers surplus. On a temporary basis, a lease price below costs can be used to increase consumers surplus (at the cost of the incumbent's profits).

We now turn to asymmetric access prices and the lease price of the incumbent's local loop. Recall from Subsection 6.2.2 that asymmetric access price regulation can be used to increase the entrant's profits, consumers surplus, and welfare.

As a starting point, consider cost-based access prices. A lease price subsidy intensifies competition between incumbent and entrant to the effect that prices are lower and consumers surplus is higher. Per-minute prices under cost-based access prices and a lease price subsidy are depicted in Figure 6.7.

Figure 6.7   LLU: per-minute prices under regulation with cost-based access and lease price subsidy (six periods)

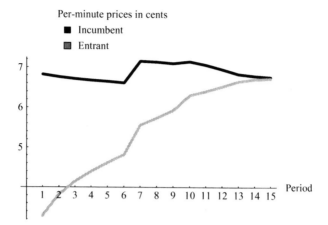

Figure 6.8   LLU: per-minute prices under regulation with asymmetric access prices (nine periods) and lease price subsidy (six periods)

In combining a lease price subsidy and asymmetric access price regulation in early periods, the regulator can stimulate competition. In all our simulations, we observe that the entrant's profits increase under a lease price subsidy (under cost-based, reciprocal access price, or asymmetric access price regulation). Post-entry competition is enhanced to the effect that an entrant gains market share more easily and retail markups are lower, compared with the case of either a lease price subsidy or asymmetric access price regulation. This intensified competition is good for consumers surplus. Also, the entrant benefits from such a regulatory policy; its profits increase. These higher profits provide stronger incentives to enter.

In our simulation, we consider a lease price subsidy for six periods of 5 euros and an access price markup for calls terminating on the entrant's network of 1.5 euro cents. We observe that in this case the incumbent's price is initially lower than in the first periods in which the lease price subsidy is no longer in place (see Figure 6.8). Furthermore, regulation achieves the incumbent's price in the first period, in which it enjoys a large consumer base, being very close to the price when the market has matured and regulation is cost based. This means that asymmetric wholesale price regulation can manage to control the incumbent's retail price, so that retail price regulation appears not to be needed even in early periods.[8]

Figure 6.9 reveals that the incumbent's profits are very sensitive to asymmetric regulation. The entrant's profits react positively to a higher lease price

---

[8] Clearly, such a result depends on the particular parameter constellation. As in the environments above, it will be extremely difficult for the regulator to make good predictions of the precise effects of a change in regulatory policy on market outcomes.

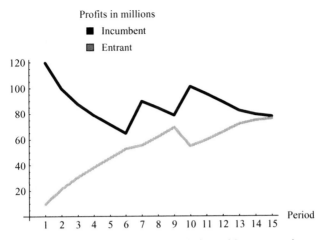

Figure 6.9   LLU: profits under regulation with asymmetric access prices (nine periods) and lease price subsidy (six periods)

subsidy but this effect is much less pronounced. The main beneficiaries are consumers. Owing to the reduction of price distortions, a lower lease price increases welfare in all our simulations. In Appendix 6.4, we compare several regulatory regimes in terms of prices, market shares, entrant's profits, and welfare; outcomes confirm the observations made above.

A lease price subsidy should not be sustained over time because the incumbent does not recover costs on the local loop, so it does not have incentives to maintain or improve the unbundled local loop. Hence, a lease price subsidy can only be a temporary measure, applied with the commitment to be phased out after a certain number of periods.

6.3   Flat fees

In this section, we consider a regulatory environment in which either both operators or only the incumbent charge zero per-minute prices, that is, one or both operators offer flat fees. In the presence of non-negligible costs of access, we will find that there are no economic virtues of such a regulatory policy. However, since they have been introduced in some market segments, it seems worthwhile taking a close look at such an environment.[9]

---

[9] For instance, the German ISDN contract by Deutsche Telekom in 2001 offers free national calls on Sundays and public holidays. Also in 2001, Lince Telecommunications in Spain offers a flat fee on all national and European off-peak calls with a limit of 600 call minutes per month. Such a contract avoids traffic congestion by limiting the total amount of call minutes under the flat fee regime. Otherwise, it shares characteristics of an unrestricted flat fee for certain demand functions. Similarly, Telefónica in Spain offers a fixed number of call minutes for off-peak calls only or peak and off-peak calls together at a flat fee.

6.3.1   Access price regulation

We will first consider facilities-based competition, in which both networks are forced to offer flat fees and networks are subject to access price regulation. The model then corresponds to our earlier analysis in Section 3.3. However, operators are forced to set per-minute prices equal to zero, and they only compete in subscription fees. Profits are:

$$\Pi_i^t = -n\left(s_i^t\right)^2 x[0]c_{i1} - ns_i^t s_j^t x[0](c_{i2} + \tau_j)$$
$$+ ns_i^t s_j^t x[0](\tau_i - c_{i3}) + ns_i(m_i - f_i). \tag{6.1}$$

We will first consider mature competition so that both networks are symmetric (with $s_i^{t-1} = \frac{1}{2}$). For given reciprocal access prices, firms maximize profits with respect to subscription fees. Profits reduce to:

$$\Pi_i^t = ns_i^t(m_i - f_i - x[0]c_{i1}).$$

One can observe that the access price does not enter the profit function. The reason is that both networks have identical demand for call minutes per consumer. Consequently, gains generated from incoming traffic at a higher access price are cancelled out by losses from off-net calls. If there exists an equilibrium with an interior solution it is uniquely determined by:

$$m_i^* = f_i + x[0]c_{i1} + Z/2.$$

Profits per customer are $Z/2$; this is the same profit level as under cost-based access price regulation with two-part tariffs (see Subsection 3.5.1). This is hardly surprising: operators compete only for subscribers, and losses from usage of the network $x[0]c_{i1}$ are fully anticipated when setting the subscription fee. This holds more generally under cost-based regulation, even if networks are asymmetric.[10]

If networks are asymmetric, again the level of the reciprocal access price does not play any role so that profits neutrality holds even for asymmetric networks. To see this, notice that profits in (6.1) can be rewritten as:

$$\Pi_i^t = n\left(s_i^{t-1} + \frac{(u_i^t - u_j^t) + (m_j - m_i)}{Z}\right)(m_i - f_i - x[0]c_{i1}).$$

---

[10] The reason is that under cost-based regulation and flat fees, markups on per-minute prices do not depend on the pricing behavior of the competitor and are symmetric. The only relevant strategic variable is the subscription fee. In general, comparing the utilities derived from a subscription to the operators, consumers decide irrespective of the level of symmetric per-minute prices (given our assumption that all consumers participate in the market).

If there exists an equilibrium with an interior solution, it is uniquely determined by:

$$m_i^* = \frac{u_i^t - u_j^t}{3} + \frac{2f_i + f_j}{3} + x[0]\frac{2c_{i1} + c_{j1}}{3} + Z\frac{1 + s_i^{t-1}}{3}.$$

Observe that under cost symmetry, an increase in the connection-dependent cost $f_i = f$ is fully passed on to consumers, formally $dm_i^*/df = 1$. Also, consumers pay the full increase of the traffic-dependent costs, formally $dm_i^*/dc_1 = x[0]$ under cost symmetry. As $u_i^t - u_j^t$ approaches zero (which happens when the entrant builds up a track record), the asymmetry on the demand side disappears because market shares also approach each other.

To summarize the analysis under reciprocal access prices, our main result has been that the access price has no effect. This implies that, in a mature market, under flat fees operators only have to be required to have reciprocal access prices; further regulation of wholesale prices is not needed.

The profit-neutrality of access prices does not hold for asymmetric access prices. To confirm this, we solve the model with asymmetries on the demand side and asymmetric access prices. For simplicity, we assume symmetry on the cost side. Period t profits can be written as (skipping the time superscript t):

$$\Pi_i = ns_i(m_i - f - x[0]c_1) + ns_i s_j x[0](\tau_i - \tau_j).$$

First-order conditions $\partial \Pi_i/\partial m_i = 0$ give a system of two equations that is linear in m_1 and m_2. Equilibrium profits are:

$$\Pi_i^* = \frac{\left(u_i^0 - u_j^0 + Z + s_i^{t-1}Z\right)^2}{9Z^2}((\tau_i - \tau_j)x[0] + Z).$$

One can observe that equilibrium profits of operator i are increasing in its access price τ_i and decreasing in the competitor's access price τ_j.[11]

The difficulty of entering the market (due to temporary asymmetries) can be alleviated by asymmetric access price regulation of the form $\tau_2 > \tau_1$. In this case, the entrant makes profits on incoming calls. The entrant receives higher profits, which makes this particular asymmetric access price regulation friendlier for the entrant than reciprocal access price regulation. As in the case of two-part tariffs, competition intensifies to the effect that consumers surplus increases.

[11] Note that this implies that there does not exist a solution in an environment in which operators set access prices non-cooperatively. That is, there does not exist a subgame perfect equilibrium in the two-stage game in which operators set access prices at stage 1 and subscription fees at stage 2.

> **Guideline 6.4:** Consider facilities-based entry. Suppose that operators compete in flat fees. In an infant market, an asymmetric access markup only for the entrant increases consumers surplus and the entrant's profits. (Similar to Guideline 4.2)

To conclude, the policy conclusions concerning terminating access prices resemble those under competition in two-part tariffs.

6.3.2   Only the incumbent charges a flat fee

One can imagine that in the early periods of competition, the regulator contemplates requiring the incumbent to charge a fixed fee, while allowing the entrant to set two-part tariffs. A priori, it is unclear if this is a good policy. It therefore makes sense to discuss it briefly.

Intuitively, the retail price policy induces the incumbent to set a higher subscription fee, as calls by its customers are free (i.e., subsidized). This gives the entrant an advantage, because it will price call minutes at the socially efficient level (if access is priced at marginal costs). Imposing flat fees on the incumbent may thus be an instrument for stimulating competition (although there are other regulatory policies which achieve the same goal).

To illustrate the results, we have run simulations in the case of an entrant starting with zero market share. See Table 6.11 for a summary of the outcome. Access prices are assumed to be cost based. One can see that the asymmetric flat-fee regime stimulates competition: higher profits for the entrant make entry more attractive *ex ante* and, given entry, the entrant's market share increases. Despite satisfying the aim of stimulating competition, this policy seems to be problematic because it reduces consumers surplus and welfare.

More generally, unless per-minute costs are negligible, imposing a flat fee on an operator leads to a welfare loss: all individual call minutes between $x[c_{11}]$ and $x[0]$ satisfy the condition that the marginal willingness to pay is below the marginal cost, hence generating a deadweight loss. To the extent that true marginal costs are not far away from zero, the corresponding deadweight loss is not large, in particular if the demand for call minutes does not drastically expand. Possibly more important, the risk of network congestion sharply increases (see Subsection 6.3.3).

To summarize, it seems problematic to require the dominant operator to set a flat fee. Nevertheless, if true marginal costs are close to zero, the welfare loss caused by the requirement for the incumbent to offer a flat fee are rather small. This is also true if both operators have to set flat fees.

Table 6.11 *Cost-based access price regulation,
comparing incumbent's flat fee with two-part tariffs*

	Π_1^1	Π_2^1	CS^1	W^1
Incumbent's flat fee	421.9	1.9	590.9	1014.7
Two-part tariffs	428.1	1.5	597.4	1027.0

6.3.3   Network congestion

The risk of network congestion may provide an important argument against flat fees, depending of course on the actual capacities of networks. Indeed, flat fees can lead to a steep increase in the demand of call minutes. This suggests that for very low per-minute prices, demand may react strongly so that a linear demand function is not an appropriate approximation on the whole range of prices. In such a case, a flat fee might lead to serious capacity problems which will be reflected in lower consumers' utilities.

Note that in the presence of network congestion, socially optimal prices have the property that per-minute prices are above true marginal costs of production. In this case, prices not only reflect costs but also the negative externality for other consumers that stems from higher demand of some consumers, which increases congestion.[12]

If congestion problems occur at the level of an operator's network then a large subscriber base relative to network capacity makes a network relatively unattractive. That is, taking this externality into account, a network competes less aggressively for consumers in its flat fee than it would do in the absence of network congestion. This leads to higher flat fees in equilibrium which also harms consumers surplus. As long as the demand for subscription is inelastic, this increase in flat fees will be neutral to welfare. However, if the participation constraint becomes binding for some consumers, welfare will also be negatively affected by this strategic effect.

6.3.4   Price cap on subscription fee

A binding price cap on the incumbent's subscription fee (that is, its flat fee) makes the incumbent more aggressive in the retail market. Consequently, the entrant sets a lower subscription fee than in the absence of retail price regulation.

---

[12] If congestion is a problem also at cost-based per-minute prices then competition under two-part tariffs would also be affected. Note that profit-maximizing operators are aware that a more congested network negatively affects the utility of their consumers. Hence, operators will take congestion partially into account.

Effects on profits and consumers surplus are qualitatively the same as under linear pricing. Welfare effects are different because the deadweight loss is not affected by prices under flat fees. From a welfare perspective, it only matters that market shares depend on retail price regulation. A lower price cap leads to a higher market share for the incumbent. This improves welfare in the early stages of competition in which the entrant lacks a full track record of quality. In addition, a slow gain in market share keeps average switching costs low. For this reason, welfare increases in our model under a lower price cap. The reasoning we have provided earlier (see, for instance, Section 6.2) for why retail price regulation may prevent entry, by making it unprofitable, also applies to flat fees.

6.3.5   Local loop unbundling and lease price regulation

Consider competition in flat fees in a market with local loop unbundling. Suppose that costs are symmetric. Operators face a regulated lease price l so that profits can be written as:

$$\Pi_1 = ns_1(m_1 - f^{\text{local-line}} - f^{\text{linecard}} - x[0]c_1) + ns_1s_2x[0](\tau_1 - \tau_2)$$
$$+ ns_2(m_2 - l - f^{\text{local-line}}),$$
$$\Pi_2 = ns_2(m_2 - l - f^{\text{linecard}} - x[0]c_1) + ns_1s_2x[0](\tau_1 - \tau_2).$$

If both operators are active in equilibrium, one obtains flat fees m_1^* and m_2^* from the first-order conditions of profit maximization. Equilibrium profits reduce to:

$$\Pi_1^* = n(l - f^{\text{local-line}})$$
$$+ n\frac{1}{9Z^2}((\tau_1 - \tau_2)x[0] + Z)\left(u_1 - u_2 + \left(1 + s_1^0\right)Z\right)^2,$$
$$\Pi_2^* = n\frac{1}{9Z^2}((\tau_2 - \tau_1)x[0] + Z)\left(u_2 - u_1 + \left(1 + s_2^0\right)Z\right)^2.$$

One can write the equilibrium values of the subscription fees as functions of the lease price l for given access prices τ_1 and τ_2. One then obtains that a higher lease price l is transmitted one-to-one into higher flat fees; formally, $dm_1^*[l]/dl = 1$ and $dm_2^*[l]/dl = 1$. This implies that the marginal consumer is not affected by the lease price so that market shares do not respond to lease price regulation. From the above equilibrium profits, we see that a higher lease price leads to higher profits for the incumbent and leaves the entrant's profits unchanged. Formally, $d\Pi_1^*[l]/dl = n$ and $d\Pi_2^*[l]/dl = 0$.

Since the entrant's profits do not respond to the lease price, lease price regulation cannot stimulate entry if firms compete in flat fees. Nevertheless, a lease price subsidy makes competition more intense, to the effect that the incumbent obtains lower profits under a lease price subsidy than under cost-based regulation. A lease price subsidy leads to a transfer of surplus from the incumbent to consumers (leaving total surplus constant). We can draw the same policy conclusions as under two-part tariffs (see Section 5.2).

6.4 Two-part tariffs with termination-based price discrimination

In this section, we explore termination-based price discrimination, that is, per-minute prices for on-net and off-net calls can be set differently.[13] A regulator may be interested in this type of pricing because the traffic-dependent costs of on-net and off-net calls (which can be seen as different services) may be different due to cost reasons, such as:

- different efficiency levels of the operators' networks;
- terminating access prices set above the traffic-dependent cost of the local loop (so that the traffic-dependent cost of an on-net call is higher than the cost of an off-net call).

Accordingly, the idea is that termination-based price discrimination may result in per-minute prices that reflect the underlying costs and access fees to a better extent than non-discriminatory prices.

In practice, price discrimination can be observed in markets for mobile-to-mobile telephony and for fixed-to-mobile/mobile-to-fixed telephony. Typically, calls from a fixed to a mobile operator are much more expensive than fixed-to-fixed or even mobile-to-mobile calls. In principle, termination-based price discrimination can also be applied to fixed telephony.

6.4.1 Balanced calling patterns: market shares and profits

Under two-part tariffs with termination-based price discrimination, each operator sets three prices: the per-minute price for on-net calls p_i^{on}; the per-minute price for off-net calls p_i^{off}; and the subscription fee f_i. In order to specify consumer demand we have to specify its calling patterns. Without termination-based price discrimination, a consumer does not need to think about whether their calls terminate on-net or off-net. Under termination-based price discrimination, a consumer typically will decide to make shorter or less frequent calls that terminate on a different network if $p_i^{off} > p_i^{on}$. The reverse holds if an off-net call minute is cheaper than an on-net call minute.

We make the assumption that calling patterns are balanced in the following sense: consumers' share of on-net call minutes corresponds to the market share

---

[13] The term "termination-based price discrimination" is consistently used in the literature and for this reason we do so as well. However, we find it somewhat confusing because price discrimination typically refers pricing the *same* good or service differently, either to the same consumer or to different consumers (see Tirole, 1988, p. 133).

of the operator to which a consumer is subscribed to, after correcting for differences in per-minute prices. That is, the individual demand for on-net calls is $s_i x[p_i^{on}]$, and the demand for off-net calls is $s_j x[p_i^{off}]$.

A balanced calling pattern is rather restrictive in terms of both the composition of an operator's consumer base and the substitutability between on-net and off-net calls given any composition of a customer base; see Section 6.4.4 for further discussion on this topic. Nevertheless, the assumption of balanced calling patterns is a useful first step in analyzing markets with termination-based price discrimination. In a straightforward manner, indirect net utility is composed of the variable net utility derived from on-net calls plus the variable net utility derived from off-net calls, plus the fixed utility minus the subscription fee. One can think of the utility of a consumer as the sum of receiver-indexed sub-utilities. Then utilities are additive in the market shares of the operators and we can write the net utility as:

$$w_i[p_i^{on}, p_i^{off}, m_i] \equiv u_i^0 + s_i \tilde{v}[p_i^{on}] + (1 - s_i)\tilde{v}[p_i^{off}] - m_i,$$

where

$$\tilde{v}[p] \equiv u[x[p]] - px[p].$$

Consumers base their decision on which network to join on market share because, for instance, at a low on-net price an operator is attractive if it has a large market share. This means that consumers' choices are affected by the market share. Therefore, termination-based price discrimination gives rise to a network externality.

Market shares are:

$$s_i = s_i^0 + \frac{w_i - w_j}{Z}.$$

Solving the equation above for s_i gives:

$$s_i = \frac{s_i^0 + \frac{1}{Z}(u_i^0 - u_j^0) + \frac{1}{Z}(v[p_i^{off}] - v[p_j^{on}]) - \frac{1}{Z}(m_i - m_j)}{1 - \frac{1}{Z}(v[p_i^{on}] + v[p_j^{on}] - v[p_i^{off}] - v[p_j^{off}])}.$$

Operator i's profits are:

$$\Pi_i[p_i^{on}, p_j^{on}, p_i^{off}, p_j^{off}, m_i, m_j]$$
$$= ns_i s_i x[p_i^{on}](p_i^{on} - c_{i1})$$
$$+ ns_i(1 - s_i)x[p_i^{off}](p_i^{off} - c_{i2} - \tau_j)$$
$$+ n(1 - s_i)s_i x[p_j^{off}](\tau_i - c_{i3}) + ns_i(m_i - f_i).$$

We will rewrite profits to depend on per-minute prices and net utilities w_i. For this we substitute m_i by $u_i^0 + s_i \tilde{v}[p_i^{on}] + (1 - s_i)\tilde{v}[p_i^{off}] - w_i$. Market shares then depend on per-minute prices and net utilities so that subscription fees do not enter the expression. We have:

$$\tilde{\Pi}_i\big[p_i^{\text{on}}, p_j^{\text{on}}, p_i^{\text{off}}, p_j^{\text{off}}, w_i, w_j\big]$$
$$= n s_i[w_i, w_j] s_i[w_i, w_j]\big(u\big[x\big[p_i^{\text{on}}\big]\big] - c_{i1} x\big[p_i^{\text{on}}\big]\big)$$
$$+ n s_i[w_i, w_j](1 - s_i[w_i, w_j])\big(u\big[x\big[p_i^{\text{off}}\big]\big] - (\tau_j + c_{i2}) x\big[p_i^{\text{off}}\big]\big)$$
$$+ n(1 - s_i[w_i, w_j]) s_i[w_i, w_j] x\big[p_j^{\text{off}}\big](\tau_i - c_{i3})$$
$$+ n s_i[w_i, w_j]\big(u_i^0 - w_i - f_i\big).$$

To determine optimal per-minute prices, we take net utility levels as given. As in the standard model of competition in two-part tariffs, again we obtain a marginal cost pricing principle. It takes the following form: operators set their on-net per-minute price equal to on-net marginal costs, that is:

$$p_i^{\text{on}*} = c_{i1},$$

and their off-net per-minute price equal to off-net perceived marginal costs, that is:

$$p_i^{\text{off}*} = c_{i2} + \tau_j.$$

This follows directly from the first-order conditions $\partial \tilde{\Pi}_i / \partial p_i^{\text{on}} = 0$ and $\partial \tilde{\Pi}_i / \partial p_i^{\text{off}} = 0$. Consequently, operator i's profits in which operator i chooses its profit-maximizing per-minute prices can be written as:

$$\Pi_i\big[p_i^{\text{on}*}, p_j^{\text{on}}, p_i^{\text{off}*}, p_j^{\text{off}}, m_i, m_j\big]$$
$$= n(1 - s_i) s_i x\big[p_j^{\text{off}}\big](\tau_i - c_{i3}) + n s_i(m_i - f_i).$$

Accordingly, operators have two sources of profits: revenues from incoming calls and from subscriptions. This is similar to competition in two-part tariffs with per-minute prices that do not discriminate between termination.

6.4.2   Reciprocal access pricing under symmetry

In this subsection, we consider access pricing in a symmetric market. We assume demand and cost symmetry: $s_i^0 = s_j^0 = \frac{1}{2}$, $u_i^0 = u_j^0$, $c_{ik} = c_{jk} = c_k$, and $f_i = f_j = f$. In this setup, we consider reciprocal access prices $\tau \equiv \tau_1 = \tau_2$. Because of the marginal cost pricing principle, market share functions can be simplified as:

$$s_i = \frac{s_i^0 + \frac{1}{z}(v[c_2 + \tau] - v[c_1]) - \frac{1}{z}(m_i - m_j)}{1 - \frac{2}{z}(v[c_1] - v[c_2 + \tau])}.$$

Note that market shares react linearly to changes in the subscription fee, that is:

$$\frac{\partial s_i}{\partial m_i} = -\frac{1}{Z - 2\,(v[c_1] - v[c_2 + \tau])}.$$

This expression is negative if τ is sufficiently small or Z sufficiently large.

The first-order conditions for profit maximization (which are a necessary condition for a symmetric interior solution) implicitly define best responses. Observing that best responses are linear in the competitor's subscription fee, one obtains solutions:

$$m_i^* = f + \frac{Z}{2} - (v[c_1] - v[c_2 + \tau]).$$

Hence, whenever there exists a symmetric equilibrium, it is characterized by the above subscription fee. One can show that an equilibrium exists if Z is sufficiently large or $\tau - c_3$ sufficiently close to zero. Furthermore, the equilibrium is unique if Z is sufficiently large or $\tau - c_3$ sufficiently close to zero or τ sufficiently small (see Appendix 6.5).

One can observe that the subscription fee is increasing in switching cost parameter Z (as in the model without termination-based price discrimination), that is, $dm_i^*/dZ > 0$. More importantly, the subscription fee is decreasing in the reciprocal access price τ, $dm_i^*/d\tau = v'[c_2 + \tau] < 0$. This result says that consumers pay lower subscription fees as the positive network externality becomes stronger ($\tau > c_3$). Intuitively, consumers become more valuable because they generate profits from incoming calls. Therefore, operators reduce their subscription fees as the access price rises.

Equilibrium profits are:

$$\Pi_i^* = \frac{n}{4}\,(x[c_2 + \tau](\tau - c_3) + Z - 2(v[c_1] - v[c_2 + \tau]))\,.$$

One can observe that equilibrium profits are not neutral to the level of the access price. A reciprocal access price above costs c_3 leads to lower profits. This is easily seen in the equation above ($\partial \Pi_i^*/\partial \tau < 0$ for all $\tau \geq c_3$).[14] The non-neutrality of profits stands in contrast to the earlier neutrality result under two-part tariffs when termination-based price discrimination is not allowed.

Under cost-based access prices, equilibrium profits coincide with the profits in a model with two-part tariffs without termination-based price discrimination. This is not surprising because in both models optimal per-minute prices are equal to true marginal costs c_1.

It is interesting to consider the case in which the operators can negotiate over the reciprocal access prices. Suppose that the access price has to be

[14] Note that $\partial \Pi_i^*/\partial \tau < 0$ is equivalent to $x'[c_2 + \tau](\tau - c_3) < 0$ which is always satisfied for $\tau \geq c_3$.

non-negative. Then, by solving $\partial \Pi_i^* / \partial \tau = 0$, it follows that the negotiated reciprocal access price is either $\tau^* = 0$ if $-c_3 x'[c_2] < x[c_2]$, or alternatively, it is implicitly defined by:[15]

$$x'[c_2 + \tau^*](\tau^* - c_3) = x[c_2 + \tau^*]. \tag{6.2}$$

Consequently, termination-based price discrimination leads to a negative network externality. Operators prefer such a regime because it makes competition soft. With linear demand we find that $\tau^* = 0$.[16] Hence, operators provide access for free to their competitor.[17] This is a "bill and keep" system for network interconnection. More generally, providing subsidized access implies that consumers effectively pay less for an off-net call than for an on-net call.

Now suppose operators set the price for terminating access on their network unilaterally. Clearly, an access price above costs generates profits from incoming calls. However, a change in the access price affects competition in the retail market. Gans and King (2001) have shown that operators set access prices τ_i above marginal costs if they compete in access prices at an initial stage and in retail prices at a later stage.[18]

To summarize, we have seen that operators set the access price below costs if determined jointly. Each operator sets its access price above costs if decisions are taken unilaterally.

6.4.3   Infant market

We have seen that in a mature market with symmetric operators, profit levels increase as the reciprocal access price is reduced. In this subsection, we consider asymmetric access price regulation in an infant market (the analysis is based on Peitz, 2001). The model with termination-based price discrimination can also be analytically solved under these more general circumstances. Replacing

---

[15] The fact that a negotiated access price is set below marginal costs has been established by Gans and King (2001).

[16] A sufficient condition for existence of equilibrium in this case is that $c_3 x[c_2] < Z - 2(v[c_1] - v[c_2])$ (see Appendix 6.5).

[17] If demand function x is not linear but strictly concave the result that $\tau^* = 0$ is confirmed; if demand is strictly convex there exists a unique interior solution $\tau^* \in (-\infty, c_3)$ (see Gans and King, 2001). Under strictly convex demand, the solution to (6.2) is either positive or operators agree on $\tau^* = 0$. Even in the former case, operators may prefer to grant their competitor free terminating access if τ^* is sufficiently low and there are traffic monitoring and billing costs.

[18] More precisely, consider the two-stage game in which, first, operators simultaneously set access prices and, next, they set two-part tariffs. Strategy spaces at the first stage have to be artificially restricted to allow only for those access prices such that an equilibrium at the second stage exists. Then, in any subgame perfect equilibrium, operators set access prices above marginal costs.

per-minute prices by marginal costs in the first-order conditions, one obtains best responses that are linear in the competitor's subscription fee. It is then straightforward to compute equilibrium prices and profits. Expressions become very lengthy and difficult to interpret, however. We focus on the case where the incumbent is subject to cost-based regulation and the entrant is allowed to charge an access markup $\tau_2 > c_3$.

Appendix 6.6 contains the complete expressions for equilibrium subscription fees. Typically, subscription fees are decreasing in the entrant's access markup. The reason is that networks are strategic complements.

We replace per-minute prices by their equilibrium values so that profits functions depend only on subscription fees. Note that the incumbent's marginal profits are only affected by the access price through changes in the market share; one can show that $\partial^2\Pi_1/\partial m_1 \partial \tau_2 < 0$ (see Appendix 6.6), so that the incumbent's best response function is shifted inward by a higher access price τ_2. A change in the access markup affects the entrant's profits (and marginal profits) also through incoming traffic. Intuitively, the entrant gains more from additional consumers if the access markup is higher. Nevertheless, its marginal profits decline, because at a lower price it serves more consumers and this is more attractive if the access markup is larger. We find that, for a higher access markup, the entrant prices more aggressively given the subscription fee of the incumbent.[19] In other words, the entrant's best response is also shifted inward by a higher access price τ_2. Since networks are strategic complements, equilibrium subscription fees are decreasing in the entrant's access price.

Intuition suggests that equilibrium profits are decreasing in the entrant's access price for the incumbent and increasing for the entrant. We have confirmed this intuition for our standard parameter configuration. Figure 6.10 shows profits in million euros.[20]

Consequently, our general message that asymmetric regulation stimulates entry also holds under termination-based price discrimination. It also typically increases consumers surplus: this holds if the negative welfare effect owing to the incumbent's higher off-net per-minute price and lower market share is overcompensated by the gain from more intense competition.[21] Loosely speaking, consumers and the entrant gain if the competitive effect dominates the distortionary effect in the wholesale market.

---

[19] Formally, one has to show that $\partial^2\Pi_2/\partial m_2 \partial \tau_2 < 0$. This property is satisfied for $\tau_2 - c_3$ sufficiently small and $s_2 \leq \frac{1}{3}$ (see Appendix 6.6).

[20] Although we have closed-form solutions for equilibrium prices and profits, these expressions are too complicated to lead to general conclusions without parameter restrictions.

[21] Recall that due to a lower market share of the incumbent consumers incur, on average, lower switching costs.

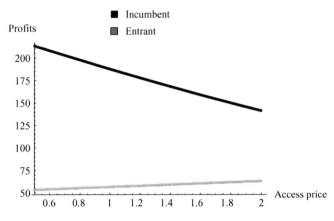

Figure 6.10   Profits given the entrant's access price

Guideline 6.5: Consider facilities-based entry. Suppose that operators compete in two-part tariffs with termination-based price discrimination. In an infant market, an asymmetric access markup only for the entrant increases consumers surplus and the entrant's profits. (Similar to Guideline 4.2)

6.4.4   Unbalanced calling patterns

In Subsection 6.4.1, we pointed out that balanced calling patterns are not necessarily a good approximation of real calling patterns in a market with termination-based price discrimination. In particular, two properties are needed so that calling patterns are balanced:
- consumers do not form clusters or closely connected groups of friends, relatives, or colleagues (making more frequent calls within these groups than to outsiders);
- on-net calls cannot be substituted by off-net calls.

The first requirement can be problematic because there are economic gains from coordination among customers. In particular, termination-based price discrimination gives rise to endogenous network externalities. When an on-net call is cheaper than an off-net call, consumers can increase their net utilities by coordinating with others to subscribe to the same network operator. If members of a school class, employees of a company, or a group of friends are subscribed to the same network, they are more likely to make on-net calls than the distribution of market shares suggests. Calling patterns will, to a certain extent, resemble the links that are maintained in these groups: consumers make most calls to persons with whom they maintain links, and many fewer to other people.

If consumers coordinate their subscription decisions, it may become easier for an entrant to obtain new subscribers. This is because the network externality is likely to be less pronounced than in the model with balanced calling patterns. If most calls are made within groups, then the entrant operator, in order to benefit from positive network externalities (supposing that off-net calls are more expensive than on-net calls), only has to attract the consumers within this group and a small customer base is hardly a disadvantage. The formal analysis of communication networks, in which links between consumers are explicitly modeled, would very much complicate the analysis. We do not expect that such an extension would add substantial new insights to our qualitative results.

The second requirement for balanced calling patterns may also conflict with realism. If off-net calls are more expensive than on-net calls, consumers may not only want to make shorter or less frequent calls off-net than on-net. They may, in addition, want to substitute some off-net calls by on-net calls. This type of substitution will not be perfect, but the implicit assumption that there is no substitution at all seems a bit strong. For example, a consumer may just want to chat to a friend, irrespective of the person. If "chatting" is the main objective, the consumer will always choose a friend that is on-net, provided that it is cheaper to make on-net calls. In this example, substitution is perfect.

If all consumers are "chatters" and off-net calls are more expensive than on-net calls, the two networks are completely disconnected. Consequently, no off-net calls are made. The operators then compete for subscribers that make only on-net calls. In this extreme case, the network externality is absent. In general, if consumers make only part of their calls in the role of a chatter some network externality is present. Profits from incoming traffic are lower than under balanced calling patterns but still strictly positive (assuming that wholesale prices are above marginal costs). Demand reacts less sensitively to changes in subscription rates, compared to a situation of balanced calling patterns. Nevertheless, the qualitative results that we have derived under balanced calling patterns remain valid.

6.5   Summary

In this chapter, we looked at competitive situations that are different from our regular set-up of competition in two-part tariffs (analyzed in the previous chapters). In particular, we considered linear pricing and flat fees as alternatives for competition in two-part tariffs and, given a situation of two-part tariffs, we considered termination-based price discrimination. We remark that the guidelines recapitulated below apply only within the setting in which they were obtained. These settings are characterized by, for instance, the entry mode, the nature of price competition, and an unsegmented market.

Firstly, consider facilities-based entry, and suppose that operators exert market power through per-minute prices. This is particularly the case if they compete on linear prices instead of two-part tariffs. With regard to terminating access prices, the following guidelines were formulated:

• In an infant and a mature market, a reciprocal access markup reduces consumers surplus. In an infant market, it also reduces the entrant's profits. (Guideline 6.1)
• In an infant market, an asymmetric access markup only for the entrant increases consumers surplus and the entrant's profits. (Guideline 6.2)

Secondly, consider entry based on local loop unbundling, and again suppose that operators exert market power through per-minute prices. The following result, obtained under competition in two-part tariffs (see Guideline 5.1), is robust:

• A lease price markup relaxes competition. In an infant and a mature market, a cost-based lease price allows the incumbent to recover its connection-dependent costs. Supposing that the lease price has to recover these costs, a cost-based lease price maximizes consumers surplus. On a temporary basis, a lease price below costs can be used to increase consumers surplus, but this comes at the cost of the incumbent's profits. (Guideline 6.3)

Thirdly, consider facilities-based entry, and suppose that operators compete in flat fees:

• In an infant market, an asymmetric access markup only for the entrant increases consumers surplus and the entrant's profits. (Guideline 6.4)

Finally, consider facilities-based entry, and suppose that operators compete in two-part tariffs with termination-based price discrimination, that is, they are allowed to set different per-minute prices for on-net and off-net calls. Although fixed operators that are subject to regulation may not (yet) be allowed to price discriminate, these types of pricing strategies are quite relevant in practice (e.g. fixed–mobile call termination). It allows operators to set per-minute prices at their exact traffic-dependent cost level, instead of pricing at the level of perceived marginal costs (which is an average). The following guideline was obtained:

• In an infant market, an asymmetric access markup only for the entrant increases consumers surplus and the entrant's profits. (Guideline 6.5)

An important lesson that can be drawn from this chapter is that the policy implications we obtained earlier on asymmetric access price regulation, such that only the entrant is allowed to charge an access markup in an infant market, is robust. It does not only apply if operators compete two-part tariffs, but also in other situations of price competition.

To conclude, we briefly discuss to what extent the profit-neutrality result under two-part tariffs (if the demand for subscriptions is inelastic) is a general property. Consider reciprocal access price regulation. If the operators compete on two-part tariffs, then a higher reciprocal access price leaves profits unaffected in a mature market. If they compete on flat fees, this is also the case in an infant market. If they compete on linear prices, a higher reciprocal access price increases both operators' profits in a mature market. Furthermore, if the operators compete on two-part tariffs and are allowed to set termination-based per-minute prices, then a higher reciprocal access price may decrease profits. Thus, profit neutrality crucially depends on the nature of price competition. Regulators and competition authorities concerned with the risk of collusion through access prices, should therefore assess to what extent operators exert market power through subscription fees.

In Chapters 3 to 6, we assumed that the market is unsegmented. In the following two chapters, we will consider a segmented market, looking at the contrasting situations where the entrant does not and does use a targeted entry strategy.

APPENDIX 6.1: LINEAR PRICING AND GLOBAL MAXIMIZERS

We report plots of profit functions given the competitors equilibrium price. Note that our plots are only valid for positive market share. This puts an upper bound on price as can be seen from our plot of market share. The market share of operator 1 is between 0 and 1. It remains 1 for prices below the critical price such that market share becomes 1. It necessarily remains 0 for prices above the first intersection of the market share function with the price axis. Note that in a very asymmetric market the customer base might still be positive when individual demand of call minutes turns to zero. The latter is the case when the price is equal to parameter a (which in our simulations is equal to 20). For higher prices, profits are zero and the profit plots are not valid.

Here, we document profits and market shares under a deviation in periods 1 and 15 for a reciprocal access markup of 1.5 euro cents under our parameter constellations. It is straightforward to observe from Figures 6.11 to 6.18 that the simulation outcomes are global maximizers, and hence equilibria. Note that the restriction that market shares lie between 0 and 1, imposes restrictions on the relevant range of prices. On this price range, profit functions are single peaked.

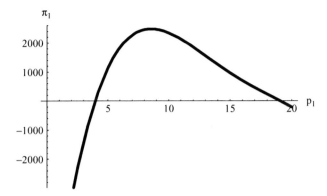

Figure 6.11   Incumbent's deviation profits in period 1

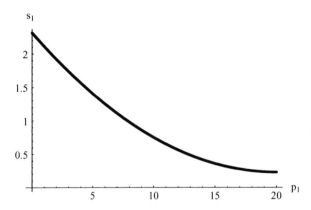

Figure 6.12   Incumbent's deviation market share in period 1

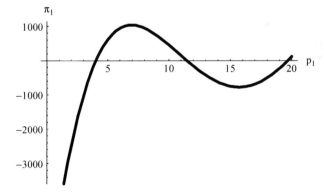

Figure 6.13   Incumbent's deviation profits in period 15

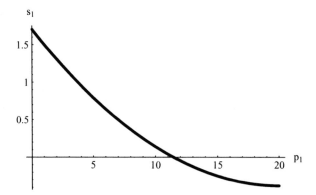

Figure 6.14   Incumbent's deviation market share in period 15

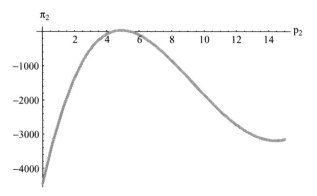

Figure 6.15   Entrant's deviation profits in period 1

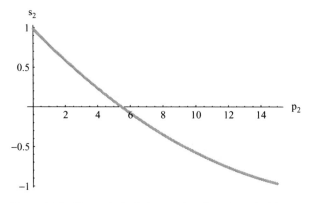

Figure 6.16   Entrant's deviation market share in period 1

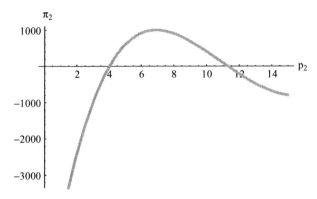

Figure 6.17   Entrant's deviation profits in period 15

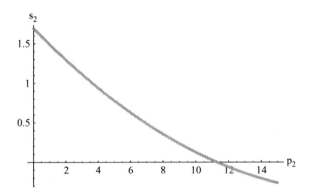

Figure 6.18   Entrant's deviation market share in period 15

APPENDIX 6.2: MONOTONE COMPARATIVE STATICS UNDER LINEAR PRICING

Part 1: Cross-derivatives and monotone comparative statics

Suppose for the moment that operators offer strategic complements as products, formally $\partial^2 \Pi_i / \partial p_i \partial p_j > 0$. Accordingly, one can say that the pricing game is "supermodular."[22] If, in addition, $\partial^2 \Pi_1 / \partial p_1 \partial \tau_2 \leq 0$ and $\partial^2 \Pi_2 / \partial p_2 \partial \tau_2 \leq 0$, while one of the inequalities is a strict one, then the pricing game exhibits strictly monotone comparative statics, namely $dp_i[\tau_2]/d\tau_2 < 0$, $i = 1, 2$. Note that if marginal profits decrease in the parameter, then an increase of the parameter values moves best responses inward. (Analogously, if $\partial^2 \Pi_1 / \partial p_1 \partial \tau_1 \geq 0$ and $\partial^2 \Pi_2 / \partial p_2 \partial \tau_1 \geq 0$, with one of the two inequalities strict, the pricing

[22] This part of the appendix is based on Peitz (2001). On strategic Complementarity, see Bulow, Geanakoplos, and Klemperer (1985). On supermodular games, see Milgrom and Roberts (1990) and Vives (1990).

game exhibits strictly monotone comparative statics, namely $dp_i[\tau_1]/d\tau_1 > 0$, $i = 1, 2$.)

Clearly, in models of telecommunications markets such as ours, cross deriva-
tives $\partial^2 \Pi_i/\partial p_i \partial p_j$ are not always globally strictly positive. More generally, best
responses are not always increasing. Nevertheless, for the local monotone com-
parative statics, it is sufficient to show that cross-derivatives are strictly positive
when evaluated at equilibrium prices.

> **Lemma** Assume that profit functions are thrice continuously
> differentiable (in p_1, p_2, τ_2). Suppose that for a given value $\tilde{\tau}_2$
> there exists a locally unique equilibrium with prices $\tilde{p}_1$ and $\tilde{p}_2$. If
> $\partial^2 \Pi_1/\partial p_1 \partial \tau_2 < 0$ and $\partial^2 \Pi_2/\partial p_2 \partial \tau_2 < 0$, both evaluated at the point
> $(\tilde{p}_1, \tilde{p}_2, \tilde{\tau}_2)$, and:
>
> $$\left. \frac{\partial^2 \Pi_i[p_1, p_2]}{\partial p_i \partial p_j} \right|_{p_1=\tilde{p}_1, p_2=\tilde{p}_2} > 0,$$
>
> prices are locally decreasing, that is,[23]
>
> $$\left. \frac{d\tilde{p}_i[\tau_2]}{d\tau_2} \right|_{\tau_2=\tilde{\tau}_2} < 0.$$

To apply the lemma, note first that in our model an increase in the entrant's
access price always decreases the entrant's marginal profits if $s_1^* > s_2^*$; we have
that:

$$\frac{\partial^2 \Pi_2}{\partial p_2 \partial \tau_2} = -(s_1 - s_2) \frac{x[p_1]x[p_2]}{Z} < 0.$$

The change of marginal profits of the incumbent is of ambiguous sign:

$$\frac{\partial^2 \Pi_1}{\partial p_1 \partial \tau_2} = -(s_1 - s_2) \frac{x[p_1]^2}{Z} + s_1 s_2 (-x'[p_1]).$$

Nevertheless, as long as the market is sufficiently asymmetric, that is, s_2^* is
sufficiently small, we find $\partial^2 \Pi_2/\partial p_2 \partial \tau_2 < 0$ in a neighborhood around the
equilibrium. To apply the lemma for local monotone comparative statics, it
remains to be checked that cross derivatives $\partial^2 \Pi_i[p_1, p_2]/\partial p_i \partial p_j$ are positive,

---

[23] With the results in the literature it is straightforward to prove this lemma. It goes as follows.
Restrict the strategy space to a neighborhood around the equilibrium so that cross derivatives are
positive, which forms a product of closed intervals. Hence, we have constructed a supermodular
game. We furthermore know that there exists a strategy space (that is, a product of closed
intervals) for which the equilibrium is unique; for this, note that best responses intersect at the
equilibrium and are continuous. Considering now a neighborhood around the parameter $\tilde{\tau}_2$ we
obtain the same qualitative result. Then the theory of supermodular games gives us the monotone
comparative statics result as stated. For this, we make use of the monotone comparative statics
results of supermodular games (see, for instance, Milgrom and Roberts, 1990).

evaluated at equilibrium prices. Note that in all the simulations reported in this section we always found that in equilibrium goods are (locally) strong strategic complements and therefore the lemma applies. Note also that the lemma can be applied to other regulatory regimes. Part 2 of this appendix contains evaluated cross-derivatives for the first period under three different regulatory regimes.

Part 2: Evaluation of cross-derivatives
In this part we derive first-period cross-derivatives in equilibrium for three regulatory regimes: (i) cost-based regulation; (ii) symmetric access price regulation with a markup of 1.5; and (iii) asymmetric access price regulation with a markup of 1.5 in favor of the entrant. We look at the price region $[0, 10] \times [0, 10]$.

As can be seen from Figures 6.19 to 6.24, there exists a rather large area in which cross derivatives are strictly positive. It should be noted, however, that there do exist prices at which cross derivatives are negative. This is most obvious for operator 1 under asymmetric access price regulation.

(i) $\qquad \dfrac{\partial^2 \Pi_1[p_1, p_2]}{\partial p_1 \partial p_2}\bigg|_{p_1=p_1^*, p_2=p_2^*} \approx 56.2 > 0$

$\qquad \dfrac{\partial^2 \Pi_2[p_1, p_2]}{\partial p_2 \partial p_1}\bigg|_{p_1=p_1^*, p_2=p_2^*} \approx 98.7 > 0$

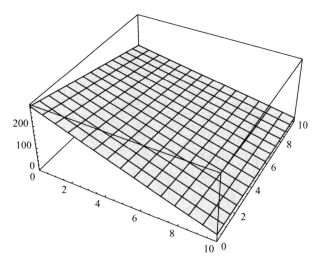

Figure 6.19   Cost-based regulation: cross derivative of operator 1's profits in period 1

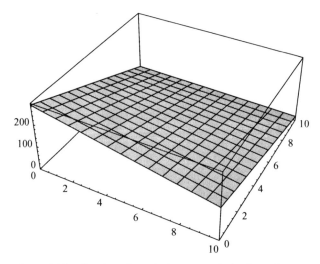

Figure 6.20   Cost-based regulation: cross derivatives of operator 2's profits in period 1

(ii)
$$\frac{\partial^2 \Pi_1[p_1, p_2]}{\partial p_1 \partial p_2}\Bigg|_{p_1 = p_1^*, p_2 = p_2^*} \approx 39.4 > 0$$

$$\frac{\partial^2 \Pi_2[p_1, p_2]}{\partial p_2 \partial p_1}\Bigg|_{p_1 = p_1^*, p_2 = p_2^*} \approx 99.4 > 0$$

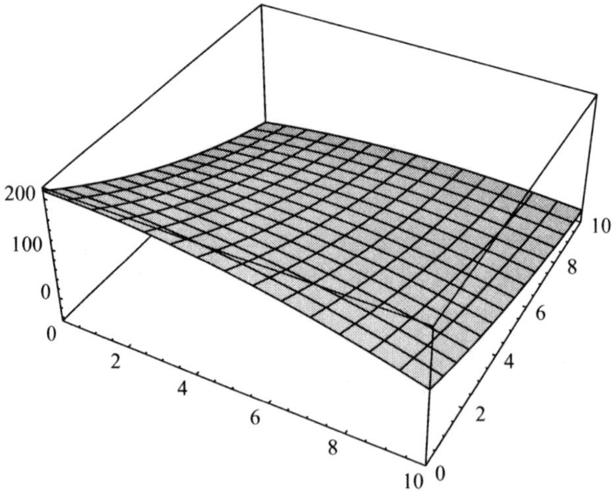

Figure 6.21   Symmetric access price regulation: cross derivatives of operator 1's profits in period 1

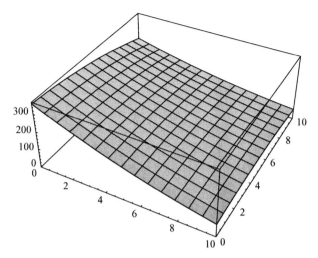

Figure 6.22   Symmetric access price regulation: cross derivatives of operator 2's profits in period 1

(iii)

$$\frac{\partial^2 \Pi_1[p_1, p_2]}{\partial p_1 \partial p_2}\bigg|_{p_1=p_1^*, p_2=p_2^*} \approx 6.76 > 0$$

$$\frac{\partial^2 \Pi_2[p_1, p_2]}{\partial p_2 \partial p_1}\bigg|_{p_1=p_1^*, p_2=p_2^*} \approx 216.5 > 0$$

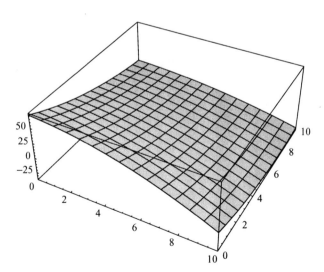

Figure 6.23   Asymmetric access price regulation: cross derivatives of operator 1's profits in period 1

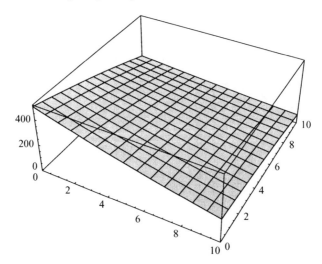

Figure 6.24   Asymmetric access price regulation: cross derivatives of operator 2's profits in period 1

APPENDIX 6.3: LINEAR PRICING – RECIPROCAL ACCESS PRICES AND LOCAL
LOOP UNBUNDLING

Table 6.12 shows prices and entrant's market share in the following four regulatory regimes: (i) cost-based access and unbundling; (ii) cost-based access and

Table 6.12 *Linear pricing with reciprocal access prices and local loop unbundling*

	Cost-based access and unbundling	Cost-based access and lease price markup	Reciprocal access markup and cost-based unbundling	Reciprocal access markup and lease price markup
p_1^1	8.20	9.23	8.55	9.56
p_1^2	8.04	9.12	8.38	9.49
p_1^3	7.91	9.08	8.24	9.42
p_1^4	7.81	9.00	8.11	9.34
p_2^1	4.58	5.62	4.91	5.99
p_2^2	4.92	5.89	5.20	6.19
p_2^3	5.15	6.11	5.40	6.38
p_2^4	5.34	6.31	5.58	6.57
s_2^1	9.7	5.6	8.6	3.8
s_2^2	15.5	9.8	14.2	7.4
s_2^3	19.5	13.4	18.4	10.9
s_2^4	22.8	16.8	21.8	14.4

lease price markup (10 euros); (iii) reciprocal access markup (1.5 euro cents) and cost-based unbundling; and (iv) reciprocal access markup (1.5 euro cents) and lease price markup (10 euros). Regulatory regimes (i) and (iii) correspond to regulatory regimes under facilities-based entry.

APPENDIX 6.4: LINEAR PRICING–ASYMMETRIC ACCESS PRICES AND LOCAL LOOP UNBUNDLING

Table 6.13 shows prices and entrant's market share and profits, as well as welfare, in the following four regulatory regimes: (i) cost-based access and unbundling; (ii) cost-based access and lease price subsidy (5 euros); (iii) asymmetric access price regulation (markup of 1.5 euro cents for the entrant) and cost-based unbundling; and (iv) asymmetric access price regulation (markup of 1.5 euro cents for the entrant) and lease price subsidy (5 euros). Regulatory regimes (i) and (iii) correspond to regulatory regimes under facilities-based entry.

APPENDIX 6.5: EXISTENCE AND UNIQUENESS UNDER TERMINATION-BASED PRICE DISCRIMINATION AND RECIPROCAL ACCESS PRICES

To show existence of equilibrium, it is sufficient to show that profit functions are concave. The condition for concavity, $\partial^2 \Pi_i / \partial m_i^2 < 0$, is equivalent to:

$$-2\left(\frac{\partial s_i}{\partial m_i}\right)^2 x\left[p_j^{\text{off}}\right](\tau - c_3) + 2\frac{\partial s_i}{\partial m_i} < 0.$$

Hence, one obtains:

$$-\frac{1}{Z - 2\left(v[c_1] - v[c_2 + \tau]\right)} x[c_2 + \tau](\tau - c_3) - 1 < 0,$$

given the competitor's optimal off-net per-minute price. This condition is satisfied for Z sufficiently large or $\tau - c_3$ sufficiently close to zero. Together with the fact that there exists a solution to the first-order conditions, this shows the existence of an equilibrium.

The argument for uniqueness of equilibrium then goes as follows: first note that in any equilibrium the marginal cost pricing principle holds. Best responses have a slope between 0 and 1 for Z sufficiently large or $\tau - c_3$ sufficiently close to zero (as observed by Laffont, Rey, and Tirole, 1998b). Note that this implies uniqueness of equilibrium. This argument relies neither on symmetry on the demand and cost side nor on reciprocal access prices. Under asymmetric access prices, there exists a unique equilibrium if Z is sufficiently large or if $\tau_1 - c_3$ and $\tau_2 - c_3$ are sufficiently close to zero.

Under symmetry, uniqueness of equilibrium can alternatively be shown as follows. Consider cross derivatives $\partial^2 \Pi_i / \partial m_i \partial m_j$. The condition for strategic

Table 6.13 *Linear pricing with asymmetric access prices and local loop unbundling*

	Cost-based access and unbundling	Cost-based access and lease price subsidy	Asymmetric access price regulation and cost-based unbundling	Asymmetric access price regulation and lease price subsidy
p_1^1	8.20	7.68	7.34	6.82
p_1^2	8.04	7.48	7.30	6.76
p_1^3	7.91	7.34	7.26	6.71
p_1^4	7.81	7.22	7.24	6.68
p_2^1	4.58	4.09	3.76	3.28
p_2^2	4.92	4.44	4.27	3.82
p_2^3	5.15	4.68	4.61	4.15
p_2^4	5.34	4.85	4.87	4.40
s_2^1	9.7	11.1	12.4	13.4
s_2^2	15.5	17.3	19.0	20.2
s_2^3	19.5	21.4	23.1	24.4
s_2^4	22.8	24.7	26.3	27.5
Π_2^1	3.8	5.1	8.1	9.8
Π_2^2	9.3	12.1	18.2	21.5
Π_2^3	14.4	18.2	26.4	30.7
Π_2^4	19.3	23.7	33.5	38.4
W^1	740.0	751.9	758.1	768.0
W^2	740.6	752.6	755.0	765.0
W^3	741.9	754.0	753.9	764.1
W^4	744.1	756.3	754.4	764.9

complementarity, $\partial^2 \Pi_i / \partial m_i \partial m_j > 0$, translates into:

$$-\frac{2}{Z - 2\left(v[c_1] - v[c_2 + \tau]\right)} x[c_2 + \tau](\tau - c_3) - 1 < 0, \qquad (6.3)$$

which is a stronger condition than the condition for concavity above. This condition is satisfied for Z sufficiently large or $\tau - c_3$ sufficiently close to zero. Suppose inequality (6.3) holds. Because the marginal cost pricing principle holds, we have seen that there exists a unique symmetric equilibrium in our model. Because of strategic complementarity, there do not exist asymmetric equilibria and the equilibrium is unique (see, for instance, Peitz, 1999). In addition, for per-minute prices equal to marginal costs the game in which operators set subscription fees is dominance solvable.

APPENDIX 6.6: SUBSCRIPTION FEES UNDER TERMINATION-BASED PRICE
DISCRIMINATION AND ASYMMETRIC REGULATION; MONOTONE
COMPARATIVE STATICS

The material of this appendix is adopted from Peitz (2001). We assume cost
symmetry.

Part 1: Characterization of equilibrium

We report the unique equilibrium candidate for the first period. In later periods
s_i^0 and u_i^0 have to be replaced by s_i^t and u_i^t respectively. An interior equilibrium is
characterized by per-minute prices $p_1^{on*} = p_2^{on*} = c_1$, $p_1^{off*} = c_2 + \tau_2$, $p_2^{off*} =
c_1$, and subscription fees:

$$
\begin{aligned}
m_1^* = f &+ \frac{Z - (v[c_1] - v[c_2 + \tau_2])}{3Z - 3(v[c_1] - v[c_2 + \tau_2]) + 2(\tau_2 - c_3)x[c_2 + \tau_2]} \\
&\times \left(u_1^0 - u_2^0 - 2(v[c_1] - v[c_2 + \tau_2])\right) \\
&+ (\tau_2 - c_3)x[c_2 + \tau_2] + \left(1 + s_1^0\right)Z), \quad \text{and}
\end{aligned}
$$

$$
\begin{aligned}
m_2^* = f &+ \frac{1}{3Z - 3(v[c_1] - v[c_2 + \tau_2]) + 2(\tau_2 - c_3)x[c_2 + \tau_2]} \\
&\times \left((u_2^0 - u_1^0)(-(v[c_1] - v[c_2 + \tau_2]) + 2(\tau_2 - c_3)x[c_2 + \tau_2] + Z\right) \\
&+ (v[c_1] - v[c_2 + \tau_2])^2 + \left(2 - s_1^0\right)Z^2 \\
&+ \left((3 - s_1^0)(v[c_1] - v[c_2 + \tau_2]) + 2\left(1 - s_1^0\right)(\tau_2 - c_3)x[c_2 + \tau_2]\right)Z).
\end{aligned}
$$

Part 2: Monotone comparative statics

For monotone comparative statics, we first check the conditions for strategic
complementarity, $\partial^2 \Pi_1 / \partial m_1 \partial m_2 > 0$ and $\partial^2 \Pi_2 / \partial m_2 \partial m_1 > 0$. We then check
that $\partial^2 \Pi_1 / \partial m_1 \partial \tau_2 < 0$ and $\partial^2 \Pi_2 / \partial m_2 \partial \tau_2 < 0$. It will be useful to evaluate the
following expressions:

$$
\frac{\partial s_1}{\partial m_1} = \frac{\partial s_2}{\partial m_2} = -\frac{1}{Z - (v[c_1] - v[c_2 + \tau_2])} < 0.
$$

For interior solutions, market share declines in the subscription fee. Further
useful expressions are:

$$
\frac{\partial s_1}{\partial \tau_2} = -\frac{\partial s_2}{\partial \tau_2} = -\frac{s_2 x[c_2 + \tau_2]}{Z - (v[c_1] - v[c_2 + \tau_2])} < 0,
$$

$$
\frac{\partial^2 s_1}{\partial m_1 \partial \tau_2} = \frac{\partial^2 s_2}{\partial m_2 \partial \tau_2} = -\frac{x[c_2 + \tau_2]}{(Z - (v[c_1] - v[c_2 + \tau_2]))^2} < 0.
$$

We find that networks are strategic complements under termination-based price discrimination and asymmetric regulation because:

$$\frac{\partial^2 \Pi_1}{\partial m_1 \partial m_2} = \frac{\partial s_1}{\partial m_2} = -\frac{\partial s_2}{\partial m_2} > 0,$$

$$\frac{\partial^2 \Pi_2}{\partial m_2 \partial m_1} = \frac{\partial s_2}{\partial m_1}\left(1 + 2\left(-\frac{\partial s_2}{\partial m_2}\right)x[c_2 + \tau_2](\tau_2 - c_3)\right) > 0.$$

Furthermore, we obtain monotonicity of the incumbent's marginal profits in τ_2:

$$\frac{\partial^2 \Pi_1}{\partial m_1 \partial \tau_2} = \frac{\partial s_1}{\partial \tau_2} + (m_1 - f)\frac{\partial^2 s_1}{\partial m_1 \partial \tau_2} < 0.$$

The change of the incumbent's marginal profits in the access price can be written as:

$$\frac{\partial^2 \Pi_2}{\partial m_2 \partial \tau_2} = \frac{\partial^2 s_2}{\partial m_2 \partial \tau_2}(m_2 - f) + \left(\frac{\partial s_2}{\partial \tau_2} + (1 - 2s_2)\frac{\partial s_2}{\partial m_2}x[c_2 + \tau_2]\right)$$

$$+ (\tau_2 - c_3)\left(\left((1 - 2s_2)\frac{\partial^2 s_2}{\partial m_2 \partial \tau_2} - 2\frac{\partial s_2}{\partial \tau_2}\frac{\partial s_2}{\partial m_2}\right)x[c_2 + \tau_2]\right.$$

$$\left. + (1 - 2s_2)\frac{\partial s_2}{\partial m_2}x'[c_2 + \tau_2]\right).$$

The first term is negative while the third term becomes arbitrarily small for $\tau_2 - c_3$ sufficiently close to zero. The second term can be written as:

$$-\frac{(1 - 3s_2)x[c_2 + \tau_2]}{Z - (v[c_1] - v[c_2 + \tau_2])} \leq 0 \quad \text{for} \quad s_2 \leq \frac{1}{3}.$$

This shows that subscription fees are decreasing in the entrant's access price τ_2, at least for $\tau_2 - c_3$ sufficiently close to zero and $s_2 \leq \frac{1}{3}$.

7 Non-targeted entry in a segmented market

7.1 Introduction

In this chapter, we extend the model of facilities-based competition from Chapters 3 and 4 to a situation with a segmented market and various possibilities of consumer heterogeneity. In particular, we suppose that there are two different market segments, such as residential customers and business customers. Some other possibilities are: an urban and a rural segment; a fixed and a mobile segment; or two different countries. Operators can distinguish the segments and, if regulation permits, are able to choose different pricing strategies for the two segments.

Throughout this chapter, we assume that the market segmentation is crude enough for operators to be able to tell the segments apart and to address them in different ways. Operators are able to observe a certain signal related to a customer's identity and know their preferences. For example, it can be observed whether a customer subscribes as a private person or on behalf of a company. Accordingly, we focus on "third-degree" price discrimination.[1]

Note that within a segment or sub-market, customers may exhibit a whole range of different traits that cannot be directly observed by firms. In reality, one often observes that firms use implicit or "second-degree" price discrimination: they select indirectly between customer types by offering different packages. For example, mobile operators typically offer a variety of contracts (a "menu"), aiming at self-selection of the different consumer types. Usually, implicit price discrimination requires a complex analysis and may lead to a wide variety of contracts.[2] By restricting the analysis to third-degree price discrimination, we can ignore non-linear prices that are different from two-part tariffs.

This chapter explores how differences between the segments may affect operators' pricing decisions, and to what extent consumers may benefit or suffer from price discrimination. The central question that we want to address is to

---

[1] For an explanation of different types of price discrimination, see Tirole (1988, ch. 3).

[2] The difference, compared with explicit price discrimination, is that the menu of contracts has to be compatible with consumers' preferences and their implied incentives to choose certain contracts ("incentive-compatibility" constraints).

what extent the regulator has to take market segmentation and operators' pricing strategies into account; here we are interested in the role of access price regulation. To answer this question, we will recall results from earlier chapters on non-segmented markets. Also, we will re-examine the profit-neutrality result, according to which the level of a reciprocal access price does not affect operators' profits levels (see Chapter 3 and Armstrong, 2001). We will see that our results from Chapter 3 hold in a segmented market as well. Nevertheless, it is shown that profits in one segment do respond to access prices, even with symmetric operators.

In a segmented market for voice telephony, one has to make assumptions about consumers' *calling patterns*. For instance, if the market is split into a residential segment and a business segment, do residential consumers on average make more calls to other residential consumers than to firms? Do firms exhibit a bias toward making calls to consumers? We will introduce and analyze several cases of calling patterns, in order to better understand the role of calling patterns as well as to assess the sensitivity of the results.

The rest of this chapter is organized as follows. Section 7.2 presents the model of facilities-based competition enriched with a segmented market. It also explains how one can incorporate calling patterns into the model. The main part of this chapter is Section 7.3, in which the regulator allows both operators to price discriminate. Such a situation where the regulator does not impose restrictions on operators with regard to pricing is a natural starting point of the analysis. Various calling patterns and asymmetries between the segments (e.g. demand-related) or operators (e.g. cost-related) are discussed, using results from simulation. Our main concern is the role of terminating access prices. The general lesson of that section is that in an infant market, in order to stimulate competition and increase consumers surplus in a particular segment, access markups for the entrant in *both* segments are the "best" choice. The reason is that a segment-specific access markup tends to reduce consumers surplus in the other segment, an effect that will be undesirable in general. Then Section 7.4 explores how competition is affected if only the incumbent is not allowed to price discriminate, and if both firms have to set uniform prices. Such regulatory constraints are currently in place in many countries, and it is important to understand their consequences. Finally, Section 7.5 summarizes the findings of the chapter.

7.2   The model with a segmented market

We adapt the model of facilities-based competition of Chapters 3 and 4 to incorporate a segmented market. Suppose that the market consists of two segments, called segments 1 and 2. The total market consists, as before, of (a continuum with mass) n consumers. Denote a segment by a superscript k. The relative size of segment $k = 1, 2$ is denoted by fraction α^k. Each operator targets both segments. Accordingly, entry is not targeted to one of the segments (Chapter 8 addresses targeted entry).

The operators can distinguish the two segments and set different prices for them.[3] This situation is usually called explicit or third-degree price discrimination. Although, in reality, operators are not always able to observe signals of all customer traits, we have situations in mind where this is possible. In the introduction, several examples were given.

Apart from customers belonging to different segments, we also allow for different characteristics between the segments. Residential and business customers may have different demand and utility parameters, and perhaps also different switching costs. For example, a company's demand for telephone services may be bigger and less elastic than the demand of a residential consumer. In other examples, other differences may be more important. If one distinguishes between consumers living in rural and urban areas, then they are likely to have different fixed connection costs.

Some new notation is needed to distinguish the segments. Since we discuss competition either in the first period or in a mature market, we drop the time superscript. In principle, all cost and demand parameters can be segment specific; the superscript k refers to segment k. On the demand side, these include individual demand parameters a^k and b^k, fixed-utility parameters u_i^{0k}, and switching-cost parameter Z^k. On the cost side, these include marginal costs c_{i1}^k, c_{i2}^k and connection-dependent fixed cost f_i^k. We also allow for segment-specific access prices τ_i^k. Finally, two-part tariffs under explicit price discrimination are denoted by subscription fee m_i^k and per-minute price p_i^k.

In the situations of entry that are explored in this chapter, we abstract from fixed-utility differences between the operators (except in Subsection 7.3.4).[4] Following the presentation of Chapter 3, we focus on the outcomes of competition in the first period and in a mature market. Recall that, in a non-segmented market, the entrant obtains a market share of $\frac{1}{3}$ if terminating access prices are cost-based (see Subsection 3.5.1). It is straightforward to show that this is also the case in our model of a segmented market.

Each segment in itself can be described as before. In addition, however, segments are linked with each other as follows. Consumers typically not only make calls within their own segment, but also to consumers in the other segment. Similar to the way consumers make on-net and off-net calls, the nature of these links is described by consumers' calling patterns. Recall that, in previous

---

[3] We consider retail price discrimination as the natural point of departure, as it imposes less restrictions on the operators.

[4] Recall that, in Chapter 4, we assumed that the entrant needs to build a track record to offer a similar fixed utility level as the incumbent. Therefore, quantitative comparisons with the outcomes of Chapter 4 cannot be made.

Table 7.1 *Call minutes in a segmented market*

To:		
From:	$i = 1, k = 1$	$i = 1, k = 2$
$i = 1, k = 1$	$n\alpha^1\beta^{11}(s_1^1)^2 x^1[p_1^1]$	$n\alpha^1\beta^{12}s_1^1 s_1^2 x^1[p_1^1]$
$i = 1, k = 2$	$n\alpha^2\beta^{21}s_1^1 s_1^2 x^2[p_1^2]$	$n\alpha^2\beta^{22}(s_1^2)^2 x^2[p_1^2]$
$i = 2, k = 1$	$n\alpha^1\beta^{11}s_1^1 s_2^1 x^1[p_2^1]$	$n\alpha^1\beta^{12}s_1^2 s_2^1 x^1[p_2^1]$
$i = 2, k = 2$	$n\alpha^2\beta^{21}s_1^1 s_2^2 x^2[p_2^2]$	$n\alpha^2\beta^{22}s_1^2 s_2^2 x^2[p_2^2]$

To:		
From:	$i = 2, k = 1$	$i = 2, k = 2$
$i = 1, k = 1$	$n\alpha^1\beta^{11}s_1^1 s_2^1 x^1[p_1^1]$	$n\alpha^1\beta^{12}s_1^1 s_2^2 x^1[p_1^1]$
$i = 1, k = 2$	$n\alpha^2\beta^{21}s_1^2 s_2^1 x^2[p_1^2]$	$n\alpha^2\beta^{22}s_1^2 s_2^2 x^2[p_1^2]$
$i = 2, k = 1$	$n\alpha^1\beta^{11}(s_2^1)^2 x^1[p_2^1]$	$n\alpha^1\beta^{12}s_2^1 s_2^2 x^1[p_2^1]$
$i = 2, k = 2$	$n\alpha^2\beta^{21}s_2^1 s_2^2 x^2[p_2^2]$	$n\alpha^2\beta^{22}(s_2^2)^2 x^2[p_2^2]$

chapters, we assumed that the numbers of on-net and off-net calls are proportionate to market shares (balanced calling patterns). As a start, we will extend the assumption of balanced calling patterns (see also Subsection 3.2.3) to a segmented market. Later (in Section 7.3), we introduce different calling patterns.

Calling patterns that extend to calls between the segments are incorporated into the model by defining consumers' inclinations to make calls to people within their own or in the other segment. The probability that a call which originates on segment k terminates on segment l is denoted by β^{kl}. Hence $\beta^{kk} + \beta^{kl} = 1$, where $l \neq k$. A call that remains within the same segment is called "on-segment," a call that terminates on the other segment is called "off-segment." Table 7.1 gives an overview of the traffic flows between segments and networks.

To simplify the notation, we define ζ_i^{kl} as a function of all retail prices, that gives the volume of (off-net) calls that originate on operator i's network within segment $k = 1, 2$ and terminate on the network of operator $j \neq i$ within segment $l = 1, 2$. Accordingly (suppressing all the arguments of function ζ_i^{kl}):

$$\zeta_i^{kl} \equiv n\alpha^k \beta^{kl} s_i^k s_j^l x^k [p_i^k], \text{ where } j \neq i.$$

One can extend the notion of a balanced calling pattern, as it was defined for a market with homogeneous customers, to a segmented market as follows.

A calling pattern is said to be balanced if, for a given per-minute price p that is the same for all consumers in the market, each operator's network generates as many off-net calls as it receives as incoming calls from the other network:

$$\sum_{k,l} \zeta_1^{kl} = \sum_{k,l} \zeta_2^{kl}.$$

Equivalently, the traffic volumes of each operator's incoming and off-net calls have the same size, aggregated over consumer types. It is straightforward to check that one can simplify this equality as:

$$\frac{\beta^{12}}{\beta^{21}} = \frac{\alpha^2 x^2[p]}{\alpha^1 x^1[p]}.$$

As a starting point of the analysis, we will use a "uniform" calling pattern, in which consumers are, in a statistical sense, indifferent about whom they call. Any call that is being made is directed to any individual consumer, whether on-net or off-net, whether on-segment or off-segment, with equal probabilities. Accordingly, consumers have no "specific" preferences with regard to on-net or off-net customers, or with regard to the segments. On an aggregate level, the probability of calling someone on a given network within a certain segment is proportional to the size of the group of customers that fall into that category. In the model, a calling pattern is uniform if $\beta^{kl} = \alpha^l$ for all $k, l = 1, 2$. The interpretation is that consumers' exogenous preferences to call to someone in a certain segment are proportional to the segment sizes.

Notice that a balanced calling pattern implies that probabilities β^{kl} implicitly depend on individual demand functions $x^1[p]$ and $x^2[p]$. By definition, this is not the case for uniform calling patterns. In particular, a balanced calling pattern is equivalent to a uniform calling pattern if $x^1[p] = x^2[p]$ for all p, that is, consumers in different segments have the same demand function. If $x^1[p] > x^2[p]$ then a uniform calling pattern implies that segment 2, which is characterized by lower individual demand for call minutes, has more calls terminating on it than originating from it.

7.3   Price discrimination

Throughout this section, we assume that both operators are allowed to set different prices for the two segments. Using this assumption, we explore the role of segment-specific access prices and differences between the segments. As a starting point (Subsections 7.3.1 and 7.3.2), the calling pattern is assumed to be uniform. Subsection 7.3.3 then explores different calling patterns. Subsection 7.3.4 looks at other demand asymmetries, and Subsection 7.3.5 at cost asymmetries.

7.3.1   Observations in a symmetric market

To have some benchmark results for later reference, we will start by looking at symmetric parameter constellations. That is, market segments are identical, operators are identical, and, in a symmetric equilibrium, they choose prices $p^1 \equiv p_1^k = p_2^k$ and $m^1 \equiv m_1^k = m_2^k$, $k = 1, 2$. Also, in equilibrium, $s_1^k = s_2^k$, $k = 1, 2$.

A first observation is that, depending on the calling pattern, the operators may not price discriminate with respect to per-minute prices, even if terminating access prices are different in the two segments. To see this, notice that in equilibrium, operator i's per-minute price in segment k is equal to the perceived marginal cost in segment k (see Chapter 3). That is, for $l \neq k$ and $j \neq i$:

$$p_i^{k*} = s_i^k \beta^{kk} c_1 + s_i^l \beta^{kl} c_1 + s_j^k \beta^{kk} (c_2 + \tau_j^k) + s_j^l \beta^{kl} (c_2 + \tau_j^l). \quad (7.1)$$

One can check that independent of market shares, if $\beta^{11} = \beta^{21}$ and $\beta^{22} = \beta^{12}$, then it follows directly that $p_i^{1*} = p_i^{2*}$ for each operator $i = 1, 2$. This is the case if, for instance, the calling pattern is uniform, that is, $\beta^{kk} = \beta^{lk} = \alpha^k$. Accordingly, under a uniform calling pattern, the operators do not set segment-specific per-minute prices in equilibrium.[5]

How do terminating access prices influence profit levels? Does the profit-neutrality result hold in a segmented market where the regulator can impose access prices that are different for the segments? Suppose that access prices in each segment are reciprocal, that is:

$$\tau^k \equiv \tau_1^k = \tau_2^k, k = 1, 2.$$

An incoming call that terminates in segment k generates net revenues $\tau^k - c_3$ per minute for the operator handling the delivery of the call. Taking into account the opportunity cost c_3, if a call is terminated by the other operator, an off-net call that terminates in segment k has costs $\tau^k - c_3$ for the operator with the network where the call originates. Therefore, one can show that operator i's net access revenues, where $i \neq j$, are equal to:

$$\sum_{k,l} \zeta_j^{kl}(\tau^l - c_3) + \sum_{k,l} \zeta_i^{kl}(-\tau^l + c_3)$$

$$= n\alpha^2 \beta^{21} x^2 [p^2](\tau^1 - c_3)(s_j^2 s_i^1 - s_i^2 s_j^1)$$

$$+ n\alpha^1 \beta^{12} x^1 [p^1](\tau^2 - c_3)(s_j^1 s_i^2 - s_i^1 s_j^2).$$

In a symmetric equilibrium, this expression is equal to zero, since operators have equal market shares in both segments. Using this expression, one can show that profits do not depend on the level of reciprocal access prices. In

---

[5] The same holds for certain types of "segment-i biased" calling patterns, which will be defined later.

fact, an operator's total profits in a symmetric equilibrium are equal to $nZ/4$ (see Subsection 3.3.2 for a similar derivation). Note that this holds for access prices that are uniform over the segments[6] ($\tau^1 = \tau^2$) as well as for segment-specific access prices ($\tau^1 \neq \tau^2$). Furthermore, this profit-neutrality result does not depend on the calling pattern nor on the relative segment sizes.

It is important to notice that profits in a segment do depend on access prices. For example, consider a reciprocal access markup in segment 2 only, and compare this to a situation of cost-based access prices in both segments. Then market share in segment 2 becomes relatively more valuable compared to segment 1, because incoming calls in segment 2 generate access revenues. Consequently, the operators compete more vigorously for customers in segment 2, leading to lower subscription fees m_1^2 and m_2^2, as well as reduced profits Π_1^2 and Π_2^2; it is straightforward to verify this.

Consumers surplus, aggregate as well as per segment, is not neutral to access prices. The reciprocal access markup in segment 2 leads to an increase of CS^2, and a decrease in CS^1. Any gain in profits in segment 1 exactly offsets the downward pressure on profits in segment 2 (as follows from profit-neutrality). In particular, the operators behave less aggressively in segment 1 because lost customers still generate profits when they make off-net calls to the other segment. Consequently, customers in segment 1 are worse off. Overall, we observe that total consumers surplus $CS^1 + CS^2$ decreases. Since consumers surplus is lower and profits are constant, welfare is lower than under cost-based access prices.[7] A segment-specific access markup is less detrimental to welfare than a uniform markup of the same magnitude, because the average distortion of per-minute prices is smaller. Finally, we remark that in equilibrium, if access prices are asymmetric across segments, operators set equal per-minute prices for the two segments. The reason is that the balanced calling pattern leads to equal perceived marginal costs for calls originating in each of the segments.[8]

Postponing more precise policy implications to the next subsection, we conclude at this point that access prices matter in a segmented market. The neutral effect on total profits notwithstanding, segment-specific access prices affect retail prices and consumers surplus within the segments in different ways.

---

[6] In a segmented market, this profit-neutrality result also holds under second-degree price discrimination where operators choose menus of contracts consisting of fixed charges and quantity, and explicitly or implicitly price discriminate (see Dessein, 2000). In Dessein's model, this follows from considering a unilateral ε-deviation from a symmetric equilibrium in the fixed charges for both segments (see also Armstrong, 2001). Poletti and Wright (2000) extend Dessein's model to allow for a binding consumer participation constraint and show that profits can be increasing in the access price. This implies that access price regulation may be needed in a mature market even if operators compete in non-linear prices. See also Schiff (2001).

[7] Recall that an access markup leads to perceived marginal costs above true marginal costs, so that there arises a deadweight loss.

[8] Recall that segments are symmetric, so that uniform calling patterns are also balanced.

Table 7.2 *Reciprocal access prices in a mature market*

	–	$\tau_1^1, \tau_1^2, \tau_2^1, \tau_2^2$	τ_1^1, τ_2^1	τ_1^2, τ_2^2
		Markups in:		
$p_1^1 = p_2^1$	2.000	2.250	2.125	2.125
$p_1^2 = p_2^2$	2.000	2.250	2.125	2.125
$m_1^1 = m_2^1$	5000.0	4861.3	4720.7	5139.7
$m_1^2 = m_2^2$	5000.0	4722.7	5069.8	4650.9
$\Pi_1^1 = \Pi_2^1$	60.0	61.4	58.6	62.8
$\Pi_1^2 = \Pi_2^2$	60.0	58.6	61.4	57.2
CS^1	405.0	399.4	410.6	393.8
CS^2	202.5	208.0	196.9	213.7

In our view, the profit-neutrality result is not a general result, since it was derived under strong symmetry assumptions which are unlikely to be met in reality. For instance, in the following subsection we demonstrate that profits are not neutral to changes in access prices if the operators initially have unequal market shares. This implies that in the early stages of competition, access price regulation can have a strong impact on the development of entry in the market.

7.3.2   Segment-specific demand

Consider the following asymmetry between the two segments: for a given per-minute price, customers in segment 2 make half the number of calls of customers in segment 1. We incorporate this assumption into the model, where $x^k[p] = (a^k - p)/b^k$, by setting $b^1 = 0.016$ and $b^2 = 0.032$. Then segment 1 can be referred to as the high-volume segment, segment 2 as the low-volume segment. Otherwise, we use the standard parameter configuration from Chapter 3. As a starting point, the calling pattern is assumed to be uniform. For the sake of exposition, we will only consider cost-based access prices (equal to $c_3 = 0.5$) and access prices that include a markup of 0.5 euro cents.

Mature market   Consider a mature market, that is, each operator's initial market share in each segment is 50 percent. We are interested in knowing how reciprocal, possibly segment-specific, access prices affect competition. Table 7.2 summarizes simulation results of four cases, where a "markup" always refers to an access price equal to 1.0.

Notice from Table 7.2 that an access markup, even if it applies to a single segment only, simultaneously increases per-minute prices in both segments. It does not lead to different per-minute prices for the segments, as can be seen from equation (7.1). As before, access markups distort calling behavior away from the first-best outcome and hence reduce total consumers surplus.

If all access prices are equal to cost, demand differences do not induce the operators to set segment-specific subscription fees, as one can see in Table 7.2. To understand why this happens, notice that along the operators' best response functions, the net revenues generated from on-net calls and from off-net calls both equal zero (see also Section 3.3). Profits are derived only from: (i) incoming traffic, which does not generate any net revenues because of cost-based access prices; and (ii) subscription fees, which do not affect a customer's individual demand for call minutes. This explains why demand differences do not affect subscription fees.

A general observation from Table 7.2 is that an access markup in a given segment makes that segment more attractive: a larger market share generates more access revenues from incoming calls. As a consequence, the operators compete more aggressively in that segment, leading to lower subscription fees. The different intensity of competition is also reflected by consumers surplus: if there is an access markup in one of the segments only, consumers in that segment are better off, compared to the case with cost-based access prices in all segments.[9]

Recall from Subsection 7.3.1 that, with identical segments, operators do not price discriminate. Here, if there is a uniform access markup in all segments (applying to $\tau_1^1, \tau_1^2, \tau_2^1, \tau_2^2$), then the demand difference does lead to price discrimination, that is, operators set different subscription fees for each segment. Competition is more intense in segment 2, the low-volume segment, because more calls terminate in that segment than originate from it. Because incoming calls contribute to profits whereas originating calls do not, operators care more about gaining market share in the low-volume segment than in the other segment. Because of this strategic effect, operators make less profits in segment 2 ($\Pi_1^2 = \Pi_2^2 = 58.6$) than in the other segment ($\Pi_1^1 = \Pi_2^1 = 61.4$), where demand is larger.

The policy implications from the analysis above are straightforward. Note that in each of the access regimes in the table, each operator i's level of total profits, $\Pi_i^1 + \Pi_i^2$, does not depend on access prices. Hence, the profit-neutrality result still holds. However, this does not mean that policy should not be concerned with access prices. Firstly, access markups introduce a social cost because they distort the demand for call minutes. Next, in order to improve consumers surplus in a particular segment i, the regulator might impose access markups in that segment only. This reduces, however, consumers surplus in the other segment. Thus, there is an undesirable spillover effect from supporting one

---

[9] Because demand parameter b affects utility levels, one cannot directly compare CS^2 with CS^1.

Table 7.3 *Segment-specific access prices in an infant market*

		Markups in:		
	–	$\tau_1^1, \tau_1^2, \tau_2^1, \tau_2^2$	τ_2^1, τ_2^2	τ_2^2
p_1^1	2.000	2.167	2.167	2.083
p_1^2	2.000	2.167	2.167	2.083
p_2^1	2.000	2.333	2.000	2.000
p_2^2	2.000	2.333	2.000	2.000
m_1^1	6000.0	5952.3	5721.1	6000.0
m_1^2	6000.0	5767.8	5721.2	5720.0
m_2^1	4000.0	3768.2	3907.4	4093.4
m_2^2	4000.0	3675.8	3814.4	3766.8
Π_1^1	106.7	109.1	99.2	106.7
Π_1^2	106.7	104.2	99.2	99.2
Π_2^1	26.7	27.3	29.2	27.9
Π_2^2	26.7	26.1	27.9	27.3
CS^1	378.3	372.8	382.0	374.6
CS^2	175.8	181.4	183.3	185.2

segment through access price regulation. From the viewpoint of a regulator which does not have a preference for a particular segment and does not want to disadvantage other segments, cost-based access prices perform best in a mature market, whether imposed by regulation or established through negotiations.

The following guideline summarizes the analysis so far.

> **Guideline 7.1:** Consider a segmented market with non-targeted facilities-based competition. In a mature market, a segment-specific, reciprocal access markup increases consumers surplus in that segment, but decreases consumers surplus in the other segment. Cost-based terminating access prices maximize welfare and consumers surplus.

Infant market Next we analyze how the equilibrium outcomes and policy implications change if the market is not mature, but the entrant's initial market share in each segment is zero. See Table 7.3 for a summary of simulation outcomes for different access price regimes.

Table 7.3 shows that the profit-neutrality result does not hold in a market characterized by asymmetric market shares. In particular, comparing cost-based access prices with uniform, reciprocal access markups (all access prices $\tau_1^1, \tau_1^2, \tau_2^1, \tau_2^2$ above costs), one can see that the incumbent's total profits are lower in the latter case.

On a more general level, our reasoning in the case of mature markets still applies. That is, if there are uniform and reciprocal access markups, then operators compete more aggressively in the low-volume segment, which is the segment with a net inflow of calls. This is again explained by the fact that the low-volume segment generates more revenues from incoming calls.

The last two columns in Table 7.3 give the outcomes for two asymmetric access price regimes. In both cases, the incumbent is forced to set its access prices equal to marginal cost. In the first of these regimes, the entrant is allowed to charge access markups that are the same for both segments. In the second one, the entrant's access price is above cost only in segment 2, the low-volume segment, but cost-based in the other segment.

Firstly, suppose that τ_2^1 and τ_2^2 are above marginal cost. Similar to our results in a non-segmented market, asymmetric access price regulation increases the entrant's profits and reduces the incumbent's profits compared to cost-based regulation. Also, consumers surplus increases in both market segments. This increase is more pronounced in the low-volume segment, which is the segment with a net inflow of calls. Welfare is hardly affected because market shares are relatively insensitive to access markups and the deadweight loss is rather small.

Secondly, suppose that only τ_2^2 is above marginal costs (see the last column of Table 7.3). A straightforward observation is that customers in segment 2 benefit. As we have seen before, competition in segment 2 becomes more intense, driving down subscription fees m_1^2 and m_2^2. Conversely, customers in segment 1 are worse off, since competition in this segment is relaxed. In fact, consumers surplus in segment 1, CS^1, is even lower than in the case of cost-based access prices. This is possible because the entrant behaves less aggressively in segment 1; any lost consumer in this segment generates profits from incoming calls in the other segment.

We have seen that stimulating competition and increasing consumers surplus in segment 2 is most effectively done by allowing a markup in τ_2^2 only, but this goes together with a reduction of CS^1. Access markups for the entrant in both segments are somewhat less effective for consumers in segment 2, but raise consumers' surplus in segment 1 as well. Therefore, if the regulator wants to avoid spillover effects between the segments, the preferred access policy involves a uniform access markup (i.e., the same markup in both segments) for the entrant. We thus have an extension of Guideline 4.2.

> **Guideline 7.2:** Consider a segmented market with non-targeted facilities-based competition. In an infant market, asymmetric access markups only for the entrant in both segments increase consumers surplus and the entrant's profits. It is roughly neutral for welfare. A segment-specific access markup only for the entrant increases consumers surplus in that segment, but decreases consumers surplus in the other segment. (Extension of Guideline 4.2)

To conclude, note that the two guidelines in this subsection were derived by allowing for different individual demand functions for each segment. In the rest of this chapter, we will see that they apply also to situations with additional asymmetries and under different calling patterns.

7.3.3   The role of calling patterns

So far, we have only looked at uniform calling patterns. Obviously, there is an infinite number of other possibilities.[10] To assess the robustness of our results, we will consider two different calling patterns: *home-biased* and *segment-i-biased* calling patterns, which are explained below. But first we make a general observation.

In equilibrium, the sum of profits derived from on-net and off-net calls is zero.[11] Therefore, only subscriptions and incoming calls contribute to an operator's profits. Hence, one can simplify operator i's profits in segment 1 as follows:

$$\Pi_i^{1*} = n\alpha^1 s_i^{1*}\left(m_i^{1*} - f^1\right)$$
$$+ n\left(\alpha^1 s_i^{1*} s_j^{1*} \beta^{11} x\left[p_j^{1*}\right] + \alpha^2 s_i^{1*} s_j^{2*} \beta^{21} x\left[p_j^{2*}\right]\right)\left(\tau - c_3^1\right).$$

One can see that the calling pattern (described by β^{11} and β^{21}) directly enters into the profit function for a segment. In general, they also affect profits in a segment through per-minute prices and subscription fees.

Under unbalanced calling patterns and segment-specific demand, profits in a segment depend on terminating access prices. The reason is that one segment has a net inflow of incoming calls which makes market share in this segment more attractive, inducing operators to compete more aggressively for customers in this segment. Hence, if calling patterns are not balanced, consumers in a

---

[10] Work on competition in two-part tariffs with unbalanced calling patterns is also presented in Dessein (1999b).

[11] This follows from the fact that in equilibrium, per-minute prices are set equal to perceived marginal costs. See also Subsection 3.3.1.

segment with a net inflow of calls face lower subscription fees than those in a segment with a net outflow of calls.

Home-biased calling patterns   If a consumer who makes a call is most likely to call someone within the same segment, then we say that calling patterns are *home-biased*. In the model, this corresponds to call probabilities that are more than proportionate to the segment sizes, that is, $\beta^{kk} > \alpha^k$ for $k = 1, 2$. In the extreme case that $\beta^{11} = \beta^{22} = 1$, consumers never make calls to the other segment. If that is the case, the segments do not need to be interconnected. This situation corresponds to a model of telecommunications competition with multi-market contact. For example, two operators compete with each other in two different countries (corresponding to the segments), and residents of one country never make calls to residents of the other country. As an example of a home-biased calling pattern, we will consider simulations for the case $\beta^{11} = \beta^{22} = 0.8$.

Segment-i-biased calling patterns   If there is a bias towards a particular segment in the market compared to the case of uniform calling patterns, we say that calling patterns are *segment-i-biased*.[12] For example, consumers in *both* segments are inclined to make relatively more calls to a particular segment k, that is, $\beta^{1k} > \alpha^k$ and $\beta^{2k} > \alpha^k$ for a given $k = 1, 2$. Another example is that only consumers in a particular segment k are inclined to make relatively more calls within their own segment, that is, $\beta^{kk} > \alpha^k$, while calling patterns of consumers in the other segment do not exhibit such a bias. This corresponds, for instance, to a situation in which residential customers are most likely to make calls to other residential customers, while business customers' on-segment and off-segment calls are proportionate to the segment sizes. In our simulations, we will consider the segment-1-biased calling pattern described by $\beta^{11} = \beta^{21} = 0.8$ and the segment-2-biased calling pattern described by $\beta^{12} = \beta^{22} = 0.8$. Notice that these cases do not price discriminate with respect to per-minute prices (see the discussion after equation (7.1) in Subsection 7.3.1).

These calling patterns will be explored under different access regimes, both in a mature market and an infant market. In both cases, we stick to our assumption that $b^1 = 0.016$ and $b^2 = 0.032$, that is, as before, segment 1 can be referred to as the high-volume segment, and segment 2 as the low-volume segment. As in the rest of this chapter, we restrict the analysis to access markups of 0.5 euro cents. We start with a discussion of a mature-market situation.

[12] If $x^1[p] > x^2[p]$, then the positive net inflow of calls for segment 2 is higher under segment-2-biased than under uniform calling patterns.

Table 7.4 *Reciprocal access markups in both segments: calling patterns in a mature market*

	Calling pattern			
	Uniform	Home-biased	Segment-1-biased	Segment-2-biased
$p_1^1 = p_2^1$	2.25	2.25	2.25	2.25
$p_1^2 = p_2^2$	2.25	2.25	2.25	2.25
$m_1^1 = m_2^1$	4861.3	4778.1	4611.7	5110.9
$m_1^2 = m_2^2$	4722.7	4805.9	4972.3	4473.1
$\Pi_1^1 = \Pi_2^1$	61.4	60.6	58.9	63.9
$\Pi_1^2 = \Pi_2^2$	58.6	59.4	61.1	56.1
CS^1	399.4	402.7	409.4	389.4
CS^2	208.0	204.7	198.0	218.0

Mature market   Table 7.4 summarizes the simulation results for the selected calling patterns if access prices are reciprocal and include the same markups in both segments.

Compare the outcomes obtained under a uniform calling pattern with those obtained under a home-biased calling pattern. If customers are more inclined to communicate with customers within their own segment, as in the case of the home-biased pattern, then fewer calls leave the segment where they originate. Therefore, both operators receive more incoming calls in the high-volume segment, and less in the other segment. Since there is a reciprocal access markup which is uniform across segments, competition is more intense in segment 1. As a consequence, the operators set lower subscription fees for customers in segment 1. Nevertheless, because incoming calls are an important profit driver, segment 1 profits may be higher than segment 2 profits, as indeed happens in our simulations. Notice that the reverse holds for segment 2: competition for low-demand customers is less intense, resulting in higher subscription fees.

Again compared to the case with uniform calling patterns, consumers in segment 1 are better off due to more intense competition, whereas customers in segment 2 see that their surplus is reduced. This follows directly from the subscription fees that are chosen in equilibrium if the calling pattern is home-biased. In fact, such a calling pattern reinforces our earlier observations that demand differences between the segments affect competition and consumers surplus within each segment.

We now move on to compare segment-i-biased calling patterns with the uniform calling pattern (see the last two columns in Table 7.4). On a general level,

Table 7.5 *Reciprocal access markups in the low-volume segment:
calling patterns in a mature market*

	Calling pattern			
	Uniform	Home-biased	Segment-1-biased	Segment-2-biased
$p_1^1 = p_2^1$	2.125	2.050	2.050	2.200
$p_1^2 = p_2^2$	2.125	2.200	2.050	2.200
$m_1^1 = m_2^1$	5139.7	5056.1	5056.1	5222.5
$m_1^2 = m_2^2$	4650.9	4776.6	4859.8	4443.8
$\Pi_1^1 = \Pi_2^1$	62.8	61.1	61.1	64.5
$\Pi_1^2 = \Pi_2^2$	57.2	58.9	58.9	55.6
CS^1	393.8	400.5	400.5	387.2
CS^2	213.7	207.0	207.0	220.3

a tendency of consumers to make more calls to customers in segment i "shifts" competition to segment i. Given that there is an access markup, operators find that segment more valuable because it attracts more incoming traffic than the other segment. Consequently, subscription fees in segment i are lower than under uniform calling patterns, whereas subscription fees in the other segment are higher.

Next, consider a regulatory regime with reciprocal but segment-specific access prices. In particular, suppose that there is a reciprocal access markup only in the low-volume segment 2. Table 7.5 summarizes the simulation outcomes.

For all calling patterns that are considered, subscription fees are relatively low in the low-volume segment. Again, this is because the value of incoming traffic induces the operators to compete more intensively in that segment. Depending on the calling pattern, perceived marginal costs may differ across segments so that consumers in the different segments pay different per-minute prices. See, for instance, the outcomes in the case of the home-biased calling pattern. Since the access markup only applies to calls terminating on segment 2, operators' perceived marginal costs are higher in segment 2 than in segment 1, leading to larger per-minute prices.

Another observation from Table 7.5 is that the segment-2-biased calling pattern leads to a large difference in subscription fees across segments. The reason is that the difference in demand between the segments and the nature of the calling pattern reinforce the intensifying effect on price competition.

One can draw some general lessons from these selected examples. Overall, by looking closely at the role of calling patterns if there are access markups,

Table 7.6 *Uniform reciprocal access markups: calling patterns in an infant market*

	Calling pattern			
	Uniform	Home-biased	Segment-1-biased	Segment-2-biased
p_1^1	2.167	2.167	2.167	2.167
p_1^2	2.167	2.167	2.167	2.167
p_2^1	2.333	2.333	2.333	2.333
p_2^2	2.333	2.333	2.333	2.333
m_1^1	5952.3	5869.0	5702.3	6202.3
m_1^2	5767.8	5851.2	6017.8	5517.8
m_2^1	3768.2	3684.8	3518.2	4018.2
m_2^2	3675.8	3759.1	3925.7	3425.8
Π_1^1	109.1	107.6	104.6	113.6
Π_1^2	104.2	105.7	108.6	99.7
Π_2^1	27.3	26.9	26.2	28.4
Π_2^2	26.1	26.4	27.2	25.0
CS^1	372.8	376.1	382.8	362.8
CS^2	181.4	178.1	171.4	191.4

one can conclude that deviations from the calling pattern predicted by the regulator may intensify competition in a certain segment, while relaxing it in the other one. More intense competition leads to lower subscription fees and higher consumers surplus in that segment. Nevertheless, although segment-specific access markups may be used to increase the surplus of consumers in a specific segment, a side effect is that it harms customers in the other segment. In a mature market, the regulator should therefore be aware of the calling pattern to assess the potential effects of segment-specific markups. By imposing cost-based access prices for both operators in both segments, the regulator does not need to worry about spillover effects between the segments. Hence, Guideline 7.1 remains valid.

Infant market   Next, we consider the role of calling patterns in an infant market. We start with reciprocal access price regulation (see Table 7.6). For the calling patterns under consideration, since the access markup is neither segment-specific nor operator-specific, perceived marginal costs are the same in both segments. Therefore, both operators charge the same per-minute price in both segments. Also, a large fraction of calls made by the entrant's customers

Table 7.7 *Asymmetric access markups in both segments: calling patterns in an infant market*

	Calling pattern			
	Uniform	Home-biased	Segment-1-biased	Segment-2-biased
p_1^1	2.167	2.167	2.167	2.167
p_1^2	2.167	2.167	2.167	2.167
p_2^1	2.000	2.000	2.000	2.000
p_2^2	2.000	2.000	2.000	2.000
m_1^1	5721.1	5665.4	5553.9	5888.3
m_1^2	5721.2	5777.0	5888.4	5554.1
m_2^1	3907.4	3851.7	3740.3	4074.6
m_2^2	3814.4	3870.1	3981.6	3647.2
Π_1^1	99.2	97.7	94.8	103.7
Π_1^2	99.2	100.7	103.7	94.8
Π_2^1	29.2	29.2	29.2	29.2
Π_2^2	27.9	27.9	27.9	27.9
CS^1	382.0	384.3	388.7	375.3
CS^2	183.3	181.0	176.6	190.0

terminate on the incumbent's network, so that its per-minute prices are relatively high compared to the incumbent's.

In the case of a home-biased calling pattern, relatively few calls leave each segment. Therefore, profits are more sensitive to prices in the high-volume segment (segment 1), and operators compete more aggressively in segment 1, compared to the case of uniform calling patterns. A segment-i-biased calling pattern makes competition more intense only in segment i, with the corresponding effects on profits and consumers surplus. More generally, we remark that profits and consumers surplus in a segment are sensitive to the calling pattern, whereas market shares are not.

We now turn to an assessment of the role of calling patterns if access price regulation is asymmetric across the firms. Suppose that the entrant is allowed to set access prices τ_2^1 and τ_2^2 above marginal costs, whereas the incumbent's access prices are cost-based. Compare the results in Table 7.7 with the earlier results under cost-based regulation reported in Table 7.3. Recall that if access prices are equal to marginal cost levels, the calling pattern does not affect the outcomes. One can see that, independent of the calling pattern, profits of the incumbent are lower under asymmetric access price regulation than under cost-based access price regulation. On the other hand, the entrant is better off. Depending on the calling pattern that prevails, asymmetric access regulation may affect consumers in the two segments rather differently. Moreover, subscription fees in the two segments depend heavily on the calling pattern. A calling pattern that increases the net inflow to segment i, makes competition in that segment more intense and hence leads to lower subscription fees m_1^i and m_2^i (see also the earlier discussion in the case of a uniform calling pattern). It may happen, as in the case of a segment-2-biased calling pattern, that the entrant's subscription fee in segment 1, m_2^1, increases compared to the case of cost-based access prices. Hence, competition in the other segment may become less intense, as can be explained by the demand asymmetry between the segments.

As a robustness check, we address to what extent the insights above depend on the demand difference between the segments. Recall that we assumed that segment 2 is a lower-volume demand. If consumers in both segments had the same individual demand function, then a home-biased calling pattern would yield the same outcome as a uniform calling pattern (this can easily be checked with simulations). That is, outcomes would be the same in both segments. Outcomes with segment-1-biased calling patterns would be the mirror image to outcomes with segment-2-biased calling patterns. This holds in mature and new markets, as well as under reciprocal and asymmetric access price regulation that is uniformly applied in both segments.

Finally, we are interested in knowing what role calling patterns play if the entrant is allowed to set only its access price in segment 2, τ_2^2, above marginal cost, while all other access prices are cost based. This type of access regulation may occur if the regulator wishes to stay as close as possible to cost-based regulation, but at the same time wants to stimulate competition in a particular segment (e.g. residential telephony). Table 7.8 presents the outcomes for different calling patterns. To discuss these outcomes, we will make a comparison with the results in the first column in Table 7.3 (where calling patterns do not matter).

One can observe in Table 7.8 that, regardless of the calling pattern, the incumbent's subscription fee m_1^1 in segment 1 (which is subject to cost-based regulation) is not or hardly affected by the access markup in the other segment. Because of the larger traffic-dependent costs, the incumbent's customers face higher per-minute prices p_1^1 and p_1^2.

More importantly, the access markup in segment 2 leads to an increase of the entrant's subscription fee in segment 1. The intuition behind this result is that the access markup makes the entrant more interested in incoming calls from the incumbent's network, than in calls generated by its own customers. Hence, the entrant is less eager to compete for market share in segment 1. Depending on the calling pattern, this deviation from prices under cost-based access regulation can be quite large. Consequently, consumers surplus in

Table 7.8 *Asymmetric access markup in the low-volume segment:*
calling patterns in an infant market

	Calling pattern			
	Uniform	Home-biased	Segment-1-biased	Segment-2-biased
p_1^1	2.083	2.033	2.033	2.133
p_1^2	2.083	2.133	2.033	2.133
p_2^1	2.000	2.000	2.000	2.000
p_2^2	2.000	2.000	2.000	2.000
m_1^1	6000.0	6000.0	6000.0	5999.8
m_1^2	5720.0	5776.2	5887.7	5553.3
m_2^1	4093.4	4037.4	4037.4	4149.1
m_2^2	3766.8	3850.8	3906.4	3627.9
Π_1^1	106.7	106.7	106.7	106.7
Π_1^2	99.2	100.7	103.7	94.8
Π_2^1	27.9	27.2	27.2	28.7
Π_2^2	27.3	27.7	26.9	27.7
CS^1	374.6	376.8	376.8	372.4
CS^2	185.2	181.8	179.6	190.7

segment 1 is lower if there is asymmetric access price regulation in segment 2
than under cost-based regulation.

The main message from this exercise, which also demonstrates that Guideline
7.2 is robust with regard to changes in calling patterns, is that a regulator that
intends to foster competition in segment 2, should take the detrimental effect
on consumers surplus in the other segment into account. The strength of this
spillover effect depends on the calling pattern. For instance, the stronger the bias
to make calls within the same segment, the less pronounced the effect is. Also,
a calling pattern with a segment-1 bias tends to reduce the negative impact
on segment 2. Nevertheless, a strong segment-1 bias dampens the effect of
asymmetric access price regulation in segment 2. Hence, such a calling pattern
makes it very difficult for the regulator to accomplish the goal of strengthening
competition in segment 2 by access regulation.

7.3.4   *Other demand-side asymmetries*

In this subsection, we analyze the impact of segment-specific switching costs
(affecting the intensity of competition in a segment) and of a fixed-utility
difference that is asymmetric for the operators as well as the segments.

Throughout this subsection, we assume that the calling pattern is uniform. We will see that Guidelines 7.1 and 7.2 are robust to various segment asymmetries.

Segment-specific switching costs   Recall from Chapter 3 that the maximum switching cost parameter in the model is a measure of the "stickiness" of the market: if Z increases, fewer consumers switch to an operator that cuts its price. We adopt the standard parameter configuration of Chapter 3, with the exception that we make segment 1 less sticky (the segments are identical in all other aspects). In the model, $Z_1 = 3000$ and $Z_2 = 6000$. A first observation is that competition in segment 1 is more intense than in the other segment, which is reflected by lower subscription fees m_1^1 and m_2^1.

Firstly, suppose that the market is mature. Comparing reciprocal markups (in both segments) to cost-based access prices, each operator's total and segment-specific profits are the same in the two cases.[13] To see this, recall from Section 7.2 that uniform calling patterns, combined with identical demand functions in the two segments, imply that calling patterns are balanced.

If we also introduce a demand difference between the segments ($b^1 < b^2$, as explored earlier in this chapter), then the high-volume segment 1 exhibits a net outflow of calls to the other segment. If access prices are equal to costs, this hardly affects subscription fees. More importantly, introducing a uniform and reciprocal access markup makes the low-volume consumers more attractive to the operators, leading to intensified competition in segment 2. Hence, the access markup can increase the intensity of competition in the less competitive segment (segment 2), but this is at the cost of consumers' surplus in the other segment.

Secondly, suppose that the entrant's initial market share equals zero (in both segments) and, to start with, that the segments have identical demand. Before discussing simulation results, we point out that the profit-neutrality result does not hold under reciprocal access prices: with a reciprocal and uniform access markup, both operators have lower profits than under cost-based regulation. In our simulations, however, the change in profits is relatively small.

Table 7.9 presents a summary of selected simulation outcomes if access prices are asymmetric. Again we address the question of whether the regulator should allow an asymmetric access markup in the less competitive segment, that is, allow the entrant to include a markup in τ_2^2 while regulating the other access prices at cost-based levels.

Compared to a situation with cost-based access prices, consumers in segment 1 are better off if both τ_2^1 and τ_2^2 are above costs, and worse off if only τ_2^2 is

---

[13] Total profits are typically not neutral to the level of the access markup under implicit price discrimination (whereas they remain neutral under explicit price discrimination). This holds, for instance, under unbalanced calling patterns even if consumers have the same individual demand functions in both segments (see Dessein, 1999b).

Table 7.9 *Access prices in an infant market: different intensities of competition with homogeneous demand*

	Markups in:		
	–	τ_2^1, τ_2^2	τ_2^2
p_1^1	2.000	2.167	2.083
p_1^2	2.000	2.167	2.083
p_2^1	2.000	2.000	2.000
p_2^2	2.000	2.000	2.000
m_1^1	4000.0	3628.2	3999.9
m_1^2	6000.0	5628.2	5626.7
m_2^1	3000.0	2814.6	3093.4
m_2^2	4000.0	3814.6	3720.1
Π_1^1	53.3	43.4	53.3
Π_1^2	106.7	96.7	96.7
Π_2^1	13.3	15.8	14.6
Π_2^2	26.7	29.2	27.9
CS^1	451.7	459.1	447.9
CS^2	378.3	385.7	389.5

above cost. Qualitative results and the underlying reasoning resemble those in Subsections 7.3.2 and 7.3.3. Competition in segment 1 is relaxed, which explains the reduction in consumers surplus CS^1. Customers in segment 2 are better off in both access regimes, since they benefit from more intense competition.

As a robustness check, we introduced the additional difference with regard to demand functions ($b^1 = 0.016$ and $b^2 = 0.032$). Table 7.12 in Appendix 7.1 presents a summary of simulation results. Again, we consider asymmetric access markups that favor the entrant. One can see that the qualitative effects do not fundamentally change.[14] Some effects are less pronounced because the demand asymmetry reduces the intensity of competition in segment 1.

The general message of Guidelines 7.1 and 7.2 remains valid. Segment-specific asymmetric access price regulation improves consumers surplus in the segment to which the markup for the entrant applies. An additional insight is

[14] In the simulations, the incumbent's prices are close to the prices under uniform access prices. In segment 1, with cost-based access prices, the subscription fee is close to the subscription fee that results if both segments are subject to cost-based regulation. In segment 2, with an asymmetric access markup, the subscription fee is quite close to the subscription fee that results if both segments are subject to an asymmetric access markup.

that segment-specific asymmetries in competitiveness may justify a fine-tuned regulatory policy which allows for a higher access markup for the entrant in the less competitive segment, while allowing a smaller but also positive access markup for the entrant in the other segment. We will return to the discussion of combined differences in demand and competitiveness below.

Segment-specific fixed utility levels for the entrant   Suppose that customers in the two segments have identical demand functions, so that uniform calling patterns are balanced. Consider an infant market (the entrant's market shares in each segment are equal to zero) in which the entrant offers a lower level of fixed, connection-dependent utility to customers in segment 2.[15] In particular, $u_1^1 = u_2^1 = 5000$ whereas $u_1^2 = 5000$ and $u_2^2 = 0$. As a consequence, the incumbent faces less downward pressure on its subscription fee in segment 2. Is it desirable for the regulator to stimulate competition in segment 2 by allowing only the entrant to include access markups, either in segment 2 only or in both segments?

Comparing uniform and segment-specific asymmetric access price regulation, one can again observe that segment-specific regulation does a better job in stimulating consumers surplus CS^2 (see Table 7.13 in the Appendix). On the other hand, competition in segment 1 is more relaxed in the case of a segment-specific access markup, because a lost consumer in segment 1 still generates profits from making off-net calls to segment 2. This leads to a reduction of CS^1. As we have also seen in previous simulations, uniform access markups increase consumers surplus in both segments. Since the entrant has a disadvantage in both segments, regulatory policy may favor an access markup in both segments to stimulate overall competition between operators. Note, however, that segment 2 is more asymmetric so that the incumbent enjoys more market power in this segment provided that regulation is uniform across segments (this is similar to the analysis with segment-specific switching costs). This suggests that the access markup in segment 2 should be higher than in segment 1.

Summarizing, asymmetric uniform access price regulation can, to some extent, compensate for the entrant's less favorable position in the market, stimulating competition and increasing consumers surplus in both segments.

7.3.5   Segment-specific costs

In reality, the fixed costs of connecting individual customers typically is not the same for all kinds of customers. For example, these costs may be different for customers living in urban and in rural areas, or for small and large customers.

---

[15]   See Chapter 4 for more background on this assumption.

The cost of a connection is often related to the geographical density of customers. It is therefore interesting to see how such cost asymmetries affect the outcomes of competition. Since simulation results yield model outcomes with straightforward interpretations, we will discuss the outcomes broadly, instead of presenting the details of the simulations.

To start with, we assume that traffic-independent costs are smallest in segment 1. In the simulations, we assume that $f_1^1 = f_2^1 = 1500$, while $f_1^2 = f_2^2 = 3000$. There are no other asymmetries between the segments.

The outcomes of the model are straightforward and intuitive. The cost asymmetry translates directly into lower subscription fees in segment 1, in an infant market as well as in a mature market. The reduction of subscription fees is proportionate to the fixed cost difference. Obviously, per-minute prices are not affected. Also, in an infant market, the speed of entry (i.e., the entrant's market share after period 1) is not affected; it is the same in both segments. The operators price discriminate with respect to subscription fees, reflecting that the cost of connecting customers is different across the segments.

Access prices play the same role as before. For instance, suppose that the regulator is concerned about the strong disparity in the intensities of competition in the two segments. To induce the operators to compete more intensely in segment 2, the regulator can use a reciprocal access markup in that segment only, as we have seen in several earlier examples. The intended consequence of such a segment-specific access markup is that subscription fees in segment 2 go down, but competition in segment 1 is relaxed to a certain extent. While such a regulatory intervention is roughly neutral for total consumers surplus and welfare, it does involve an increase of consumers surplus in segment 2 at the expense of consumers in segment 1. Accordingly, the earlier formulated guidelines still apply. This implies that the regulator can intervene in the wholesale market to achieve political aims such as the affordability of telephony in the high-cost segment.

Now suppose that only the entrant has a fixed cost advantage in segment 1; in the simulations, $f_2^1 = 1500$ and $f_1^1 = f_1^2 = f_2^2 = 3000$. Thus, the entrant starts with zero market share in both segments and has a cost advantage in segment 1, so that it has its main disadvantage in segment 2. Compared to the situation in which $f_2^1 = 3000$, the entrant's cost advantage and resulting lower subscription fee in segment 1, m_2^1, force the incumbent to reduce its subscription fee m_1^1 as well. Competition in segment 2 is not affected. A difference with the previous example is that now the entrant gains a larger market share in segment 1. The entrant is able to increase its profits Π_2^1. Since subscription fees decrease, consumers surplus in segment 1 increases.

To the extent that the regulator wants to neutralize a temporary disadvantage of the entrant (due to its small customer base in an infant market), regulatory intervention should concentrate on segment 2. An asymmetric access markup in segment 2 stimulates competition in that segment and may therefore be preferred to cost-based regulation. (Potential side effects of such regulation have been discussed before.)

In general, segment-specific asymmetries in traffic-independent costs naturally induce the operators to price discriminate with their subscription fees. If only the entrant has a segment-specific cost advantage, it is able to translate this into higher profits in that segment, as one would expect in an environment where operators compete in prices.

7.4   Regulatory restrictions on price discrimination

So far throughout this chapter, the operators have had the freedom to price discriminate, that is, to set segment-specific retail prices. Nevertheless, one can imagine that the regulator wants to impose constraints on price discrimination. For instance, by a uniform pricing constraint, consumers in the less competitive segment can be guaranteed the same prices as consumers in the more competitive segment. Also, in an infant market, one may wonder if entry can be stimulated by imposing the incumbent to choose uniform prices. In this section, we address whether such restrictions are indeed useful.

Mature market   To start the discussion of uniform pricing restrictions, consider a mature market. The calling pattern is uniform, while $b^1 = 0.016$ and $b^2 = 0.032$. Note that under cost-based access price regulation, operators do not have an incentive to price discriminate so that the uniform pricing restriction can only play a role if there is an access markup in at least one segment (see first column of Table 7.2). Table 7.10 summarizes simulation outcomes for three access price regimes. In each access price regime, both operators are treated identically, but there may be asymmetries across the segments stemming from segment-specific access price regulation. Our simulations show that per-minute prices are different from perceived marginal costs; this not only holds for segment-specific reciprocal access markups but even for uniform reciprocal access markups. Hence the marginal costs pricing principle (see Sections 3.3 and 7.3) is violated.

Firstly, consider a uniform reciprocal access markup. If price discrimination was allowed, both operators would set lower subscription fees in segment 2 compared to segment 1 (compare Table 7.2), because segment 2 has a net inflow of calls under uniform calling patterns. Under the uniform pricing constraint, operators cannot price discriminate between the segments. Still, consumers in segment 2 are more valuable. So how can an operator attract a consumer from segment 2 rather than segment 1? This can be done by increasing the per-minute

Table 7.10 *Reciprocal access prices in a mature market: uniform pricing*

Uniform pricing: Markups in:	Both $\tau_1^1, \tau_1^2, \tau_2^1, \tau_2^2$	Both τ_1^1, τ_2^1	Both τ_1^2, τ_2^2
$p_1^1 = p_1^2$	2.338	1.898	2.430
$p_2^1 = p_2^2$	2.338	1.898	2.430
$m_1^1 = m_1^2$	4720.3	5086.2	4645.6
$m_2^1 = m_2^2$	4720.3	5086.2	4645.6
$\Pi_1^1 = \Pi_2^1$	60.5	60.8	59.6
$\Pi_1^2 = \Pi_2^2$	59.5	59.2	60.4
$\Pi_1 = \Pi_2$	120.0	120.0	120.0
CS^1	401.1	406.1	400.0
CS^2	206.2	201.3	207.1
CS	607.3	607.5	607.2
W	827.3	827.5	827.2

price and simultaneously decreasing its subscription fee. This explains that, in equilibrium, both operators set the per-minute price above perceived marginal costs. This shows that also under two-part tariffs and in a mature market, per-minute prices and perceived marginal costs do not necessarily coincide. We have seen in Chapter 3 that with homogeneous consumers an operator uses only the subscription fee to extract profits. With consumer heterogeneity and the impossibility of targeting each segment separately, a per-minute price is above marginal costs and outgoing traffic generates profits.

Although the uniform pricing restriction affects retail prices, equilibrium profits remain unchanged. Imposing a uniform pricing restriction leads primarily to a redistribution of consumers surplus between the segments. The welfare loss due to higher per-minute prices is negligible in our simulations.

Secondly, consider segment-specific access markups. Such markups leave profits unchanged so that the profit-neutrality result is still valid in a segmented, mature market with uniform pricing. A uniform pricing restriction reduces the effectiveness of segment-specific access price regulation in stimulating competition in a particular segment (compare Tables 7.2 and 7.10). Note that if regulation attempts to improve consumers surplus in segment 1 – this is the segment in which competition is less intense under a uniform access markup – by allowing an access markup only in this segment, then each operator sets its per-minute price below perceived marginal costs.[16] Such a

---

[16] In our simulations the per-minute price is even below true marginal costs.

pricing strategy is optimal for each operator, because now consumers in segment 1 are more valuable since they generate profits from incoming calls. To attract these consumers rather than consumers in segment 2, operators have to reduce their per-minute prices and simultaneously increase their subscription fees.

The analysis above is summarized in the following guideline:

> **Guideline 7.3**: Consider a segmented market with non-targeted facilities-based competition. Suppose that there are reciprocal access markups in either one or both segments. In a mature market, imposing uniform pricing primarily leads to a redistribution of consumers surplus from the segment with lower prices to the segment with higher prices under price discrimination.

Infant market   Consider an infant market (the entrant initially has a market share of zero) with identical market segments. In particular, for the moment we drop the assumption of segment-specific individual demand functions. Suppose that the incumbent's access prices are cost based, and consider access markups for the entrant. Since the outcomes of simulation are straightforward, we will not present them but directly discuss some of the features.

Obviously, if the entrant can charge the same access markup in the two (identical) segments, the operators have no reason to price discriminate. Hence, uniform pricing restrictions are automatically satisfied. Next, consider a markup for the entrant only in segment 2. Such an asymmetry generates price pressure for the incumbent in segment 2. A uniform pricing restriction for the incumbent partially transmits this downward pressure on prices into segment 1. Consequently, consumers in segment 1 benefit from the uniform pricing restriction, whereas consumers in segment 2 are worse off. If the access markup was introduced to stimulate competition in segment 2 in the first place, a uniform pricing restriction reduces the effectiveness of such a policy in segment 2. Nevertheless, the negative effect on consumers in segment 1 is alleviated.

In our simulations, the negative effect of an access markup for the entrant in segment 2 on consumers in segment 1 is essentially neutralized through the introduction of a uniform pricing restriction when the reference is cost-based access price regulation. Consumers surplus in segment 2 increases. Therefore, such a regulatory policy can possibly achieve the aim of stimulating competition in one segment while avoiding inflicting harm on the consumers in the other segment. Similar observations can be made about forcing not just the incumbent but also the entrant to price uniformly.

Table 7.11 *Asymmetric access prices in an infant market and pricing restrictions*

Uniform pricing: Markups in:	Neither τ_2^1, τ_2^2	Incumbent τ_2^1, τ_2^2	Both τ_2^1, τ_2^2	Neither τ_2^2	Incumbent τ_2^2	Both τ_2^2
p_1^1	2.167	2.167	2.151	2.083	2.275	2.235
p_1^2	2.167	2.167	2.151	2.083	2.275	2.235
p_2^1	2.000	2.000	2.099	2.000	2.000	2.255
p_2^2	2.000	2.000	2.099	2.000	2.000	2.255
m_1^1	5721.1	5721.2	5734.2	6000.0	5702.5	5735.2
m_1^2	5721.2	5721.2	5734.2	5720.0	5702.5	5735.2
m_2^1	3907.4	3907.5	3777.8	4093.4	4052.1	3718.9
m_2^2	3814.4	3814.4	3777.8	3766.8	3812.7	3718.9
Π_1^1	99.2	99.2	98.8	106.7	105.5	104.2
Π_1^2	99.2	99.2	99.7	99.2	100.4	101.7
Π_1	198.5	198.5	198.5	205.9	205.9	205.9
Π_2^1	29.2	29.2	29.1	27.9	26.8	26.6
Π_2^2	27.9	27.9	28.0	27.3	28.5	28.6
Π_2	57.1	57.1	57.1	55.2	55.3	55.2
CS^1	382.0	382.0	382.4	374.6	377.4	378.4
CS^2	183.3	183.3	182.9	185.2	182.2	181.2
CS	565.3	565.3	565.3	559.8	559.6	559.6
W	820.8	820.8	820.8	820.8	820.7	820.7

Overall, restrictions on price discrimination, whether applied to one or both operators, do not affect total surplus in the market, and hardly affect profit levels. Nevertheless, in the case of a segment-specific access markup, a uniform pricing restriction for the incumbent increases the entrant's total profits to some extent. Also, uniform pricing restrictions tend to counterbalance asymmetric outcomes caused by segment-specific access prices. Finally, we remark that, so far, the operators set per-minute prices equal to perceived marginal costs. In the specification that follows, we will see that this is not necessarily the case.

To further assess the effects of asymmetric restrictions on retail prices, we look at an infant market and parameter constellations in which individual demand is asymmetric across segments (see Section 7.3). Suppose that the calling pattern is uniform, and let $b^1 = 0.016$ and $b^2 = 0.032$. Table 7.11 presents the simulation outcomes.

Although the asymmetric demand functions make the interpretation of the outcomes less straightforward than in the previous example, some interesting conclusions can be drawn. Again, regulatory restrictions on price discrimination, whether applied to the incumbent only or to both operators, hardly affect the operators' total profits or welfare. What does matter is that for a given access price regime, if a change from one to another retail price regime is beneficial for one customer segment, then consumers in the other segment are – to the same (or almost the same) extent – worse off. As argued for symmetric demand above, a uniform pricing restriction (on the incumbent or on both operators) together with an access markup for the entrant in a particular segment can stimulate competition in that segment while protecting consumers in the other segment (in the sense that consumers surplus in the other segment is approximately the same as under cost-based access price in both segments). In our simulations, this can be seen by comparing the fifth column of Table 7.11 with the first column of Table 7.3.

One can observe that demand asymmetries combined with a uniform pricing restriction on both operators and access markups induce the operators to deviate from the marginal cost pricing principle. It is important to understand why per-minute prices are different from perceived marginal costs. Without the uniform pricing restriction, the operators can use segment-specific subscription fees to adapt to demand differences across the segments, while at the same time using per-minute prices to generate a maximum surplus from their customers' calling behavior. With uniform prices, operators can no longer separate these goals. Instead, they use subscription fees as well as per-minute prices to cope with the asymmetries in the market.

In the case of a uniform access markup for the entrant, segment 2, with relatively more incoming calls and hence access revenues, is the most attractive segment for the entrant. Suppose that both operators have to set uniform prices. To attract consumers in segment 2 rather than in segment 1, the entrant has to increase its per-minute price and decrease its subscription fee. In an infant market with asymmetric access prices, the strategic interaction between operators is rather complicated. When both operators face the uniform pricing restriction we observe that, in equilibrium, the entrant sets its per-minute price above perceived marginal cost, and the incumbent below.

If the entrant's access markup only applies to segment 2, the entrant has even stronger incentives to attract consumers in segment 2; likewise the incumbent wants to maintain its customer base in segment 2. As a consequence, the incumbent sets its per-minute price above perceived marginal costs if it is subject to a uniform pricing constraint. Both operators set their per-minute prices above perceived marginal costs if both are subject to a uniform pricing constraint.

We conclude the discussion above with the following guideline.

> **Guideline 7.4:** Consider a segmented market with non-targeted facilities-based competition. Suppose that only the entrant is allowed to charge access markups, in either one or both segments. In an infant market, imposing uniform pricing, either on the incumbent or on both operators, primarily leads to a redistribution of consumers surplus from the segment with lower prices to the segment with higher prices under price discrimination. Given a segment-specific access markup, imposing uniform pricing can partially protect consumers in the segment without the markup from excessive prices.

7.5   Summary

The analysis in Chapters 3 to 6 was based on the assumption that the market is unsegmented. In this chapter, the model of facilities-based competition was extended to incorporate a segmented market, consisting of two segments (e.g. residential and business customers). We primarily focused on two issues, namely regulation of terminating access prices, and whether operators should be allowed to price discriminate (i.e., set different prices in the segments). These issues were explored in a situation of "non-targeted" facilities-based entry, that is, under the assumption that the entrant rolls out a network in both segments.

Four guidelines were obtained, with policy implications that are specific to segmented markets. The first two concern spillover effects caused by access price regulation if the operators are allowed to price discriminate:

- In a mature market, a segment-specific, reciprocal access markup increases consumers surplus in that segment, but decreases consumers surplus in the other segment. Cost-based terminating access prices maximize welfare and consumers surplus. (Guideline 7.1)
- In an infant market, asymmetric access markups only for the entrant in both segments increase consumers surplus and the entrant's profits. It is roughly neutral for welfare. A segment-specific access markup only for the entrant increases consumers' surplus in that segment, but decreases consumers surplus in the other segment. (Guideline 7.2)

The next two guidelines focus on price discrimination versus uniform pricing, and the way restrictions on retail pricing affect optimal access price regulation:

- Suppose that there are reciprocal access markups in either one or both segments. In a mature market, imposing uniform pricing primarily leads to a redistribution of consumers surplus from the segment with lower prices to the segment with higher prices under price discrimination. (Guideline 7.3)
- Suppose that only the entrant is allowed to charge access markups, in either one or both segments. In an infant market, imposing uniform pricing, either on the incumbent or on both operators, primarily leads to a redistribution of

consumers surplus from the segment with lower prices to the segment with higher prices under price discrimination. Given a segment-specific access markup, imposing uniform pricing can partially protect consumers in the segment without the markup from excessive prices. (Guideline 7.4)

We also addressed the role of consumers' calling patterns, that is, the "innate" inclinations of certain types of consumers to make calls to the same or other types. For instance, residential consumers may make more calls to other residential consumers than relative sizes of market segments suggest. By and large, although calling patterns may affect competition and the effectiveness of regulatory interventions (in particular, they affect spillover effects between the segments), the guidelines do not critically depend on them.

In practice, facilities-based entrants operating in a segmented market do not (yet) target all the segments of a market. Instead, they often single out a particular segment (partial entry), or target different segments in different ways (mixed entry). These entry modes are explored in the next chapter.

APPENDIX 7.1

In this appendix, we provide a robustness check with respect to individual demand in the two segments. In the simulations, the more competitive segment 1 is the high-volume segment (for the parameter constellation, see Section 7.3.4). See Tables 7.12 and 7.13.

Table 7.12 *Access prices in an infant market: different intensities of competition with heterogeneous demand*

	Markups in:		
	–	τ_2^1, τ_2^2	τ_2^2
p_1^1	2.000	2.167	2.083
p_1^2	2.000	2.167	2.083
p_2^1	2.000	2.000	2.000
p_2^2	2.000	2.000	2.000
m_1^1	4000.0	3721.1	3999.9
m_1^2	6000.0	5721.2	5720.0
m_2^1	3000.0	2907.5	3093.4
m_2^2	4000.0	3814.4	3766.8
Π_1^1	53.3	45.9	53.3
Π_1^2	106.7	99.2	99.2
Π_2^1	13.3	15.8	14.6
Π_2^2	26.7	27.9	27.3
CS^1	451.7	455.4	447.9
CS^2	175.8	183.3	185.2

Table 7.13 *Access prices in an infant market: different fixed utilities in segment 2*

	–	τ_2^1, τ_2^2	τ_2^2
		Markups in:	
p_1^1	2.000	2.097	2.014
p_1^2	2.000	2.097	2.014
p_2^1	2.000	2.000	2.000
p_2^2	2.000	2.000	2.000
m_1^1	6000.0	5549.2	6000.0
m_1^2	7666.7	7215.9	7213.9
m_2^1	4000.0	3658.2	4015.6
m_2^2	2333.3	1991.6	1896.2
s_1^1	66.7	66.7	66.7
s_1^2	94.4	94.4	94.4
Π_1^1	106.7	94.6	106.7
Π_1^2	214.1	197.0	197.0
Π_2^1	26.7	28.1	27.7
Π_2^2	0.7	1.0	0.8
CS^1	378.3	392.0	377.7
CS^2	298.7	312.4	316.2

8   Targeted entry

8.1   Introduction

In this chapter, we continue to explore entry in a segmented market. As in the previous chapter, we distinguish two types of consumers, for instance, residential and business customers, or urban and rural customers. This allows us to incorporate targeted entry in the models. For example, an entrant may wish to serve business customers but not residential customers, or alternatively, target segments in different ways (e.g. with and without network rollout).

We refer to situations in which an entrant singles out one segment as "partial entry." Alternatively, an entrant may wish to become active in both segments while rolling out a customer access network for business customers but serving residential customers by using the incumbent's local connections. We call situations in which an entrant targets the two segments in different ways "mixed entry."

We explore several types of partial entry and mixed entry. Partial entry raises regulatory concerns because the incumbent remains a monopolist in the segment where there is no entry. To protect consumers in the captive segment, retail price regulation is a necessity. Both partial and mixed entry tend to complicate regulation, because regulatory measures meant for one segment can have spillover effects to the other segment, as we have encountered in Chapter 7. We will see that the regulator can often circumvent such spillovers by allowing the incumbent to price discriminate across the segments. Moreover, situations of targeted entry are particularly relevant when discussing problems related to the provision of universal service.[1]

Targeted entry situations come closer to the real world than the more stylized entry modes that we explored in earlier chapters. For example, in the Netherlands, Versatel is an operator with a long-distance network consisting of city rings connecting the largest cities and business centers in the Benelux, and customer access networks that connect customers along its Benelux network. Moreover, Versatel does not confine its network rollout to the so-called

---

[1] For an overview on universal service, see Riordan (2001). See also Chapter 2.

Randstad only;[2] its intention is to connect several medium-sized cities in the north as well as the very south of the country. In 2000, Versatel was able to serve about 40 percent of the Dutch corporate market with DSL (digital subscriber line). Entrants MCI Worldcom, Colt, and GTS follow similar partial facilities-based entry strategies in the Netherlands. Furthermore, Energis (formerly called Enertel, a joint venture of Dutch energy companies) and Telfort (a joint venture of BT and the Dutch Railways) have long-distance backbones with national coverage. Energis serves only the corporate segment and provides another example of partial entry, whereas Telfort is active in both the residential market (through carrier-select services) and the business market. Hence, Telfort follows a mixed entry strategy which combines carrier-select-based and facilities-based entry (see DGTP, 2000). At some point, this type of operator may start serving residential customers by leasing local connections from the incumbent, or by rolling out local connections itself. The models that we analyze in this chapter come close to examples of this kind.

The rest of this chapter is organized as follows. Section 8.2 analyzes partial facilities-based entry, that is, the entrant builds a customer access network for one segment only and does not offer telephony services to the other segment. In that section, we compare uniform pricing to price discrimination by the incumbent, discuss the need to regulate the incumbent's prices in the segment with captive consumers, and then explore access price regulation. Section 8.3 analyzes partial LLU-based entry, that is, the entrant leases local connections from the incumbent in one segment of the market. There we focus on the role of the lease price of the incumbent's local connections. In Section 8.4, we assume that the entrant adopts a partial carrier-select-based entry strategy: it only targets one segment and does this by offering carrier-select services to consumers. Both retail and access price regulation are investigated. Section 8.5 discusses two important forms of mixed entry. Finally, Section 8.6 concludes by gathering together the policy guidelines of the chapter.

8.2   Partial facilities-based entry

8.2.1   Specification of the model

In this section we focus on the following type of partial facilities-based entry: the entrant rolls out local connections for customers in segment 1 (the imperfectly competitive segment, or more shortly, the competitive segment) but does not become active in segment 2 (the captive or monopoly segment). We assume that both operators have a long-distance backbone, covering both segments.[3]

---

[2] The Randstad consists of the four major cities in the Netherlands (Amsterdam, The Hague, Rotterdam, and Utrecht).

[3] The example of Energis, discussed in the introduction of this chapter, illustrates this model.

Table 8.1 *Partial facilities-based entry: the entrant's ways of access*

	Type of access	Wholesale price
Access to:		
incumbent's customers segment 1	Terminating	τ_1^1
incumbent's customers segment 2	Terminating	τ_1^2
potential customers segment 1	Direct	–
potential customers segment 2	–	–

The incumbent serves both segments of the market. Initially, its market share in segment 1 is 100 percent. Calling patterns are uniform. As an example, one can think of consumers in the monopoly segment as residential customers, and consumers in segment 1 as business customers.

To focus on the effects of retail and access price regulation, we assume in our simulations that the segments are identical except for entry: they are of equal size, that is, $\alpha^k = \frac{1}{2}$ and segment-1 customers have the same demand characteristics as segment-2 customers. Consequently, uniform calling patterns are also balanced (see Chapter 7). The traffic-dependent and connection-dependent costs are assumed to be the same for the two segments. In reality, consumers belonging to different segments usually have different traits. Abstracting from such differences, though, allows us to interpret the results in a straightforward way, without having to correct for segment-specific effects. Our numerical examples use the parameter constellation of the previous chapter. In particular, we abstract from fixed-utility differences between the operators.[4] Following the presentation of Chapter 3, we focus on the outcomes of competition in an infant and a mature market.

Concerning notation, similar to the previous chapter, operator i's per-minute price and subscription fee in segment k are denoted by p_i^k and m_i^k. Note that throughout this section, the entrant only chooses p_2^1 and m_2^1, since it is not active in segment 2. Similarly, operator i's access price for calls terminating in segment k is denoted by τ_i^k. Accordingly, τ_1^1 and τ_1^2 are the incumbent's wholesale prices, whereas τ_2^1 is the entrant's wholesale price. Table 8.1 summarizes the entrant's types of access to consumers in the different segments.[5]

8.2.2   Asymmetries between segments

Accordingly, in the model both segments are equally attractive for the entrant. In other words, within a completely symmetric setting one cannot assess which

---

[4] Recall that in Chapter 4 we assumed that the entrant needs to build a track record to offer a similar fixed utility level as the incumbent. Therefore, quantitative comparisons with the outcomes of Chapter 4 cannot be made.

[5] Recall that under direct access consumers can subscribe to the entrant.

segment is the more attractive for the entrant. Varying dimensions of asymmetry between the segments we make the following observations:

- Suppose that in segment 1 fixed and sunk costs (that are independent of the size of the subscriber base) relative to the market size of the segment are lower than in segment 2. Then segment 1 is more profitable.
- If consumers in segment 1 have higher switching costs than in segment 2, segment 1 is more attractive for the entrant. The reason is that in the less sticky segment, operators would price more aggressively; the entrant prefers the segment in which it enjoys more market power, which is the more sticky segment.
- If the two segments are subject to different regulatory policies in the presence of entry, the entrant may prefer entry in a particular segment. For instance, suppose that the incumbent is subject to retail price regulation in the segment for residential customers (to guarantee affordability of telephony services) independent of entry, while retail price regulation applies to the segment of business customers only in the absence of entry. Then entry in the segment for residential customers is less attractive because the entrant would face lower prices by the incumbent.
- Unbalanced calling patterns between segments, such as segment-1-biased calling patterns, can make segment 1 more attractive, depending on the regulatory policy (see also Chapter 7).
- If the model is extended to allow for the effects of a track record (compare Section 4.2), the entrant prefers entry into segment 1 if the lack of a track record is less of a disadvantage in this segment compared with segment 2.

Also outside the scope of the model, there may be reasons why one segment is more attractive than others. For example, in the real world, business customers may want to purchase additional services (e.g. leased lines, virtual networks, office switches), while residential customers may only be interested in voice telephony and Internet access.

8.2.3   Retail price regulation and price discrimination versus uniform pricing

Since the incumbent serves both segments, one has to distinguish two possibilities for retail pricing:

- price discrimination (prices in segments 1 and 2 may be set differently);
- uniform pricing (prices identical in the two segments).

Which of these applies depends on the regulatory regime: the regulator can force the incumbent to set uniform prices. In practice, uniform pricing is often the default situation for operators with significant market power. Notice that, in this section, uniform pricing is not relevant for the entrant's prices, as it targets only one segment.

To start with, suppose that the incumbent is allowed to choose different prices for the two segments. Then the incumbent does not face any trade-off between milking segment 2 and fighting for its position in segment 1. It can do both at the same time. To avoid monopoly pricing in the monopoly segment, it is necessary to regulate it, for instance by using price caps.

Now suppose that the incumbent is forced to choose uniform prices. Without a price cap on its subscription fee, the incumbent faces the following trade-off. On the one hand, it wants to raise prices to extract maximum surplus from consumers in the captive segment. On the other hand, it wants to reduce prices to limit its loss of market share and profits in segment 1. Accordingly, the presence of an entrant in segment 1 acts, to some extent, as a disciplinary force on the incumbent in the monopoly segment. Nevertheless, for a broad range of parameter configurations of the model, it turns out that milking segment 2, up to the level where consumers' net utility level is zero, is so attractive that the presence of an entrant in segment 1 does not affect the pricing of the incumbent. For a sufficiently high willingness to pay in segment 2, the incumbent effectively leaves segment 1 to the entrant.[6] Hence, provided that monopoly behavior in segment 2 is undesirable, it is necessary to put price caps on the incumbent's prices (at least on the subscription fee) to protect consumers in the monopoly segment. If the monopoly segment is sufficiently small compared with the competitive segment, then a uniform pricing constraint does discipline the incumbent in the competitive segment, so that the uniform pricing restriction on its own possibly achieves affordability: the incumbent's subscription fee is between the price it would set when being active in the competitive segment only and the monopoly price. Even in this latter case, competitive pressure may be insufficient from the viewpoint of the regulator so that a price cap is still needed.

> **Guideline 8.1**: Consider a segmented market with partial facilities-based entry. To protect consumers in the monopoly segment, the incumbent's subscription fee in that segment has to be regulated if the incumbent is allowed to price discriminate, and, in general, also if the incumbent has to set uniform prices.

Accordingly, if only the subscription fee $m_1 \equiv m_1^1 = m_1^2$ is restricted by a binding price cap, and the incumbent chooses a uniform per-minute price $p_1 \equiv p_1^1 = p_1^2$, then the incumbent faces no competitive pressure in segment 2 and will set a relatively high per-minute price (compared to perceived marginal

---

[6] In a more general model, where consumers range from low to high willingness to pay for a subscription, one can obtain equilibria in which only a fraction of consumers in the monopoly segment subscribe. Then entry in segment 1 would have some disciplining effect.

costs). Competition in the other segment acts, to some extent, as a counteracting force. Nevertheless, competition in segment 1 is not very intense. The entrant optimally sets its per-minute price p_2^1 equal to perceived marginal cost, but is able to charge a relatively high subscription fee m_2^1 (depending on the price cap on m_1). A per-minute price above marginal costs generates a welfare loss for all consumers who are subscribed to the incumbent.

In general, there is a strategic linkage between the two segments under uniform pricing so that conditions (and size) of the monopoly segment affect the pricing in the competitive segment. Also, the presence of the monopoly segment leads to higher prices in the competitive segment.[7] Consequently, uniform prices have an important drawback that is absent in the case of price discrimination: regulating the incumbent's prices at a higher level reduces the intensity of competition in segment 1. Conversely, decreasing the incumbent's prices reduces the entrant's profits and hence makes entry less attractive.

To the extent that a uniform pricing restriction leads to lower prices in the monopoly segment, it can be seen as a policy that avoids putting consumers in the monopoly segment (for instance, residential[8] or rural[9] customers) in a worse position than consumers in the competitive segment. It is therefore typically an ingredient of a universal service obligation. Suppose that revenues in the monopoly segment do not cover costs in the monopoly segment (for instance, because the monopoly segment is a high-cost area). Universal service with a uniform pricing restriction can thus be seen as a cross-subsidization from consumers in the competitive segment to consumers in the monopoly segment.

In terms of entry, it may be argued that the spillover effect between segments is actually an advantage: by requiring the incumbent to set uniform prices, it will compete less aggressively in the segment where entry occurs, so that entry is not discouraged. Consumers in the competitive segment, however, are worse off as competition is relaxed.

We have seen that lifting the obligation of uniform pricing from the incumbent would enable it to compete more aggressively in segments where entry has occurred.[10] It is therefore more effective to separate the protection of consumers

---

[7] These two observations hold in a variety of models: see Anton, Van der Weide, and Vettas (1998); Choné, Flochel and Perrot (2000); Valletti, Hoernig, and Barros (2002).

[8] For example, in the Netherlands, incumbent KPN is not allowed to charge different prices for residential and business customers.

[9] For example, in the UK, BT is required to price uniformly in the whole country. The British regulator Oftel defends the uniform pricing restriction as part of the universal service obligation on the grounds that uniform pricing "has delivered the benefits of competitive price levels nationally rather than just in geographic areas where competition is strongest. It has also helped to ensure that telephony is affordable in areas where the high costs of provision would otherwise disadvantage certain groups of consumers" (Oftel, 2001c, pp. 3–4). Our analysis raises doubts about such a justification of uniform pricing.

[10] One cannot deduce from this observation that uniform pricing eliminates the risk of predatory pricing,

in the captive segment from creating a comfortable atmosphere for entry in the other segment. Predatory behavior by the incumbent in segment 1 can be prevented, without generating spillover effects into the monopoly segment, by the application of general antitrust measures or by *ex ante* regulation of the incumbent's retail prices in segment 1. In the latter case, regulation is only needed temporarily, that is, until the entrant's position is strong enough.

Based on the considerations above, we make the following observation.

Guideline 8.2: Consider a segmented market with partial facilities-based entry. By allowing the incumbent to price discriminate between the segments, spillover effects of retail price regulation (from the regulated monopoly segment to the other segment) can be avoided.

In the analysis of access price regulation below, we will consider retail price discrimination as the natural point of departure, as it imposes less restrictions on the incumbent. We will take a closer look at the model and consider the simultaneous application of various regulatory instruments.

8.2.4   Cost-based prices and recovery of fixed costs in the monopoly segment

Suppose that the incumbent is allowed to price discriminate between segments 1 and 2. The incumbent's retail prices in segment 2, p_1^2 and m_1^2, have to be regulated. For simplicity, and without loss of generality, we assume that these prices are fixed by the regulator.[11] Given the regulatory regime, which also includes access prices τ_1^2, τ_1^1, and τ_2^1, the operators compete in segment 1. Hence, the incumbent chooses prices p_1^1 and m_1^1, and the entrant chooses p_2^1 and m_2^1.

As a benchmark case, consider an infant market, that is, initially $s_1^2 = 0$. Suppose that access prices are equal to the marginal cost of terminating access, that is, $\tau_1^1 = \tau_2^1 = \tau_1^2 = c_3$, and the incumbent's prices in segment 2 are also cost based, that is, $p_1^2 = c_1$ and $m_1^2 = f$. In this situation, the incumbent makes zero profits in the monopoly segment. Table 8.2 summarizes the outcome in period 1.

Given that there are fixed costs to be covered, such as the costs of maintaining and upgrading the network that connects customers in segment 2, this benchmark case does not depict a realistic situation. To guarantee the provision

---

[11] This is a shortcut for price caps that apply to the incumbent in segment 2. If these price caps are binding, price caps are equivalent to assuming that the regulator fixes the incumbent's prices.

Table 8.2 *Partial facilities-based entry: outcome under cost-based regulation in an infant market*

	Access prices	Retail prices	s_1	Π_1	Π_2	CS	W
Segment 1	$\tau_1^1 = \tau_2^1 = 0.5$	$p_1^{1*} = 2, p_2^{1*} = 2,$	0.666	106.67	26.67	378.33	511.67
		$m_1^{1*} = 6000, m_2^{1*} = 4000$					
Segment 2	$\tau_1^2 = 0.5$	$p_1^2 = 2$ and $m_1^2 = 2000$ (fixed)	1	0	–	525	525

of universal service, that is, to make sure that consumers in both segments can continue to enjoy telephony services, the regulator may grant the incumbent a certain level of profits in the monopoly segment. Below, we explore several ways to do this, while at the same time discussing the effects of retail and access price regulation on competition and consumers surplus.

To start with, we keep to the assumption that all access prices are equal to marginal costs, and explore markups in the incumbent's retail prices. We start with a markup in the per-minute price, and next discuss a markup in the subscription fee.

Allowing the incumbent to charge a markup in the per-minute price for segment 2 does not affect the outcome of competition in segment 1 (i.e., it does not influence prices, market shares, profits, and consumers surplus). There are two effects. Firstly, consumers' demand in segment 2 is distorted: because of the higher per-minute price, they make less phone calls. As a consequence, they generate less utility, and hence less surplus to divide, from their connections: there is a deadweight loss. Secondly, the incumbent now makes positive profits in segment 2.

Consider, as an example, a regulated price $p_1^2 = 2c_1 = 4$. Then the incumbent obtains in the monopoly segment $\Pi_1^2 = 80$. Consumers surplus is reduced to $CS^2 = 440$, for there is a deadweight loss as well as a transfer of surplus to the incumbent. Consequently, total surplus in the monopoly segment is reduced to $W^2 = 520$.

The deadweight loss caused by a markup in per-minute price p_1^2 can be avoided by allowing the incumbent to set m_1^2 above the fixed cost of a connection f while fixing $p_1^2 = c_1$. Then consumers' calling behavior is not distorted. There is only one effect compared to the benchmark case, which is a transfer of surplus from consumers in segment 2 to the incumbent, leading to positive profits in segment 2. For instance, if $m_1^2 = 3f$, then the incumbent makes profits $\Pi_1^2 = 160$. The outcome of competition in segment 1 is not affected at all by a markup in m_1^2.

The two cases above have in common that only consumers in segment 2 are affected. There are no spillovers into the other segment. Notice, however, that a change in p_1^2 affects the number of calls made by customers in the monopoly segment that terminate on the entrant's network in segment 1. Nevertheless, if the entrant's access price τ_2^1 is equal to marginal costs, then less incoming traffic does not lead to a reduction of profits for the entrant.

Now suppose that, to make some profits, the incumbent is allowed to charge an access markup in the monopoly segment, that is, $\tau_1^2 > c_3$, while access prices in segment 1 are still cost based. The incumbent's prices in the monopoly segment are fixed at cost-based levels, that is, $p_1^2 = c_1$ and $m_1^2 = f$. Besides the intended effect that the incumbent's profits in the monopoly segment, Π_1^2, increase, there is a spillover effect: the intensity of competition in segment 1 is reduced, in both the short and the long term. To see this, notice that the entrant, even though it is active in segment 1 only, faces a higher access price for calls terminating in segment 2. Therefore, the entrant's perceived marginal cost, which equals:

$$\alpha^2 s_1^2 (c_2 + \tau_1^2) + \alpha^1 (s_2^2 c_1 + s_1^1 (c_2 + \tau_1^1)) = \alpha^2 (c_2 + \tau_1^2) + \alpha^1 c_1,$$

increases. Hence, a higher access price leads to a higher per-minute price p_2^1 in equilibrium. As this worsens the entrant's competitive position relative to the incumbent, the latter operator is able to charge a higher subscription fee m_1^1 without losing market share. In equilibrium, the entrant charges a slightly lower subscription fee m_2^1 than under cost-based regulation. Also, the entrant's market share is reduced. The following observation is particularly important in this respect. In the long term, instead of a convergence towards equal market shares, the entrant's market share in segment 1 converges to a level below $\frac{1}{2}$, because of the persisting disadvantage of the entrant. Thus, an access markup in the monopoly segment prevents a level-playing field in the competitive segment.

As an example, consider $\tau_1^2 = c_3 + 0.5 = 1$ (all other parameters are as in the benchmark case). In period 1, equilibrium profits are equal to $\Pi_1^2 = 3.70$, $\Pi_1^1 = 114.10$, and $\Pi_2^1 = 26.65$. One can see that the entrant's profits are only slightly reduced, but also that the incumbent's profits in segment 1 substantially increase, compared to the benchmark case. Also, consumers in the monopoly segment are not worse off: $CS^2 = 525$. On the other hand, consumers in segment 1 are significantly affected, as their surplus is reduced to $CS^1 = 367.21$. Overall, there is a welfare transfer from segment 1 to segment 2. In a mature market, the picture is similar.

One can observe that a substantial markup in τ_1^2 leads to a relatively small increase in profits Π_1^2. Clearly, allowing the incumbent to include markups in its retail prices, in particular in the subscription fee, is much more effective if one wants to guarantee a certain profit level in the monopoly segment. Moreover, we have seen that retail markups in segment 2 do not reduce the intensity of competition in segment 1. We summarize these observations in the following guideline.

> **Guideline 8.3:** Consider a segmented market with partial facilities-based entry. Suppose the incumbent is allowed to price discriminate, and that the regulator wants to guarantee a minimum profit level for the incumbent in the monopoly segment. Allowing the incumbent a markup in its subscription fee in the monopoly segment avoids distortions and spillover effects (to the other segment) that occur by allowing the incumbent markups in per-minute prices or the access price in the monopoly segment.

Of course, there may be situations in which a markup in the subscription fee cannot generate enough revenues without creating distortions or violating other objectives. For example, the monopoly segment may be too small to cover the fixed costs needed to upgrade the incumbent's network. In such a situation, the markup needed in the subscription fee might simply become so large that some consumers can no longer afford a subscription. Hence, a subscription fee markup may conflict with universal service goals (that is, it might violate the requirement of affordability; see also Section 2.2). The regulator (assuming that there are no cross subsidies or tax revenues coming from "outside") may then have to combine a subscription fee markup with markups in either the per-minute price or the access price in the monopoly segment.

For example, in the Netherlands, the regulator Opta requires the incumbent to offer a contract (among others) with a sufficiently low subscription fee. Accordingly, consumers with small budgets can, in principle, always afford a subscription. Hence, they are not cut off from the outside world, but they pay more to make phone calls. Alternatively, a regulator may allow for a markup in the access price for that segment. By doing so, the regulator is imposing a per-minute tax on calls from other segments to the monopoly segment to generate extra revenues. The negative consequences of this type of regulation have been analyzed above.

We conclude with a remark on uniform pricing and its implications for competition. Based on the discussion above, one can see that a straightforward way to generate extra revenues for the incumbent is to allow a markup on the subscription fee in the other segment as well. Suppose that a higher regulated subscription fee of the incumbent in both segments leads to higher equilibrium profits of the incumbent in the competitive segment (this is the case in our simulations). Then, by imposing uniform pricing on the incumbent's per-minute prices and by fixing the incumbent's subscription fee in both segments at the same level, prices can be kept lower in the monopoly segment than under regulation of the subscription fee that applies only to the monopoly segment. At the same time, the incumbent's profits are kept unchanged. The reverse holds in the competitive segment: competition is relaxed so that the entrant receives higher profits and consumers surplus in this segment is reduced. By such regulation, the regulator is effectively introducing cross-subsidization in the market: consumers in the competitive segment partly finance a certain profit level for the incumbent so that it can recover fixed costs from the monopoly segment.

8.2.5   Access price regulation in the competitive segment

We will now explore the role of access prices in the competitive segment. In particular, we analyze how access markups in segment 1 affect competition.

Suppose that there is a reciprocal access markup in segment 1, that is, $\tau_1^1 = \tau_2^1 > c_3$, while the access price in the monopoly segment is equal to marginal cost, that is, $\tau_1^2 = c_3$. The outcome of competition in segment 1 then strongly resembles the outcome in a model with a non-segmented market (see the model with homogeneous consumers in Section 3.5), but there are important differences as well. In particular:

- A certain fraction of the calls originating in segment 1 will terminate in the monopoly segment. Since the access price in the latter segment is equal to the marginal cost of termination, both operators' perceived marginal cost levels in segment 1 are lower than in a model without the monopoly segment. Therefore, per-minute prices in segment 1 are also lower, again compared to a model of an non-segmented market. As a consequence, the operators offer more value to consumers and can, to a certain extent, increase subscription fees.
- The existence of the monopoly segment intensifies competition for market share in segment 1. To see this, notice that market share becomes more valuable for the entrant: it increases the number of incoming calls from segment 2 and hence generates extra profits. The resulting downward pressure on subscription fees reduces profits, but at the same time the entrant's profits go up as the entrant receives more incoming calls from the monopoly segment. It can be shown that these effects exactly offset one another, so that profits Π_2^1 do not change.

The downward pressure on subscription fees due to more intense competition outweighs the effect that lower per-minute prices have in easing the pressure on subscription fees. Hence, the existence of a monopoly segment leads to lower subscription fees in the segment with facilities-based entry.

For the incumbent, calls originating from consumers in segment 2 and terminating on its own network in segment 1 are, in fact, on-net calls that do not generate access revenues. Because the incumbent suffers from more intense competition if there is a reciprocal access markup in segment 1, its profits in segment 1, Π_1^1, decrease.

In the benchmark case of cost-based access and retail price regulation (Table 8.2), the monopoly segment does not affect segment 1 because there are no access markups. Compared to the benchmark case, how is the incumbent's overall profit level affected by the reciprocal access markup in segment 1? It is straightforward to see that the access markup increases its traffic-dependent costs in segment 2, and hence reduces profits Π_1^2. As a consequence, the incumbent's total profits also go down.

Consumers in the monopoly segment are not affected by the access markup in segment 1, given that retail prices remain regulated at the same levels as under cost-based regulation.[12] For consumers in segment 1, however, the picture changes significantly. On the one hand, they make fewer calls due to higher per-minute prices, and hence generate less surplus from calls. This effect is rather small, though. On the other hand, they benefit substantially from the reduced subscription fees. Suppose, as an example, that $\tau_1^1 = \tau_2^1 = c_3 + 0.5 = 1$ and prices in segment 2 are cost based, and consider the outcome in period 1. Then $CS^1 = 389.58$, compared with $CS^1 = 378.33$ under cost-based regulation. Overall, welfare is hardly affected: $W = 1036.65$, compared with $W = 1036.67$ under cost-based regulation. The welfare loss is explained by the deadweight loss, which is caused by the increase in per-minute prices in segment 1.

The effects of a reciprocal access markup in segment 1 described above also hold in a mature market, when market shares converge to $\frac{1}{2}$ for each operator. We remark, however, that these long-term effects are somewhat hypothetical, given that it is not unlikely that entry in segment 2 occurs in the meantime (see Section 8.5 on mixed entry below).

Summarizing, the existence of a monopoly segment combined with reciprocal access markups in the segment where entry occurs, leads to an interesting interaction between the segments. These effects are mainly caused by the fact that market share in segment 1 becomes more valuable for both operators, because the existence of segment 2 generates extra incoming traffic for the entrant and outgoing traffic for the incumbent. We can summarize our insights as follows.

> **Guideline 8.4**: Consider a segmented market with partial facilities-based entry. Suppose the incumbent is allowed to price discriminate while retail prices are fixed in the monopoly segment. In an infant and a mature market, a reciprocal access markup in the competitive segment intensifies competition and increases consumers surplus in that segment. They affect neither consumers surplus in the regulated monopoly segment nor the entrant's profits.

---

[12] This type of regulation implies that operator 1 makes losses in the monopoly segment, since $\tau_1^2 = c_3$. Given cost-based access in the monopoly segment, if the regulator wants the incumbent at least to cover its connection-dependent and traffic-dependent costs in the monopoly segment it has to adjust the regulated retail prices in this segment (e.g. by allowing for a subscription fee markup). This has the effect that consumers in the monopoly segment are negatively affected by a reciprocal access markup in the competitive segment.

This guideline reflects an important difference to the policy implications for an unsegmented market. Recall from Chapter 4 that in a model of facilities-based entry in a non-segmented market, a reciprocal access markup is neutral to both operators' profits in the long run. Here, we observe that a reciprocal access markup in the competitive segment reduces the incumbent's profits.

Instead of considering a reciprocal access markup in the competitive segment suppose that only the entrant is allowed to charge an access markup, that is, $\tau_1^1 = \tau_1^2 = c_3$ and $\tau_2^1 > c_3$. Then a similar result with respect to consumers surplus is obtained. The existence of the monopoly segment again leads to lower subscription fees than in a model of a non-segmented market, just as we have seen above. Moreover, an asymmetric markup for the entrant increases only the incumbent's perceived marginal cost, and hence its per-minute price p_1^1, putting the incumbent at a disadvantage. Therefore, compared with the case with reciprocal access markups, the entrant obtains higher profits.

Compared with asymmetric access price regulation in a non-segmented market (see Sections 3.5 and 4.5), the entrant makes profits not only from calls that originate from segment 1, but also from calls that originate from segment 2. Asymmetric access price regulation is thus a powerful tool to stimulate entry in segment 1. Clearly, such regulation has to be phased out as the entrant gains market share.

> **Guideline 8.5:** Consider a segmented market with partial facilities-based entry. Suppose the incumbent is allowed to price discriminate while retail prices are fixed in the monopoly segment. In an infant market, an asymmetric access markup only for the entrant increases consumers surplus in the competitive segment and the entrant's profits. (Consumers surplus in the monopoly segment is not affected.)

Suppose the incumbent is forced to set uniform prices $p_1 \equiv p_1^1 = p_1^2$ and $m_1 \equiv m_1^1 = m_1^2$. Then access markups in segment 1 necessarily affect retail prices (and consumers surplus) in segment 2. Here, the incumbent's subscription fee is fixed because, with uniform pricing, the incumbent's subscription fee also typically has to be regulated (see Guideline 8.1). Simulations show that a reciprocal access markup in segment 1 increases consumers surplus not only in segment 1, but also in segment 2, if the incumbent cannot price discriminate. This is also true in case of an asymmetric access markup in segment 1 (for the entrant only), again given a uniform pricing regime. In both situations of access markups, the entrant's profits increase. Hence, the guidelines' policy implications are robust to the pricing regime in the retail market.

8.3   Partial LLU-based entry

In this section we discuss partial entry based on local loop unbundling: the entrant leases unbundled local connections from the incumbent in segment 1 but does not enter segment 2. In the sense that such a strategy requires less investment by the entrant, this can be seen as a more cautious entry strategy than partial facilities-based entry.

As we will see, the results if the incumbent can price discriminate are in line with those obtained in Section 5.2, where we explored LLU-based entry in a market with homogeneous customers. Also, the policy implications with respect to terminating access prices obtained in Section 8.2 apply here as well, and will therefore not be repeated. Because of that, we will keep this section relatively short, without providing detailed analysis or reporting simulation results. We restrict the analysis to regulation of the lease price of the local loop.[13]

We assume, as in the previous section, that the entrant has a long-distance backbone and the incumbent serves both segments of the market. Initially, the incumbent's market share in segment 1 is 100 percent. Table 8.3 gives an overview of the entrant's ways of access in the model.

Suppose that the incumbent is allowed to price discriminate, while its retail prices in segment 2 are fixed by the regulator at cost-based levels. More generally, the regulator can safely guarantee the incumbent a positive profit level in segment 2 by allowing for a markup in subscription fee m_1^2. Then terminating access prices play exactly the same role as in a situation of partial facilities-based entry. Therefore, Guidelines 8.3 to 8.5 in Section 8.2 also apply here.

The crucial difference to partial facilities-based entry is that the entrant leases the incumbent's local loops for its customers in segment 1. How does the level of the lease price affect competition in this entry situation? As a benchmark case, suppose that the lease price of the local loop is cost based, that is, $l = f^{\text{local-line}}$. Then both operators face exactly the same connection-dependent fixed costs as in a situation of partial facilities-based entry. Denote equilibrium subscription fees in segment 1 in this case by $m_1^{1*} = \hat{m}_1$ and $m_2^{1*} = \hat{m}_2$.

Now consider a markup in the lease price, so that the entrant has to pay $l > f^{\text{local-line}}$ in each period. One can then show, and simulations confirm, that in equilibrium, $m_1^{1*} = \hat{m}_1 + l - f^{\text{local-line}}$ and $m_2^{1*} = \hat{m}_2 + l - f^{\text{local-line}}$. Per-minute prices are not affected by a markup in the lease price. Only the incumbent's profits increase due to the markup. The entrant is able to pass on its increased traffic-dependent cost to its customers, so that its profits remain constant.[14] Market shares are not affected. Effectively, a lease price above cost

---

[13] A simulation program of the model is included on the Cambridge University Press Web site, http://uk.cambridge.org/resources/0521808375; the interested reader can perform simulations to obtain numerical results.

[14] We assume that the markup in the line rental is not so high that consumers in segment 1 no longer buy a subscription. In other words, their willingness to pay is sufficiently large to cover the markup.

Table 8.3 *Partial LLU-based entry: the entrant's ways of access*

	Type of access	Wholesale price
Access to:		
incumbent's customers segment 1	Terminating	τ_1^1
incumbent's customers segment 2	Terminating	τ_1^2
potential customers segment 1	Direct (LLU)	l (per customer)
potential customers segment 2	–	–

can be seen as a monetary transfer from consumers in segment 1 to the incumbent. Therefore, to maximize consumers surplus in a given situation of partial LLU-based entry, the lease price should be cost based.

This result holds independent of access prices. Furthermore, we observe that adding a monopoly segment for the incumbent does not affect the results obtained in Section 5.2 on LLU-based entry in a non-segmented market. To see why this is the case, notice that local loop unbundling does not affect the value of an additional subscriber for each operator if a higher lease price is passed on to consumers.

To confirm the robustness of the results on LLU-based entry of Section 5.2, we formulate the following guideline.

> **Guideline 8.6**: Consider a segmented market with partial LLU-based entry. In an infant and a mature market, a cost-based lease price allows the incumbent to recover its connection-dependent costs. A lease price below costs can (temporarily) be used to increase consumers surplus at the cost of the incumbent's profits. (Similar to Guideline 5.1)

Notice that, in principle, a markup in the line rental can be used to generate revenues to cover the fixed cost of the network in the monopoly segment. For instance, suppose that the regulator cannot or does not want to set a markup on the subscription fee for consumers in segment 2 to generate revenues to cover fixed and sunk costs. Then the regulator may want to allow the incumbent to use the revenues from a markup in the lease price in segment 1 to partially finance the costs of network maintenance in the monopoly segment.

Partially or fully replacing a markup in the subscription fee in segment 2 by a markup in the lease price, such that the incumbent's profits remain constant, leaves the entrant's profits and welfare unchanged. It amounts to a transfer from consumers in segment 1 to consumers in segment 2. Given that we have seen that a lease price markup is neutral for the entrant and for welfare, this may be a better solution than allowing the incumbent to charge an access markup in segment 2, since the latter has negative side effects (recall the insights obtained in Section 8.2).

To conclude this section, we address to what extent the obtained results change if the regulator requires the incumbent to set uniform prices $p_1 \equiv p_1^1 = p_1^2$ and $m_1 \equiv m_1^1 = m_1^2$. Recall that the subscription fee m_1 typically has to be regulated (see also Subsection 8.2.2). With price discrimination, operators could react to a markup in the lease price by increasing subscription fees in segment 1. With uniform pricing, the incumbent can only react with its per-minute price p_1(to the extent that p_1 is not regulated). Hence, consumers in segment 2 are also affected. The entrant, on the other hand, will still set p_2^1 equal to perceived marginal cost, but will increase its subscription fee m_2^1. Simulations show that a markup in the lease price relaxes competition in segment 1 (showing up in higher prices p_1 and m_2^1), while consumers surplus is reduced in both segments. The policy implication (see Guideline 8.6 above) remains that the lease price should be cost based.

8.4   Partial carrier-select-based entry

For an entrant that does not want to roll out its own customer access network, carrier-select-based entry can be a sensible alternative to leasing the incumbent's local lines. In this section, we address partial entry based on originating access to the incumbent's network. The entrant offers carrier-select (or preselect) services to consumers in segment 1, while it does not enter segment 2.

The results that are obtained if the incumbent can price discriminate are straightforward, given the insights in Section 5.3 on carrier-select-based entry in a market with homogeneous customers. Therefore, this section has been kept relatively brief.[15] We assume that there are no capacity shortages in the incumbent's points of interconnection. For an analysis that includes capacity shortages for interconnection capacity (in an unsegmented market), see Section 5.3.

The assumptions that underlie the analysis are as follows. The entrant has a long-distance backbone. The incumbent serves both segments of the market, and its market share in segment 1 is 100 percent. The incumbent is allowed to price discriminate. It charges an originating access price δ_1^1 for calls made by the entrant's customers, and a terminating access price τ_1^k for incoming calls terminating to its customers belonging to segment $k = 1, 2$. Table 8.4 summarizes the entrant's ways of access in the model.[16]

---

[15] A simulation program for the model in this section is available on the Cambridge University Press Web site, http://uk.cambridge.org/resources/0521808375.

[16] Recall that originating access is a form of indirect access, i.e., consumers cannot subscribe to the entrant.

Table 8.4 *Partial carrier-select-based entry: the entrant's ways of access*

	Type of access	Wholesale price
Access to:		
incumbent's customers segment 1	Terminating	τ_1^1
incumbent's customers segment 2	Terminating	τ_1^2
potential customers segment 1	Originating	δ_1^1
potential customers segment 2	–	–

To protect captive consumers, the regulator has to put price caps on the incumbent's retail prices in segment 2, for the incumbent does not face any downward pressure from competition in that segment. We assume therefore, without loss of generality with regard to the policy implications, that these prices are fixed at cost-based levels. Again, recall that the regulator can guarantee the incumbent positive profits in segment 2 by allowing for a markup in, preferably, the subscription fee. Because all customers, including the entrant's, have to pay a subscription fee to the incumbent, the regulator also has to put a price cap on m_1^1. Suppose that this subscription fee is set at the fixed cost of a connection f. The operators compete by choosing per-minute prices in segment 1. The incumbent's prices in segment 2, as well as its subscription fee in segment 1, have to be regulated.

> **Guideline 8.7**: Consider a segmented market with partial carrier-select-based entry. To protect consumers from excessive pricing, the incumbent's subscription fees in both segments have to be regulated.

Because the incumbent can price discriminate, all of the regulated prices can be fixed at the associated cost levels. Notice in particular that, because the incumbent is allowed to price discriminate, regulation of its per-minute price in segment 2 does not affect competition in segment 1.

Now we turn to the level of originating and terminating access prices. For off-net calls that stay within segment 1, the entrant has to pay $\delta_1^1 + \tau_1^1$ per minute to the incumbent, while the wholesale price for calls to the other segment is $\delta_1^1 + \tau_1^2$. Hence, both the incumbent's originating access price δ_1^1 and both of its terminating access prices τ_1^2 and τ_1^1 directly increase the entrant's perceived marginal costs. An increase in any of these access prices translates into a higher per-minute price p_2^1, which in turn relieves the competitive pressure on the incumbent, which can increase p_1^1. Consequently, markups in the incumbent's access prices reduce the entrant's profits and distort calling behavior in segment 1, leading to a lower surplus for consumers in this segment. If the incumbent's originating and terminating access prices are cost based, welfare is maximized. Also, consumers surplus is maximized under the constraint that access prices have at least to cover marginal costs.

To summarize our findings, we formulate the following guideline.

> **Guideline 8.8**: Consider a segmented market with partial carrier-select-based entry. In an infant and a mature market, cost-based originating and terminating access prices maximize consumers surplus and welfare. (Similar to Guideline 5.3)

To complete the discussion of partial carrier-select-based entry, suppose that the incumbent has to set uniform prices and that the subscription fee is regulated (while its per-minute price is not regulated). Accordingly, its subscription fee $m_1 \equiv m_1^1 = m_1^2$ is fixed by the regulator, while it can choose $p_1 \equiv p_1^1 = p_1^2$. Compared to a regime of price discrimination which leaves the subscription fee in segment 1 unregulated, per-minute prices in segment 1 increase, while consumers in the captive segment benefit from a somewhat lower per-minute price. Accordingly, consumers surplus increases in the captive segment, but decreases in segment 1. Because price competition is relaxed, the entrant's profits increase. Again, in a regime of uniform retail prices, access markups directly lead to higher per-minute prices, thus reducing consumers' surplus in both segments. Access markups also reduce the entrant's profits, similar to a regime that allows for price discrimination. Summarizing, the policy implications obtained earlier remain unchanged if the regulator imposes uniform pricing.

8.5   Mixed entry

This section discusses two forms of mixed entry. It is meant to complement the earlier sections, so that the reader gets a complete overview of the most relevant entry situations and the associated regulatory issues. We will not present simulation results.[17]

The section complements the discussion of regulatory spillover effects and pricing regimes in previous sections: different entry settings provide new illustrations that regulation induced by a particular type of entry in one segment

---

[17] Simulation programs for the two models in this section are available at the Cambridge University Press Web site, http://uk.cambridge.org/resources/0521808375.

Table 8.5 *Mixed facilities-based and LLU-based entry:
the entrant's ways of access*

	Type of access	Wholesale price
Access to:		
incumbent's customers segment 1	Terminating	τ_1^1
incumbent's customers segment 2	Terminating	τ_1^2
potential customers segment 1	Direct	–
potential customers segment 2	Direct (LLU)	l (per customer)

may have spillover effects to the other segment, especially if the incumbent is
forced to choose uniform prices.

8.5.1   Mixed facilities-based and LLU-based entry

Consider an entrant that targets customers in segment 1 by rolling out local
connections and consumers in segment 2 by leasing the incumbent's local lines.
For instance, the entrant finds it worthwhile to invest in a customer access
network for the business segment, but has decided not to do the same for the
residential segment, possibly because the segments are not equally profitable.
Instead, it leases parts of the incumbent's existing network to target residential
consumers. Thus, a mixed entry strategy can be useful for operators which may
wish to serve smaller customers without incurring the big investment cost of
network rollout, in addition to directly connecting to bigger clients. Table 8.5
summarizes the entrant's access to consumers under mixed facilities-based and
unbundling-based entry.

A mixed entry strategy may prevail over a number of periods only; alternatively, it may be a long-term outcome in case a duplication of the local loop is
privately too costly in a certain segment. Note that regulation can encourage or
discourage the duplication of the local loop. The regulator may want to discourage it in those segments in which facilities-based competition is not socially
desirable (such as typically for rural consumers). To this end, the regulator would
need to know the social costs and benefits of the duplication of infrastructure.
It can then choose its regulatory instruments such that the operators implement
the socially optimal investment at the local loop.

Furthermore, we analyze the effect of the lease price charged by the incumbent in segment 2 on competition in both segments. Suppose that there
is an increase in the lease price above the fixed cost of a local connection
f. The entrant then faces a higher connection-dependent cost in segment 2.
If the incumbent is allowed to price discriminate, then the increase in the

line rental leads to inflated subscription fees in segment 2 without generating spillover effects (e.g. a softening of competition) in the other segment. Also, a markup in the line rental reduces consumers surplus and the entrant's profits in segment 2. These results apply both in the case of an infant market (where the entrant starts with zero market share) and in the case of a mature market.

Now suppose that the regulator imposes uniform pricing on the incumbent. Just as in the case above, where the incumbent was allowed to price discriminate, an increase in the lease price leads to higher subscription fees in segment 2. A difference is that the incumbent's inflated subscription fee now also applies to segment 1. Accordingly, the entrant faces less price pressure in that segment, allowing it to increase its subscription fee for segment-1 customers. The conclusion is that a larger markup in the lease price charged in segment 2 softens price competition in the segment with facilities-based competition (segment 1). Consumers surplus in both segments decreases. The incumbent's profits in both segments increase, whereas the entrant's profits go up in segment 1 but down in segment 2. Depending on parameter values of the model, the entrant's overall profits may increase, both in an infant and in a mature market.[18] Accordingly, in the case that not only the incumbent but also the entrant benefit from a markup in the lease price, tacit collusion poses a significant risk if the operators can freely negotiate on the level of the lease price.[19]

Summarizing, our earlier policy guideline (see Guideline 8.6) that the lease price of the local loop should be equal to its underlying cost, remains unchanged. In the case that the incumbent is obliged to charge uniform prices, the motivation is even more compelling because a markup in the line rental softens competition in the other segment. In addition, if the lease price is determined by negotiations between the operators, it is crucial that the regulator closely monitors these negotiations, to reduce the risk of tacit collusion via the lease price. Hence, we obtain the following two guidelines.

> **Guideline 8.9:** Consider a segmented market with mixed facilities-based and LLU-based entry. In an infant and a mature market, a cost-based lease price of the incumbent's local loop allows the incumbent to recover its connection-dependent costs. Under the constraint that the lease price has to recover these costs, a cost-based lease price maximizes consumers surplus. (Similar to Guideline 5.1)

---

[18] This can easily be confirmed in simulations by choosing the relative size of segment 2 large enough, e.g. $\alpha^2 = 0.8$.

[19] If both operators have to set uniform prices, then a lease price markup increases the incumbent's profits but leaves the entrant's (total) profits unchanged.

> **Guideline 8.10**: Consider a segmented market with mixed facilities-based and LLU-based entry. If the incumbent is not allowed to price discriminate, the lease price can possibly be used as an instrument of tacit collusion. By allowing the incumbent to price discriminate, this risk of tacit collusion can be avoided.

8.5.2   Mixed facilities-based and carrier-select-based entry

Consider now an entrant that targets segment-1 customers with its own access network and segment-2 customers by offering carrier-select-based voice telephony. An example of this type of entry is provided by Telfort in the Netherlands (see the examples discussed in Section 8.1). Telfort targets business customers in certain areas of the country by directly connecting them to its long-distance backbone, while offering carrier-select voice telephony to residential consumers. Table 8.6 summarizes the entrant's ways of access in the model.

Suppose that the incumbent is allowed to set different retail prices for the two segments. Since customers in segment 2, who choose to make calls through the entrant's long-distance network, have to keep their subscription to the incumbent, the latter operator does not face downward pressure on its segment-2 subscription fee. A price cap is therefore necessary.

Alternatively, suppose that the regulator imposes uniform pricing on the incumbent. The incumbent's incentive to milk consumers in segment 2 by a high subscription fee is partly offset by a loss in market share in segment 1, implying lower profits in that segment. Nevertheless, if willingness to pay is sufficiently high in segment 2, and if that segment is of significant size, the gains from an increase of profits in segment 2 are so strong that the incumbent sets a "high" subscription fee in both segments. Therefore, regulation of the incumbent's

Table 8.6 *Mixed facilities-based and carrier-select-based entry: the entrant's ways of access*

	Type of access	Wholesale price
Access to:		
incumbent's customers segment 1	Terminating	τ_1^1
incumbent's customers segment 2	Terminating	τ_1^2
potential customers segment 1	Direct	–
potential customers segment 2	Originating	δ_1^2

subscription fee is necessary.[20] Without a price cap, if all consumers have the same willingness to pay, the incumbent even reduces consumers surplus in segment 2 to zero. It then possibly leaves the other segment to the entrant. We summarize the discussion above, which applies in an infant market as well as in a mature market, as follows.

> **Guideline 8.11**: Consider a segmented market with mixed facilities-based and carrier-select-based entry. In an infant and a mature market, to protect consumers from excessive pricing, the incumbent's subscription fee in the segment with carrier-select competition has to be regulated if the incumbent is allowed to price discriminate, and, in general, also if the incumbent has to set uniform prices.

Notice that with uniform pricing, a lower price cap on the incumbent's subscription fee intensifies competition in segment 1. This makes facilities-based entry in segment 1 less attractive although it is good for segment-1 customers. Hence, one can observe that, compared to the non-segmented-market model of carrier-select-based entry (see Section 5.3), the presence of an additional segment with facilities-based competition introduces a trade-off between protecting consumers in the carrier-select segment and stimulating facilities-based entry in the other segment. This trade-off was absent in the non-segmented market model, and is also absent if the incumbent is allowed to price discriminate.

What is the optimal level of the originating access price from a regulatory point of view? Suppose that the incumbent's subscription fee is fixed, while it can freely set its per-minute price. If price discrimination is allowed, the originating access price charged by the incumbent in segment 2 should be cost based; the motivation is similar to that discussed in Sections 5.3 and 8.4. In the case of uniform pricing, there is an additional argument in favor of a cost-based access price. The reason is that there is a spillover effect between the segments with regard to the originating access price. An increase in the originating access price leads to an inflation of the entrant's per-minute price in segment 2. In turn, the incumbent raises its (uniform) per-minute price above marginal costs, and the entrant is able to increase its subscription fee in segment 1. Accordingly, segment-1 customers experience softer price competition. The conclusion is that consumers in segment 1 also suffer from a markup on originating access in segment 2. Finally, notice that a markup increases the entrant's profits in segment 1, and decreases its profits in segment 2.[21] To the extent that the former effect

---

[20] This can easily be confirmed by simulations under a broad range of different parameters, in particular segment sizes.

[21] Which effect dominates depends on the relative importance of the two segments. Notice that this may change over time, as the entrant gains market share.

dominates, the originating access price can be used as an instrument of tacit collusion.

Guideline 8.12: Consider a segmented market with mixed facilities-based and carrier-select-based entry. In an infant and a mature market, a cost-based originating access price prevents a deadweight loss and reduction of consumers surplus. It also avoids the risk of tacit collusion through the originating access price. Moreover, by allowing the incumbent to price discriminate between the segments, spillover effects of retail price regulation can be avoided.

8.6   Summary

Compared to Chapter 7, which also discussed entry in a segmented market, this chapter focused on entry modes that come closer to situations that can be observed in practice. Whereas in the previous chapter we looked at non-targeted facilities-based competition, here we have explored a range of strategies allowing entrants to single out a particular segment (partial entry), or target different segments in different ways (mixed entry).

To start with, we recapitulate the guidelines derived in different situations of partial entry. Firstly, consider a segmented market with partial facilities-based entry. For instance, an entrant may only be interested in business customers, and leave the residential segment to the incumbent. It rolls out a customer access network for its customers. Although the regulator will be glad that there is competition in one segment, it still has an important task in the monopoly segment, and also has to assess how regulatory choices aiming at one segment affect the other one. As the following guidelines speak for themselves, we recapitulate them without further comments.

- To protect consumers in the monopoly segment, the incumbent's subscription fee in that segment has to be regulated if the incumbent is allowed to price discriminate, and, in general, also if the incumbent has to set uniform prices. (Guideline 8.1)
- By allowing the incumbent to price discriminate between the segments, spillover effects of retail price regulation (from the regulated monopoly segment to the other segment) can be avoided. (Guideline 8.2)
- Suppose the incumbent is allowed to price discriminate, and that the regulator wants to guarantee a minimum profit level for the incumbent in the monopoly segment. Allowing the incumbent a markup in its subscription fee in the monopoly segment avoids distortions and spillover effects that occur by allowing the incumbent markups in per-minute prices or the access price in the monopoly segment. (Guideline 8.3)

- Suppose the incumbent is allowed to price discriminate while retail prices are fixed in the monopoly segment. In an infant and a mature market, a reciprocal access markup in the competitive segment intensifies competition and increases consumers surplus in that segment. It affects neither consumers surplus in the regulated monopoly segment nor the entrant's profits. (Guideline 8.4)
- Suppose the incumbent is allowed to price discriminate while retail prices are fixed in the monopoly segment. In an infant market, an asymmetric access markup only for the entrant increases consumers surplus in the competitive segment and the entrant's profits. (Consumers surplus in the monopoly segment is not affected.) (Guideline 8.5)

An entrant targeting a particular segment may not want to roll out a customer access network. Consider therefore, in a segmented market, as a second mode of targeted entry, partial LLU-based entry. The following guideline addresses the lease price of the local loop.

- In an infant and a mature market, a cost-based lease price allows the incumbent to recover its connection-dependent costs. A lease price below costs can (temporarily) be used to increase consumers surplus at the cost of the incumbent's profits. (Guideline 8.6)

Thirdly, as another alternative for an entrant that does not wish to roll out its own local network, consider a carrier-select-based entrant targeting one segment only. The following guidelines are relevant for the incumbent's subscription fee, as well as its originating and terminating access prices.

- To protect consumers from excessive pricing, the incumbent's subscription fees in both segments have to be regulated. (Guideline 8.7)
- In an infant and a mature market, cost-based originating and terminating access prices maximize consumers surplus and welfare. (Guideline 8.8)

Now suppose that the entrant targets both segments, but in different ways (mixed entry). Firstly, consider a segmented market with mixed facilities-based and LLU-based entry. The lease price of the local loop is the variable that raises a particular regulatory concern that was not present in previous situations of local loop unbundling, namely that the lease price can be used as an instrument of tacit collusion. The following guidelines were obtained.

- In an infant and a mature market, a cost-based lease price of the incumbent's local loop allows the incumbent to recover its connection-dependent costs. Under the constraint that the lease price has to recover these costs, a cost-based lease price maximizes consumers surplus. (Guideline 8.9)
- If the incumbent is not allowed to price discriminate, the lease price can possibly be used as an instrument of tacit collusion. By allowing the incumbent to price discriminate, this risk of tacit collusion can be avoided. (Guideline 8.10)

One can observe that the risk of tacit collusion through the lease price does not occur if price discrimination between the segments is allowed. This demonstrates (again) how important it is for the regulator to be aware of the interaction between the wholesale and resale market, and also between the segments.

Secondly, suppose that there is an entrant that adopts a mix of facilities-based and carrier-select-based entry. This situation provides another illustration of the role of a uniform pricing restriction imposed on the incumbent.

- In an infant and a mature market, to protect consumers from excessive pricing, the incumbent's subscription fee in the segment with carrier-select competition has to be regulated if the incumbent is allowed to price discriminate, and, in general, also if the incumbent has to set uniform prices. (Guideline 8.11)
- In an infant and a mature market, a cost-based originating access price prevents a deadweight loss and reduction of consumers surplus. It also avoids the risk of tacit collusion through the originating access price. Moreover, by allowing the incumbent to price discriminate between the segments, spillover effects of retail price regulation can be avoided. (Guideline 8.12)

As one can see from these guidelines, the analysis of a variety of targeted-entry situations generates a coherent pattern of policy implications. At a more general level, the results confirm the insights derived for situations of a non-segmented market in Chapters 3 to 6.

We conclude this summary with a caveat that also applies to earlier chapters (in particular to Chapters 4 and 5, see Section 5.4). The guidelines were obtained within the setting of a particular entry situation. Given a certain entry mode, the guidelines aim at stimulating entry and ensuring that consumers are not exploited in segments in which entry has not taken place, or in which the entrant is at a disadvantage (so that the competitive pressure on the incumbent's prices is weak). Nevertheless, the regulator typically acts within the broader context of juggling with all types of entry that may occur simultaneously or sequentially over time. In reality, entry strategies are endogenous and depend on the regulatory policy. For example, the regulator may want to stimulate carrier-select-based and local loop unbundling immediately after liberalization by enforcing cost-based wholesale prices for these entry modes. Later, the regulator may aim at the emergence of facilities-based competition in most segments by making the former two entry modes more costly for entrants. Hence, given such dynamic regulatory objectives, cost-based wholesale prices are not necessarily desirable in the long term. Cost-based originating access to the incumbent's network may be needed to stimulate competition in the short term, while sunset clauses can stimulate investments in infrastructure in the longer term, so that deregulation can take place at a later stage. The next chapter, which concludes the book, contains more discussion on this topic.

9 Concluding remarks

In this book, we have tried to provide answers to the multi-faceted question of how to regulate telecommunications markets. It is our hope that the analysis and guidelines contribute to policy and regulation that aim at stimulating and fostering competition, such that consumers are able to benefit from it.

We have addressed a wide range of different situations of entry and strategic interaction between operators, using models of the theory of industrial organization. These types of models have proved to be very useful for exploring the complex environments characterized by network structures, which are quite different from many product markets.

In our analysis (Chapters 3 to 8), we derived guidelines for policy, applied to different modes of entry (facilities-based, local-loop unbundling, carrier-select, and targeted entry) and modes of price competition (two-part tariffs, linear prices, flat fees, price discrimination, uniform pricing, and termination-based price discrimination). We will not repeat these guidelines here, since they were recapitulated and discussed in the conclusion of each of those chapters. We do, however, wish to point out here that several guidelines appear to be quite general. For instance, the same policy implications for access price regulation in infant markets emerge from different modes of competition. Overall, the complete set of guidelines gives a coherent picture of retail and access price regulation. Also, the guidelines do not crucially depend on the input parameters that were used in the simulations. We are therefore confident that the models deliver robust results.

Unfortunately, our models cannot describe reality in complete detail. Nevertheless, in uncovering general principles they can be used to better understand cause-and-effect relationships in telecommunications, so that one gains a clear idea of the advantages and disadvantages of certain regulatory interventions.

In the models we isolated certain entry modes and pricing strategies and derived guidelines for access price and retail price regulation. From a broader perspective, some regulatory policy referred to by guidelines may conflict with certain policy goals. For example, whereas a cost-based access pricing rule may be optimal for consumers *ex post* (i.e., after investment and entry decisions have been taken), it may *ex ante* discourage operators from rolling out networks themselves or upgrading them to deliver higher quality (more on this below).

In the formulation of the guidelines we concentrated on the important issue of investment incentives for entrant operators by taking entrants' profits explicitly into account. Below we take a look at some of the issues that received less attention: entry of inefficient entrants; the heterogeneity of operators and the dependence of operators' market strategies on regulation; the formulation of regulatory policy in the presence of market uncertainty; operators' investment decisions when facing regulatory uncertainty; the full or partial replacement of regulation by competition policy; and, finally, the convergence of communications and information services and its impact on regulation.

9.1   Efficient versus inefficient entrants

In the models explored in this book, it was implicit that entry is successful if the entrant can make profits that are sufficient to cover its cost of entry. The analysis has not addressed the question how to achieve efficient entry and how to avoid inefficient entry.[1] Throughout most of the analysis, we have postulated that in the long term operators are equally efficient. If some of the asymmetries between operators persist over time, the regulator has to worry about inefficient entry.

Consider the hypothetical case that (equally efficient) entrants compete all their profits away. In this case, under cost-based access pricing rules an inefficient entrant cannot make positive profits so that only efficient entrants enter (see also Subsection 2.3.2).

More realistic models incorporate the fact that entrant operators do not offer perfect substitutes. For instance, we assumed that competition is imperfect due to the presence of consumer switching costs. Then, even under cost-based regulation, operators with different cost levels can all enjoy positive profits – we believe that this property holds in many segments of telecommunications markets. When entry is endogenous, while there are significant sunk costs, a less efficient operator will not necessarily be replaced by a more efficient one.[2] Hence, even cost-based access price regulation cannot necessarily achieve welfare-maximizing facilities-based entry. Consequently, we do not always expect efficient entry in a telecommunications market characterized by imperfect competition.

Many of the guidelines derived from the analysis in infant markets focused on asymmetric access price regulation. Regulatory authorities must keep in mind that allowing an access markup (on a temporary basis) only to the entrant may

---

[1] For a discussion on inefficient entry, see Armstrong (2000b).

[2] If new services create added value for some customers, this positive effect has to be taken into account when answering the question which of the potential entrants should enter to maximize welfare.

attract less efficient entrants. In other words, regulatory policy cannot ignore the issue of inefficient entry because providing a temporary advantage to entrants gives early, inefficient arrivals the possibility of making (higher) profits. This can have long-term effects if later efficiency improvements are too costly to carry out.

A related problem of inefficient entry is that an entrant may not select the most efficient entry mode because of regulatory intervention. For instance, if unbundling is made attractive by setting a low lease price, facilities-based entry may not occur even though this may be efficient (see Section 5.4). More generally, regulation affects investment decisions so that the regulator has to be concerned about the impact of regulatory policy on infrastructure investment in telecommunications markets (see also below).

9.2   Operators' market strategies and regulation

As has been emphasized in the introduction of the book, entrants are a hetero-geneous lot. They were categorized according to whether entry was facilities based, LLU based, or resale based at the local loop, and these entry modes were compared in Section 5.4. We saw that regulation may strongly affect the incentives on whether and how to enter a market or market segment. Entry decisions depend not only on regulation that applies at the moment of entry, but also on the expected future regulatory policy until infrastructure investments become obsolete or contracts expire.

Chapter 8 explored entry by operators that target different segments by differ-ent market strategies. Clearly, regulation must address segment-specific techno-logical constraints, since they may induce targeted entry strategies. For instance, entry is less likely to be facilities based in high-cost segments (unless regulation favors investment in those areas). It is therefore important that regulators assess which segments, in the short or longer term, are most suitable for facilities-based competition (implying a duplication of the incumbent's infrastructure). Such segments may need only a light-handed regulation, if any at all, once the market has sufficiently matured.

In certain market segments, such as rural areas, network duplication may be too costly. Nevertheless, LLU-based and resale-based competitors may dis-cipline the incumbent, so that retail price regulation may not be needed in a mature market, unless political motives play a role.

Investments may be so costly that services are offered by the incumbent only because it is required to do so under a universal service obligation. In such high-cost segments, regulation of retail prices may remain necessary.

Given the heterogeneity among operators, perhaps political motives and con-straints are one of the main problems in designing a sound regulatory policy. In particular, regulation asking for universal service forces the operator in question to offer services below costs in high-cost areas if these services are not afford-able otherwise. A uniform pricing restriction then leads to a cross-subsidization from low-cost to high-cost areas or segments. This implies that low-cost seg-ments, which without regulation directed at the high-cost segments would at most need a light regulation, are affected and possibly require heavier regulation (see Chapters 7 and 8). A discussion of which of the universal service goals are really justified and whether they should not be better financed by government transfers seems desirable: less demanding universal service obligations together with outside financing help to reduce the regulatory burden in telecommunica-tions markets. Universal service obligations possibly make entry into high-cost areas less attractive and into low-cost areas more attractive;[3] this holds in partic-ular if a uniform pricing constraint is imposed. Therefore, the implementation of a universal service obligation may affect entry and thus the market structure which materializes.

Apart from political motives, regulation is affected by complex entry patterns. Given the current uncertainty with respect to the evolution of the industry, it is unclear to what extent technology favors operators that are active in several segments because of economies of scale and scope. It is conceivable that spe-cialized entrants temporarily or even permanently find profitable niches and market segments (Subsection 2.2.2 provided some examples of niche strategies for the Netherlands).

In the near future, it may then become useful to distinguish operators based on the services that they offer, in addition to the distinction based on how they access consumers and their networks. For example, there may be entrants offering low-end services (e.g. selling capacity as a commodity) or selling high-end services (such as customized network services for large firms). As operator–customer relationships become more important, it may become more difficult for a single operator to target many different consumer groups at the same time. This may lead to further services-oriented specialization. Operators, which may share parts of a network with complementary operators, then specialize in offering services to particular segments. In effect, services offered by one operator are substitutes to those offered by some competitors and complements to those offered by others.

In a world of specialized operators targeting specific segments of the mar-ket, access is and will remain an important issue. Firstly, facilities-based and unbundling-based entry increases the need for network interconnection. Secondly, as the market becomes more fragmented, terminating access becomes more important because operators need access to customers in the segments that they do not target.

---

[3] A similar point is made by Farrell and Katz (1998), who discuss the universal service obligations in the US.

9.3   Market uncertainty and regulatory response

In our models, we abstracted from the initial uncertainty faced by the regulator concerning the evolution of the market. We implicitly modeled the regulator as having perfect foresight concerning the strategic interaction among operators in all periods.

Given the uncertain nature of technological progress in telecommunications and the rapid change of market structure, it is impossible to precisely forecast the success of entrants in the different segments of the telecommunications market. The existence of market uncertainty has important implications for the design of regulatory policy, as outlined below.

As a general problem, note that price regulation can give rise to regulatory capture and regulatory takings.[4] These are particularly likely if the uncertainty is large and if reviews of the regulatory pricing rules are not frequent.

In this book, we have repeatedly argued that regulation in an infant market should be different from regulation in a mature market. In a world without uncertainty this implies that the use of sunset clauses and other time constraints on regulation enable the regulator to commit to asymmetric regulation until a certain market structure prevails and to symmetric regulation afterwards.

In an uncertain world, sunset clauses that are not conditional on market structure have the disadvantage that the predicted market structure may fail to materialize, so that regulation is not *ex post* optimal in the regulator's view. Therefore, the regulator may find it more attractive to implement a more flexible policy that depends on realized market outcomes such as market shares. The European Union has taken such a stance: operators with significant market power, essentially defined as operators with more than 25 percent market share (exceptions to the rule are possible), are subject to heavier regulation than other operators. However, such outcome-based regulation may have negative effects on competition. For instance, if the replacement of asymmetric by reciprocal access prices depends on market outcomes, operators can strategically exploit the endogeneity of regulatory variables by taking into account the effect of their decisions on the relevant market outcomes.[5] A market-share-based criterion of regulation gives incentives to incumbents and entrants to behave less aggressively: the incumbent prefers a rapid replacement of asymmetric regulation and the entrant the opposite.

The previous discussion shows that, in an uncertain world, sunset clauses may lead to an *ex post* inefficient regulatory policy if they are not conditional on market outcomes, but only time dependent. On the other hand, outcome-based regulation is prone to be strategically exploited by operators. Hence, the

---

[4] For a discussion of regulatory capture and regulatory takings, see Laffont and Tirole (2000).
[5] This seems to have happened in the UK during the duopoly period (1982–1991).

regulator faces a trade-off in its design of regulatory policy which is affected by the degree of the regulator's uncertainty and the ability of operators to influence market outcomes. Less uncertainty about market parameters makes a less flexible time frame more appealing to the regulator; the extreme case would be to commit to sunset clauses that do not respond to market outcomes. If it is relatively costly or difficult for operators to influence market outcomes on which regulated prices or constraints that are imposed by regulation depend, a flexible, that is, outcome-dependent, regulatory policy is more appealing.

9.4   Dynamic investment and regulatory uncertainty

Throughout the book, we presumed that regulatory policy was known by the operators in advance. However, if regulatory principles are not announced early or if the regulator cannot precommit to such principles, operators face regulatory uncertainty when taking investment decisions. In particular, entrants may start more cautiously to see which regulation applies in the segments with competition to update their beliefs about regulation that will prevail in other market segments. The consequence of such staggered entry is a delay in investment. As a result, the market as a whole matures more slowly, that is, entrants choose a smaller coverage, or roll out a less elaborate network, than without regulatory uncertainty. This increases the need for heavy regulation for two reasons. Firstly, larger parts of the market remain a monopoly; and secondly, regulatory uncertainty favors entry modes in which sunk costs are low. This implies that overall regulatory uncertainty creates a bias in favor of resale-based entry and against facilities-based entry.

In reality, telecommunications markets are segmented and some segments mature earlier than others. Also, entrants may plan investments such that they target some segments earlier than others. If investments are delayed in a particular segment due to regulatory uncertainty, this can, in effect, also delay investments in other segments. This happens, for instance, if entrants follow a step-by-step procedure according to which they enter the next segment only if entry in the previous segment was successful.

In our discussion so far we have distinguished between an incumbent which already has sunk its investment costs and entrants which have to take their entry decisions and the respective investment decisions (at least with regard to customer access networks). This seems a good description of the liberalized markets for fixed voice telephony in Europe. In other markets or market segments in which new services are offered (see below), incumbency does not mean that the required investments have already been made. In such markets one faces the general problem of R&D-intensive industries: after investments have been sunk, a competitive market is preferable, implying that the price for access should be low; before investments have been sunk, one wants to give incentives to undertake such investments, which can be done by a high access price to secure future rents for the firm that has invested.[6]

9.5 Regulation versus competition policy

A key function of the regulatory frameworks that are in place in Europe and the US is to manage the transition from the former monopolistic nature of the market to self-sustained competition. During this transition, consumers still have to be protected from the risk that incumbents abuse their dominant positions. Regulation is to be lifted step by step, to make more room for competition policy. This should occur when competition policy becomes more effective at preventing abuse of dominant positions than regulation. Of course, in reality there is no "switch" from regulation to competition policy, but rather a transition during which regulation and competition policy gradually change roles.[7]

Certain market segments such as mobile telephony in many countries do not have the feature that a single incumbent with a large installed consumer base dominates the market. In these segments, it is easier to make the case in favor of the application of competition policy.

In this book, we have not addressed the pros and cons of *ex ante*, sector-specific regulation versus *ex post*, general competition policy and law.[8] For the sake of exposition, we implicitly assumed that regulation (instead of competition policy) has the possibility of dealing with all relevant access prices, retail price caps, restrictions on retail price structures, and so on.

We wish to point out that there are substantial differences between regulation and competition policy. Regulation is designed to deal with the rather special features of telecommunications markets, such as originating and terminating access to networks. Regulators therefore have to be well informed about the underlying technology. This is probably an advantage, as it may result in targeted, effective interventions. Also, regulation is prescriptive, and tends to lean heavily on the implementation of specific price controls (e.g. regulated prices and price caps). Hence, it provides very direct instruments.

A drawback of regulation is that the larger the complexity and uncertainty in a market, the larger the risk of unintended consequences of regulatory intervention. For example, consider the spillover effects from intervening in a particular market segment to other segments, encountered in Chapters 7 and 8, or the possibilities of new technologies that were not taken into account when

---

[6] For a more detailed discussion, see Valletti (2001).

[7] In most countries, competition policy is thought to supplement *ex ante* regulation. For instance, the UK regulator Oftel provides guidelines on the application of competition policy to telecommunications markets; see Oftel (2000f).

[8] Some discussion on this issue is provided by Bourreau and Dogan (2001) and Laffont and Tirole (2000, Chapter 7).

designing the regulatory framework. Furthermore, firms may experience regulation as being too interventionist in the market.[9]

Whereas regulation is meant to eliminate existing dominant positions during the transition phase of the market, competition policy tries to prevent or punish abuses of dominant positions. Competition policy is generic and typically applies to all sectors of the economy. It may therefore not always be able to cope with problems that are specific for a certain sector or technology.

Competition policy is an *ex post* approach, that is, a harm-based approach. It is therefore much less immediate than regulatory intervention. If a firm behaves anti-competitively, inflicting harm on competitors or consumers, then that firm can be penalized afterwards if its conduct is found to have had adverse effects. Hence, competition policy can be seen as a threat to firms that are considering abuse of market power. Arguably, an advantage of such an *ex post* approach is that competition authorities only have to assess behavior after the alleged abuse has taken place, which requires less information than regulatory intervention. A disadvantage is that the damage (e.g. entrants exiting the market or refraining from additional investments, or excessive prices paid by consumers) often cannot be repaired.

Because of the special characteristics of network industries, it is not quite clear whether *ex ante* regulation can ever be withdrawn completely. Nevertheless, it is likely that it will not be long before competition policy will start playing a more important role than *ex ante* regulation in most telecommunications sectors.

9.6   Beyond fixed voice telephony

Although fixed voice telephony based on circuit-switched networks still has a strong foothold and should not be dismissed as a relic of the past, it is clear that other technologies are quickly gaining ground. To put our analysis in perspective, we will briefly discuss some of these developments (see also Chapter 2).

Network structures are changing rapidly, and traditional and new operators are introducing innovative services. Computer technology allows operators to make their networks more "intelligent," in the sense that they can develop smart services that reside in the network instead of at networks' endpoints. A simple example is voice mail. Whereas in the past, consumers had to plug in answering machines, nowadays operators offer message recording and playback services with their own network technologies. Furthermore, compression techniques make it possible to send more information through traditional phone lines, which is a step towards broadband communication. At present, an important

---

[9] On the other hand, it may happen that entrants, facing a bullying incumbent, complain that the regulator has too little powers at its disposal if regulators do not have the authority to implement certain types of regulation.

issue is whether entrants that have unbundled access to incumbents' local loops will be able to offer the same type of services that incumbents can offer. This depends critically on the nature of access to local switches (e.g. the point of access in the hierarchy of the network is an important factor).

For many people in the developed world, mobile telephony is now as common as fixed telephony. Consumers who find a subscription to a fixed line too expensive can buy cheap, prepaid mobile phones without subscriptions. This possibility of substitution does not mean that fixed and mobile services are, or will ever be, perfect substitutes. The reason is that people typically use mobile phones when they are mobile, that is, they cannot be reached by other means (e.g. because there is no fixed line, or because callers do not know the telephone number of fixed lines in the direct vicinity of called persons). Hence, the complementary nature of fixed and mobile telephony will remain important for regulators to take into account (see Oftel, 2000d). Regulators and competition authorities concerned with fixed voice telephony should take the resulting interactions between the fixed and mobile sector into account.

A specific example concerns termination rates for traffic from fixed to mobile networks. Although mobile operators may be fiercely competing to attract mobile subscribers, they hardly have incentives to reduce fixed–mobile access prices, since the termination of calls incoming from fixed networks is a bottleneck service. Consequently, fixed subscribers currently pay excessive per-minute price for calls to mobile subscribers, although concerned regulators have started to look at this problem.

Packet-switched technology (see also Chapter 2), on which the Internet infrastructure is based, has introduced an alternative for the public switched telephony network. It is already possible to make phone calls over the Internet, although the sound quality can be inferior if there are capacity bottlenecks (reducing the speed of transmission) somewhere in the chain of network connections. At some point, however, these problems may vanish so that the Internet backbone can become available as a serious contender for regular telecommunications services. Since current regulation is typically based on laws specifically designed to deal with traditional network architectures, there is a risk that regulation becomes, to a certain extent, biased. If operators with certain new technologies are subject to fewer regulatory constraints, investment incentives are distorted in favor of such technologies.

During the last ten to twenty years, the links of the telecommunications industry with other industries have become more prominent (see Fransman, 2001), for example with the industries producing equipment and software for networks (the necessary inputs for network operators). New links have also emerged, largely as the result of recent technological changes. Firstly, there is a link with connectivity-related services (e.g. Internet access, e-mail, and Web hosting). Most network operators are able to use their infrastructure and connections with other networks to offer these types of services. Secondly, there is a link with the industries where services "on top" of connectivity services (e.g. Web browsers and search engines) or "in between" connectivity and applications (e.g. electronic payment systems) are developed. Thirdly, there is a link with applications industries (e.g. content, online banking, e-commerce). As, for instance, consumers use their telephone lines to access the Internet and buy online services, clearly the "old" telecommunications industry is rapidly becoming more interdependent with other industries. These industries range from computer manufacturing to media and entertainment.

This often-invoked process of "convergence," that also refers to the interchangeability of networks to deliver data, may have implications for policy directed towards fixed voice telephony.[10] As noted earlier in this chapter, telecommunications laws usually pertain to traditional network architectures. Hence, regulation might become void if these networks are no longer used. Alternatively, existing networks may be used in different ways than envisaged when the current regulatory framework was designed. Whereas regulation is primarily geared towards voice telephony, consumers are also using their fixed lines to access the Internet. In the recent past, this has led to problems of capacity shortages of incumbents' points of interconnection, in particular in cases where consumers used carrier-select operators to access the Internet.[11] One of the factors contributing to these problems was that an individual consumer's demand for Internet access minutes is quite different from his demand for regular call minutes, even though regulation cannot distinguish between these types of call minutes.[12] More generally, one can expect an increasing number of possibilities for using and upgrading existing networks for innovative services. This may increase the risk that existing access regulation becomes obsolete or that unexpected regulatory hurdles emerge.

Importantly in the light of convergence, players that are dominant or have a monopoly position in one segment become active in other segments. For example, incumbent telecommunications operators, which may still have a dominant position because they own bottlenecks, are now offering Internet access and developing new information services. Their dominant position in fixed voice telephony may be "leveraged" to other sectors, for instance through bundling of services (see Chapter 2). Competition policy traditionally addresses the concerns of leverage and bundling but additional regulatory measures may be needed in telecommunications markets.

---

[10] Convergence can, for example, be defined as the increase in possibilities for transmitting a variety of communication services over a variety of networks (interchangeably).

[11] This problem becomes even worse when Internet service providers offer free Internet access, cross-subsidized with advertising revenues.

[12] A practical solution is to use different telephone numbers for Internet access, making it possible to recognize and divert Internet traffic.

Convergence raises questions about the current institutional structure of regulation.[13] With multiple regulators exercising oversight over several linked markets (e.g. telecommunications and broadcasting), it is difficult to guarantee consistent regulation. From an institutional point of view, a response to deal with linked markets is to extend regulation into sectors linking with telecommunications, possibly resulting in a common regulatory framework for all electronic communications networks and services (including broadcasting and media sectors).

The discussion above, on a range of topics that are highly relevant for telecommunications markets, suggests that a need for active competition policy and regulation will persist in the future.

---

[13] For some discussion on this topic, see Armstrong (2000a).

Parameter input: facilities-based competition

Complementary to "Regulation and Entry into Telecommunications Markets" by Paul de Bijl and Martin Peitz

■ About this notebook

This version 3 July 2000.
This file contains parameter input for all models with one customer type.

> *The grey cells in this notebook contain user input and may be changed.*

■ Time horizon

■ Number of periods

```
imax = 1;
```

```
reghorizon = imax;
```

Discount factor of operators:

```
investdiscount = 1;
```

Discount factor of regulator:

```
regdiscount = 1;
```

■ Demand

■ Size of the market

```
market = 8000000;
```

252

- Consumers possibly derive a constant utility from being connected to an operator's network

```
constutility = 5000;
```

- Number of periods in which the entrant can build a track-record for high quality:

```
track = 12;
```

- Individual utility and demand for call minutes (can be skipped)

Individual utility from making telephone calls:

```
u[z_] := a z - (b z^2) / 2
```

Remark: marginal utility is non-decreasing only if $x \leq a/b$, which will automatically be satisfied for non-negative prices (see the demand function below).
Individual consumer's demand function for call minutes:

```
x[p_] := Extract[Solve[D[u[z], z] == p, z], 1][[1, 2]]
```

The demand function is as follows:

```
Simplify[x[p]]
```

$$\frac{a - p}{b}$$

- Demand parameters

```
a = 20;
b = 0.016;
```

- Switching cost parameter

```
z = 6000;
```

■ Initial market shares

```
initialshare1 = 1;
initialshare2 = 0;
```

Market shares must add up to 1:

```
initialshare1 + initialshare2 == 1
```

```
True
```

253

```
φφ1[0] = initialshare1;
φφ2[0] = initialshare2;
```

■ Infrastructure

■ Traffic-dependent costs operator 1

Marginal cost of an on-net call (local loop – long-distance network – local loop)

```
c11 = 2;
```

Marginal cost of an off-net call (local loop – long-distance network)

```
c12 = 1.5;
```

Marginal cost of an incoming call (local loop)

```
c13 = 0.5;
```

■ Traffic-dependent costs operator 2

Marginal cost of an on-net call (local loop – long-distance network – local loop)

```
c21 = 2;
```

Marginal cost of an off-net call (local loop – long-distance network)

```
c22 = 1.5;
```

Marginal cost of an incoming call (local loop)

```
c23 = 0.5;
```

Marginal cost of a call by a carrier-select operator (long-distance network)

```
c24 = 0;
```

■ Fixed costs

Fixed cost of single local connection (local line and linecard)

```
f1 = 2000;
f2 = 2000;
```

■ Regulatory regime

- Separate price caps on subscription fees and per-minute prices

```
capp1 = 3;
capm1 = 10000;
```

- Prices of terminating access to local loop

```
ta1[i_] := c13
ta2[i_] := c23
```

Program: facilities-based competition

Complementary to "Regulation and Entry into Telecommunications Markets"
by Paul de Bijl and Martin Peitz

■ Model assumptions

Facilities-based entry: the entrant has a long-distance backbone with the same coverage as the incumbent's backbone.
The operators compete in two-part tariffs.
Separate price caps on per-minute price and subscription fee possible.

■ Starting values

$$pp1[0] = c11 + (1 - 0.9 \, initialshare1) \, (ta2[1] - c13)$$

$$pp2[0] = c21 + 0.9 \, initialshare1 \, (ta1[1] - c23)$$

$$mm1[0] = f1 + 0.9 \, initialshare1 \, z - 0.9 \, initialshare1 \, x[pp1[0]] \, (c12 + ta2[1] - c11)$$

$$mm2[0] =$$
$$f2 + (1 - 0.9 \, initialshare1) \, z - (1 - 0.9 \, initialshare1) \, x[pp2[0]] \, (c22 + ta1[1] - c21)$$

■ Scaling

All calculations are done in cents.

```
monunit = 100;
```

During the calculations, the size of the market is normalized to 1. Results are presented in millions of the monetary unit.

```
fin = 10 ^ 6;
scale = market / (monunit fin);
```

In the presentation of certain results, numbers smaller than **dx** are replaced by 0. While checking if the f.o.c.s are equal to 0, values smaller than **dxfoc** are replaced by 0.

```
dx = 10 ^ (-5);
dxfoc = 10 ^ (-6);
```

■ Indirect utility function

```
u0[1, i_] := constutility
u0[2, i_] := constutility

v[p_, m_, firm_, i_] := u0[firm, i] + u[x[p]] - x[p] p - m
```

■ Market shares

```
φ1[p1_, p2_, m1_, m2_, i_] := φφ1[i - 1] + (v[p1, m1, 1, i] - v[p2, m2, 2, i]) / Z

φ2[p1_, p2_, m1_, m2_, i_] := φφ2[i - 1] + (v[p2, m2, 2, i] - v[p1, m1, 1, i]) / Z
```

■ Call probabilities

■ Firm 1

On-net calls

```
probonnet1[p1_, p2_, m1_, m2_, i_] := φ1[p1, p2, m1, m2, i]
```

Off-net calls

```
proboffnet1[p1_, p2_, m1_, m2_, i_] := φ2[p1, p2, m1, m2, i]
```

■ Firm 2

On-net calls

```
probonnet2[p1_, p2_, m1_, m2_, i_] := φ2[p1, p2, m1, m2, i]
```

Off-net calls

```
proboffnet2[p1_, p2_, m1_, m2_, i_] := φ1[p1, p2, m1, m2, i]
```

■ Profit functions

■ Firm 1

On-net calls

```
onnet1[p1_, p2_, m1_, m2_, i_] :=
    φ1[p1, p2, m1, m2, i] x[p1] probonnet1[p1, p2, m1, m2, i] (p1 - c11)
```

Off-net calls

```
offnet1[p1_, p2_, m1_, m2_, i_] :=
 φ1[p1, p2, m1, m2, i] x[p1] proboffnet1[p1, p2, m1, m2, i] (p1 - c12 - ta2[i])
```

Incoming calls from the other operator

```
incoming1[p1_, p2_, m1_, m2_, i_] :=
 φ2[p1, p2, m1, m2, i] x[p2] proboffnet2[p1, p2, m1, m2, i] (ta1[i] - c13)
```

Traffic-independent revenues

```
subscriptions1[p1_, p2_, m1_, m2_, i_] := φ1[p1, p2, m1, m2, i] (m1 - f1)
```

Profits (gross of fixed costs)

```
π1[p1_, p2_, m1_, m2_, i_] := onnet1[p1, p2, m1, m2, i] + offnet1[p1, p2, m1, m2, i] +
 incoming1[p1, p2, m1, m2, i] + subscriptions1[p1, p2, m1, m2, i]
```

Net access revenues (in terms of money flows)

```
tar1[p1_, p2_, m1_, m2_, i_] :=
 φ1[p1, p2, m1, m2, i] x[p1] proboffnet1[p1, p2, m1, m2, i] (-ta2[i]) +
 φ2[p1, p2, m1, m2, i] x[p2] proboffnet2[p1, p2, m1, m2, i] (ta1[i])
```

Net access revenues (received revenues net of costs)

```
nettar1[p1_, p2_, m1_, m2_, i_] :=
 φ2[p1, p2, m1, m2, i] x[p2] proboffnet2[p1, p2, m1, m2, i] (ta1[i] - c13)
```

Perceived marginal costs

```
pmc1[p1_, p2_, m1_, m2_, i_] :=
 probonnet1[p1, p2, m1, m2, i] c11 + proboffnet1[p1, p2, m1, m2, i] (c12 + ta2[i])
```

▪ Firm 2

On-net calls

```
onnet2[p1_, p2_, m1_, m2_, i_] :=
 φ2[p1, p2, m1, m2, i] x[p2] probonnet2[p1, p2, m1, m2, i] (p2 - c21)
```

Off-net calls

```
offnet2[p1_, p2_, m1_, m2_, i_] :=
 φ2[p1, p2, m1, m2, i] x[p2] proboffnet2[p1, p2, m1, m2, i] (p2 - c22 - ta1[i])
```

Incoming calls from the other operator

```
incoming2[p1_, p2_, m1_, m2_, i_] :=
 φ1[p1, p2, m1, m2, i] x[p1] proboffnet1[p1, p2, m1, m2, i] (ta2[i] - c23)
```

Traffic-independent revenues

```
subscriptions2[p1_, p2_, m1_, m2_, i_] := φ2[p1, p2, m1, m2, i] (m2 - f2)
```

Profits (gross of fixed costs)

```
π2[p1_, p2_, m1_, m2_, i_] := onnet2[p1, p2, m1, m2, i] + offnet2[p1, p2, m1, m2, i] +
 incoming2[p1, p2, m1, m2, i] + subscriptions2[p1, p2, m1, m2, i]
```

258

Net access revenues (in terms of money flows)

```
tar2[p1_, p2_, m1_, m2_, i_] :=
  φ2[p1, p2, m1, m2, i] x[p2] proboffnet2[p1, p2, m1, m2, i] (-ta1[i]) +
    φ1[p1, p2, m1, m2, i] x[p1] proboffnet1[p1, p2, m1, m2, i] (ta2[i])
```

Net access revenues (received revenues net of costs)

```
nettar2[p1_, p2_, m1_, m2_, i_] :=
  φ1[p1, p2, m1, m2, i] x[p1] proboffnet1[p1, p2, m1, m2, i] (ta2[i] - c23)
```

Perceived marginal costs

```
pmc2[p1_, p2_, m1_, m2_, i_] :=
  probonnet2[p1, p2, m1, m2, i] c21 + proboffnet2[p1, p2, m1, m2, i] (c22 + ta1[i])
```

■ Surplus

Consumers' surplus:

```
cs[p1_, p2_, m1_, m2_, i_] :=
  scale (φ1[p1, p2, m1, m2, i] v[p1, m1, 1, i] + φ2[p1, p2, m1, m2, i] v[p2, m2, 2, i] -

    (v[p2, m2, 2, i] - v[p1, m1, 1, i])²
    ─────────────────────────────────────
                    2 z                    )
```

Producers' surplus:

```
ps[p1_, p2_, m1_, m2_, i_] := scale (π1[p1, p2, m1, m2, i] + π2[p1, p2, m1, m2, i])
```

Welfare:

```
welfare[p1_, p2_, m1_, m2_, i_] := cs[p1, p2, m1, m2, i] + ps[p1, p2, m1, m2, i]
```

259

■ Calculation of Nash equilibrium

```
i = 1;

g11[p1_, p2_, m1_, m2_, i] = D[π1[p1, p2, m1, m2, i], p1];
g12[p1_, p2_, m1_, m2_, i] = D[π1[p1, p2, m1, m2, i], m1];
g21[p1_, p2_, m1_, m2_, i] = D[π2[p1, p2, m1, m2, i], p2];
g22[p1_, p2_, m1_, m2_, i] = D[π2[p1, p2, m1, m2, i], m2];

g111[p1_, p2_, m1_, m2_, i] = D[g11[p1, p2, m1, m2, i], p1];
g112[p1_, p2_, m1_, m2_, i] = D[g11[p1, p2, m1, m2, i], m1];
g122[p1_, p2_, m1_, m2_, i] = D[g12[p1, p2, m1, m2, i], m1];
g211[p1_, p2_, m1_, m2_, i] = D[g21[p1, p2, m1, m2, i], p2];
g212[p1_, p2_, m1_, m2_, i] = D[g21[p1, p2, m1, m2, i], m2];
g222[p1_, p2_, m1_, m2_, i] = D[g22[p1, p2, m1, m2, i], m2];

equil0 := FindRoot[
    {g11[p1, p2, m1, m2, i] == 0,
     g12[p1, p2, m1, m2, i] == 0,
     g21[p1, p2, m1, m2, i] == 0,
     g22[p1, p2, m1, m2, i] == 0},
    {p1, pp1[i - 1]}, {p2, pp2[i - 1]},
    {m1, mm1[i - 1]}, {m2, mm2[i - 1]},
    MaxIterations -> 50];

equil1 := FindRoot[
    {g11[p1, p2, capm1, m2, i] == 0,
     g21[p1, p2, capm1, m2, i] == 0,
     g22[p1, p2, capm1, m2, i] == 0},
    {p1, 1.01 pp1[i - 1]}, {p2, 1.01 pp2[i - 1]},
    {m2, 1.01 mm2[i - 1]},
    MaxIterations -> 50];

equil2 := FindRoot[
    {g12[capp1, p2, m1, m2, i] == 0,
     g21[capp1, p2, m1, m2, i],
     g22[capp1, p2, m1, m2, i] == 0},
    {m1, 1.01 mm1[i - 1]}, {p2, 1.01 pp2[i - 1]},
    {m2, 1.01 mm2[i - 1]},
    MaxIterations -> 50];

equil3 := FindRoot[
    {g21[capp1, p2, capm1, m2, i] == 0,
     g22[capp1, p2, capm1, m2, i] == 0},
    {m2, 1.01 mm2[i - 1]}, {p2, 1.01 pp2[i - 1]},
    MaxIterations -> 50];


p1temp0 = p1 /. equil0;
p2temp0 = p2 /. equil0;
m1temp0 = m1 /. equil0;
m2temp0 = m2 /. equil0;

p1temp1 = p1 /. equil1;
m1temp1 = m1 /. equil1;

p1temp2 = p1 /. equil2;
m1temp2 = m1 /. equil2;
```

```
bool0 = True;
bool1 = True;
bool2 = True;

If[p1temp0 ≤ capp1 && m1temp0 ≤ capm1,
    pp1[i] = p1 /. equil0;
    pp2[i] = p2 /. equil0;
    mm1[i] = m1 /. equil0;
    mm2[i] = m2 /. equil0;
    ssoc1[i] = (g111[pp1[i], pp2[i], mm1[i], mm2[i], i] < 0 ∧
      g122[pp1[i], pp2[i], mm1[i], mm2[i], i] < 0 ∧
      g111[pp1[i], pp2[i], mm1[i], mm2[i], i] * g122[pp1[i], pp2[i], mm1[i], mm2[i], i] >
       (g112[pp1[i], pp2[i], mm1[i], mm2[i], i])^2);
    ssoc2[i] = (g211[pp1[i], pp2[i], mm1[i], mm2[i], i] < 0 ∧
      g222[pp1[i], pp2[i], mm1[i], mm2[i], i] < 0 ∧
      g211[pp1[i], pp2[i], mm1[i], mm2[i], i] * g222[pp1[i], pp2[i], mm1[i], mm2[i], i] >
       (g212[pp1[i], pp2[i], mm1[i], mm2[i], i])^2);
  info[i] = "None of the price caps are binding."; Print[info[i]],
bool0 = False];

If[p1temp1 ≤ capp1 && m1temp0 > capm1,
    pp1[i] = p1 /. equil1;
    pp2[i] = p2 /. equil1;
    mm1[i] = capm1;
    mm2[i] = m2 /. equil1;
    ssoc1[i] = (g111[pp1[i], pp2[i], mm1[i], mm2[i], i] < 0);
    ssoc2[i] = (g211[pp1[i], pp2[i], mm1[i], mm2[i], i] < 0 ∧
      g222[pp1[i], pp2[i], mm1[i], mm2[i], i] < 0 ∧
      g211[pp1[i], pp2[i], mm1[i], mm2[i], i] * g222[pp1[i], pp2[i], mm1[i], mm2[i], i] >
       (g212[pp1[i], pp2[i], mm1[i], mm2[i], i])^2);
  info[i] = "Price cap on subscription fee is binding."; Print[info[i]],
bool1 = False];

If[p1temp0 > capp1 && m1temp2 ≤ capm1,
    pp1[i] = capp1;
    pp2[i] = p2 /. equil2;
    mm1[i] = m1 /. equil2;
    mm2[i] = m2 /. equil2;
    ssoc1[i] = (g122[pp1[i], pp2[i], mm1[i], mm2[i], i] < 0);
    ssoc2[i] = (g211[pp1[i], pp2[i], mm1[i], mm2[i], i] < 0 ∧
      g222[pp1[i], pp2[i], mm1[i], mm2[i], i] < 0 ∧
      g211[pp1[i], pp2[i], mm1[i], mm2[i], i] * g222[pp1[i], pp2[i], mm1[i], mm2[i], i] >
       (g212[pp1[i], pp2[i], mm1[i], mm2[i], i])^2);
  info[i] = "Price cap on per-minute price is binding."; Print[info[i]],
bool2 = False];

If[Not[bool0] && Not[bool1] && Not[bool2],
    pp1[i] = capp1;
    pp2[i] = p2 /. equil3;
    mm1[i] = capm1;
    mm2[i] = m2 /. equil3;
    ssoc1[i] = True;
    ssoc2[i] = (g211[pp1[i], pp2[i], mm1[i], mm2[i], i] < 0 ∧
      g222[pp1[i], pp2[i], mm1[i], mm2[i], i] < 0 ∧
      g211[pp1[i], pp2[i], mm1[i], mm2[i], i] * g222[pp1[i], pp2[i], mm1[i], mm2[i], i] >
       (g212[pp1[i], pp2[i], mm1[i], mm2[i], i])^2);
  info[i] = "Both price caps are binding."; Print[info[i]]];

φφ1[i] = φ1[pp1[i], pp2[i], mm1[i], mm2[i], i];
φφ2[i] = φ2[pp1[i], pp2[i], mm1[i], mm2[i], i];

Print["Ready."]
```

■ Calculations of various indicators

$$\text{sum}\pi 1 := \text{scale} \sum_{i=1}^{i\text{max}} \text{investdiscount}^i \; \pi 1 [\text{pp1}[i], \text{pp2}[i], \text{mm1}[i], \text{mm2}[i], i];$$

$$\text{sum}\pi 2 := \text{scale} \sum_{i=1}^{i\text{max}} \text{investdiscount}^i \; \pi 2 [\text{pp1}[i], \text{pp2}[i], \text{mm1}[i], \text{mm2}[i], i];$$

$$\text{sumcs} := \sum_{i=1}^{i\text{max}} \text{regdiscount}^i \; \text{cs}[\text{pp1}[i], \text{pp2}[i], \text{mm1}[i], \text{mm2}[i], i];$$

$$\text{sumps} := \sum_{i=1}^{i\text{max}} \text{regdiscount}^i \; \text{ps}[\text{pp1}[i], \text{pp2}[i], \text{mm1}[i], \text{mm2}[i], i];$$

$$\text{sumwelfare} := \sum_{i=1}^{i\text{max}} \text{regdiscount}^i \; \text{welfare}[\text{pp1}[i], \text{pp2}[i], \text{mm1}[i], \text{mm2}[i], i];$$

■ Output

```
Print[" "]
StyleForm["Checking the outcomes", FontWeight -> "Bold", FontSize -> 12]
TableForm[Table[{i, info[i]}, {i, 1, imax}],
TableHeadings -> {None, {"i", "price caps:"}}]

TableForm[Table[{i, N[Chop[g11[pp1[i], pp2[i], mm1[i], mm2[i], i], dxfoc], 1],
   N[Chop[g12[pp1[i], pp2[i], mm1[i], mm2[i], i], dxfoc], 1],
   N[Chop[g21[pp1[i], pp2[i], mm1[i], mm2[i], i], dxfoc], 1],
   N[Chop[g22[pp1[i], pp2[i], mm1[i], mm2[i], i], dxfoc], 1],
   ssoc1[i], ssoc2[i]}, {i, 1, imax}],
TableHeadings -> {None, {"i", "g11", "g12", "g21", "g22", "s.o.c. 1", "s.o.c. 2"}}]

Print[" "];
StyleForm["PARAMETER VALUES", FontWeight -> "Bold", FontSize -> 13]

StyleForm["Market size and demand", FontWeight -> "Bold", FontSize -> 12]
Print["# customers = ", EngineeringForm[market]];
Print["constant utility parameter = ", constutility];
Print["# periods to build track record for quality = ", track];
Print["demand parameter a = ", a];
Print["demand parameter b = ", b];
Print["switching cost parameter Z = ", Z];
Print[" "];

StyleForm["Costs", FontWeight -> "Bold", FontSize -> 12]
Print["Operator 1's cost levels"];
Print["c11 = ", c11, " cents"];
Print["c12 = ", c12, " cents"];
Print["c13 = ", c13, " cents"];
Print["f1 = ", f1, " cents"];
Print["Operator 2's cost levels"];
Print["c21 = ", c21, " cents"];
Print["c22 = ", c22, " cents"];
Print["c23 = ", c23, " cents"];
Print["f2 = ", f2, " cents"];
```

```
Print[" "];

StyleForm["Regulation", FontWeight -> "Bold", FontSize -> 12]
Print["price cap on per-minute price = ", cappl, " cents"];
Print["price cap on subscription fee = ", capml, " cents"];
Print["terminating access price operator 1 = ", ta1[i], " cents"];
Print["terminating access price operator 2 = ", ta2[i], " cents"];
Print[" "];
Print["-------------------------"]
StyleForm["OUTCOMES", FontWeight -> "Bold", FontSize -> 13]


StyleForm["Equilibrium prices (cents)", FontWeight -> "Bold", FontSize -> 12]
TableForm[Table[{i, NumberForm[pp1[i], 4], NumberForm[pp2[i], 4],
    NumberForm[mm1[i], 6], NumberForm[mm2[i], 6]}, {i, 1, imax}],
  TableHeadings -> {None, {"i", "p1", "p2", "m1", "m2"}}]


Print[" "]

StyleForm["Perceived marginal costs (cents)", FontWeight -> "Bold", FontSize -> 12]

TableForm[Table[{i, NumberForm[pmc1[pp1[i], pp2[i], mm1[i], mm2[i], i], 4],
    NumberForm[pmc2[pp1[i], pp2[i], mm1[i], mm2[i], i], 4]}, {i, 1, imax}],
  TableHeadings -> {None, {"i", "operator 1", "operator
2"}}]


Print[" "]

StyleForm["Terminating access revenues, money flows (millions)",
  FontWeight -> "Bold", FontSize -> 12]

TableForm[
  Table[{i, PaddedForm[Chop[scale tar1[pp1[i], pp2[i], mm1[i], mm2[i], i], dx],
    {7, 3}, SignPadding -> True],
                PaddedForm[Chop[scale tar2[pp1[i], pp2[i], mm1[i], mm2[i], i], dx],
    {7, 3}, SignPadding -> True]}, {i, 1, imax}],
  TableHeadings -> {None, {"i", "operator 1", "operator
2"}}]


Print[" "]

StyleForm["Terminating access revenues, net of traffic-dependent costs (millions)",
  FontWeight -> "Bold", FontSize -> 12]

TableForm[
  Table[{i, PaddedForm[Chop[scale nettar1[pp1[i], pp2[i], mm1[i], mm2[i], i], dx],
    {7, 3}, SignPadding -> True],
                PaddedForm[Chop[scale nettar2[pp1[i], pp2[i], mm1[i], mm2[i], i], dx],
    {7, 3}, SignPadding -> True]}, {i, 1, imax}],
  TableHeadings -> {None, {"i", "operator 1", "operator
2"}}]

Print[" "]

StyleForm["Market shares (%)", FontWeight -> "Bold", FontSize -> 12]

TableForm[Table[{i, N[100 φφ1[i], 3], N[100 φφ2[i], 3],
    If[i < imax, N[100 * (φφ1[i + 1] - φφ1[i]), 4], " "]}, {i, 0, imax}], TableHeadings ->
        {None, {"i", "operator 1", "operator 2", "Δ operator 1 (%)"}}]
```

```
Print[" "]

StyleForm["Profits operator 1 (millions)", FontWeight -> "Bold", FontSize -> 12]

TableForm[Table[{i,
    PaddedForm[scale π1[pp1[i], pp2[i], mm1[i], mm2[i], i], {7, 3}, SignPadding -> True],
    PaddedForm[Chop[scale onnet1[pp1[i], pp2[i], mm1[i], mm2[i], i], dx],
    {7, 3}, SignPadding -> True],
    PaddedForm[Chop[scale offnet1[pp1[i], pp2[i], mm1[i], mm2[i], i], dx],
    {7, 3}, SignPadding -> True],
            PaddedForm[scale incoming1[pp1[i], pp2[i], mm1[i], mm2[i], i],
    {7, 3}, SignPadding -> True],
            PaddedForm[1.000000000001 scale subscriptions1[pp1[i], pp2[i],
        mm1[i], mm2[i], i], {7, 3}, SignPadding -> True]}, {i, 1, reghorizon}],
    TableHeadings -> {None, {"i", "total", "on-net", "off-net",
    "incoming", "traffic-indep."}}]]

Print["Sum of discounted profits = ", sumπ1]


Print[" "]

StyleForm["Profits operator 2 (millions)", FontWeight -> "Bold", FontSize -> 12]

TableForm[Table[{i,
    PaddedForm[scale π2[pp1[i], pp2[i], mm1[i], mm2[i], i], {7, 3}, SignPadding -> True],
    PaddedForm[Chop[scale onnet2[pp1[i], pp2[i], mm1[i], mm2[i], i], dx],
    {7, 3}, SignPadding -> True],
    PaddedForm[Chop[scale offnet2[pp1[i], pp2[i], mm1[i], mm2[i], i], dx],
    {7, 3}, SignPadding -> True],
            PaddedForm[scale incoming2[pp1[i], pp2[i], mm1[i], mm2[i], i],
    {7, 3}, SignPadding -> True],
            PaddedForm[scale subscriptions2[pp1[i], pp2[i], mm1[i], mm2[i], i],
    {7, 3}, SignPadding -> True]}, {i, 1, reghorizon}],
    TableHeadings -> {None, {"i", "total", "on-net", "off-net",
    "incoming", "traffic-indep."}}]]

Print["Sum of discounted profits = ", sumπ2]


Print[" "]

StyleForm["Surplus (millions)", FontWeight -> "Bold", FontSize -> 12]

TableForm[Table[
    {i, PaddedForm[cs[pp1[i], pp2[i], mm1[i], mm2[i], i], {7, 3}, SignPadding -> True],
    PaddedForm[ps[pp1[i], pp2[i], mm1[i], mm2[i], i], {7, 3}, SignPadding -> True],
    PaddedForm[welfare[pp1[i], pp2[i], mm1[i], mm2[i], i],
    {7, 3}, SignPadding -> True]}, {i, 1, reghorizon}],
    TableHeadings -> {None, {"i", "consumers surplus", "producers surplus", "welfare"}}]]

Print["Sum of discounted consumers surplus = ", sumcs];


Print["Sum of discounted producers surplus = ", sumps];


Print["Sum of discounted welfare = ", sumwelfare];
```

264

Bibliography

Acton, J. P., and Vogelsang, I. (1989). Introduction (to symposium on price cap regulation). *Rand Journal of Economics*, 20, 369–372.

Anton, J., van der Weide, J., and Vettas, N. (1998). Strategic pricing and entry under universal service and cross-market price constraints. CEPR, Discussion paper 1922.

Armstrong, M. (1998). Network interconnection in telecommunications. *Economic Journal*, 108, 545–564.

(2000a). Converging communications: implications for regulation. Mimeo, Nuffield College, Oxford.

(2000b). Regulation and inefficient entry. Mimeo, Nuffield College, Oxford.

(2001). The theory of access pricing and interconnection. Forthcoming in M. Cave, S. Majumdar, and I. Vogelsang (eds.), *Handbook of Telecommunications Economics*. Amsterdam: North-Holland.

Armstrong, M., and Vickers, J. (2001). Competitive price discrimination. *Rand Journal of Economics*, 32, 579–605.

Armstrong, M., Cowan, S., and Vickers, J. (1994). *Regulatory reform: economic analysis and British experience*. Cambridge, MA: MIT Press.

Baumol, W. (1983). Some subtle issues in railroad regulation. *International Journal of Transport Economics*, 10, 341–355.

Berry, S., Levinsohn, J., and Pakes, A. (1995). Automobile prices in market equilibrium. *Econometrica*, 63, 841–890.

Biglaiser, G., and Riordan, M. (2000). Dynamics of price regulation. *Rand Journal of Economics*, 31, 744–767.

Boiteux, M. (1956). Sur la gestion des monopoles publics astreints à l'equilibre budgétaire. *Econometrica*, 24, 22–40.

Bourreau, M., and Dogan, P. (2001). Regulation and innovation in the telecommunications industry. *Telecommunications Policy*, 25, 167–184.

Bulow, J., Geanakoplos, J., and Klemperer, P. (1985). Multimarket oligopoly: strategic substitutes and strategic complements. *Journal of Political Economy*, 93, 488–511.

Cabral, L. (2000). *Introduction to industrial organization*. Cambridge, MA: MIT Press.

Cabral, L., and Riordan, M. (1989). Incentives for cost reduction under price cap regulation. *Journal of Regulatory Economics*, 1, 93–102.

Carter, M., and Wright, J. (1999a). Interconnection in network industries. *Review of Industrial Organization*, 14, 1–25.

(1999b). Local and long-distance network competition. Mimeo, University of Auckland.

(2001). Asymmetric network interconnection. Mimeo, University of Auckland.

Cave, M., Majumdar, S., Rood, H., Valletti, T., and Vogelsang, I. (2001). The relationship between access pricing regulation and infrastructure competition. Report to Opta and DG Telecommunications and Post.

Choi, J. P., and Stefanides, C. (2001). Bundling and the dynamic entry process. Mimeo, Michigan State University and Federal Reserve Bank of New York.

Choné, P., Flochel, L., and Perrot, A. (2000). Universal service obligations and competition. *Information Economics and Policy*, 12, 249–259.

De Bijl, P., and Peitz, M. (2000). Competition and regulation in telecommunications markets. Special publication (report to Opta), CPB Netherlands Bureau for Economic Policy Analysis, The Hague.

(2001a). Dynamic regulation and competition in telecommunications market – a framework for policy analysis. Mimeo, CPB Netherlands Bureau for Economic Policy Analysis.

(2001b). New competition in telecommunications markets: regulatory pricing principles, forthcoming in *Ifo-studies*.

Dessein, W. (1999a). Network competition in nonlinear pricing. Mimeo, ECARE.

(1999b). Network competition with heterogeneous calling patterns. Mimeo, ECARE.

(2000). Network competition in nonlinear pricing. Mimeo, Chicago Business School.

DGTP (2000). Netwerken in cijfers: trendrapportage over ICT-infrastructureen 2000 [Networks in numbers: trend report on ICT infrastructures 2000]. Ministerie van Verkeer en Waterstaat, The Hague.

Doganoglu, T., and Tauman, Y. (1996). Network competition with reciprocal proportional access charge rules. SUNY at Stony Brook Discussion Paper DP96-01.

Economides, N. (1989). Desirability of compatibility in the absence of network externalities. *American Economic Review*, 79, 1165–1181.

(1996). The economics of networks. *International Journal of Industrial Organization*, 14, 673–699.

(1999). The Telecommunications Act of 1996 and its impact. *Japan and the World Economy*, 11, 455–483.

(2000). US telecommunications today, April 1999. In C. Brown (ed.), *Handbook of IS Management 2000*. Boca Raton, FL: Auerbach/CRC Press.

European Commission (1987). Green Paper on the development of the common market for telecommunications services and equipment. COM(87)290, Brussels.

(1997). Green Paper on the convergence of the telecommunications, media and information technology sectors, and the implications for regulation. COM(97)623, Brussels.

(1999a). Towards a new framework for electronic communications infrastructure and associated services: the 1999 Communications Review. Communication from the Commission to the European Parliament, the Council, the Economic and Social Committee and the Committee of the Regions. COM(1999)539, Brussels.

(1999b). Status report on European Union electronic communications policy. Available at http://europa.eu.int/information_society.

(2000a). Unbundled access to the local loop. DG Information Society Working Document.

(2000b). Europe's liberalised telecommunications market – a guide to the rules of the game, Commission staff working document.

(2000c). Commission recommendation amending Commission Recommendations 98/511/EC of 29 July 1998 on Interconnection in a liberalized telecommunications market, March 2000.

(2000d). Interconnection tariffs in member states, 1 March 2000.

(2000e). Sixth report on the implementation of the telecommunications regulatory package. COM(2000)814, Brussels.

(2000f). The results of the public consultation on the 1999 Communications Review and Orientations for the new Regulatory Framework. Communication from the Commission, COM(2000)239, Brussels.

(2000g). A common regulatory framework for electronic communications networks and services. DG Information Society Working Document.

(2001). Outline of guidelines on market analysis and the calculation of market power to be adopted under Article 14 of the proposed 'Directive on a common framework for electronic communications networks and services', 24 January 2001.

European Parliament and Council (2000). Regulation (EC) No 2887/2000 of the European Parliament and of the Council of 18 December 2000 on unbundled access to the local loop. Official Journal of the European Commission, 30/12/2000, L336/4–8.

Falch, M. (1997). Cost and demand characteristics of telecom networks. In W. H. Melody (ed.), *Telecom reform: principles, policies and regulatory practices*. Lyngby: Technical University of Denmark.

Farrell, J., and Katz, M. (1998). Public policy and private investment in advanced telecommunications infrastructure. Mimeo, University of California, Berkeley.

FCC (1999). Federal Communications Commission seeks comment on price cap X-factor prescription.

(2001). Trends in telephone service. Report, August 2001.

Fransman, M. (2001). Evolution of the telecommunications industry into the Internet age. Mimeo, University of Edinburgh.

Froeb, L. M., and Werden, G. J. (1996). Simulating the effects of mergers among noncooperative oligopolists. In H. R. Varian (ed.), *Computational economics and finance: modeling and analysis with Mathematica*. New York: Springer Verlag/Telos.

Fudenberg, D., and Tirole, J. (1991). *Game theory*. Cambridge, MA: MIT Press.

Gans, J. S., and King, S. P. (2000). Mobile network competition, customer ignorance and fixed-to-mobile prices. *Information Economics and Policy*, 12, 301–328.

(2001). Using 'bill and keep' interconnect arrangements to soften network competition. *Economics Letters*, 71, 413–420.

Gibbons, R. (1992). *A primer in game theory*. Hertfordshire: Harvester Wheatsheaf.

Glass, S. (1997). *Telecommunications systems: an introductory guide*. Gilbert & Tobin, http://www.gtlaw.com.au/pubs/telcosysintroguide.html.

Green, R. (2000). Can competition replace regulation for small utility consumers? CEPR, Discussion paper 2406.

Hahn, J.-H. (1999). Network competition and interconnection with heterogeneous subscribers. Mimeo, Keele University.

Herings, P. J.-J., and Peeters, R. J. A. P. (2001). A differentiable homotopy to compute Nash equilibria of n-person games. *Economic Theory*, 18, 159–185.

Huang, C. J., and Crooke P. S. (1997). *Mathematics and Mathematica for economists*. Oxford, UK: Blackwell Publishers.

IDC (1999). De telecommunicatie diensten markt in Nederland [The telecommunications services market in the Netherlands]. Amsterdam.

Jeon, D.-S., Laffont, J.-J., and Tirole, J. (2001). On the receiver pays principle. Mimeo, IDEI, University of Toulouse.

Judd, K. (1998). *Computational economics*. Cambridge, MA: MIT Press.

Katz, M. L., and Shapiro, C. (1985). Network externalities, competition and compatibility. *American Economic Review*, 75, 424–440.

(1994). Systems competition and network effects. *Journal of Economic Perspectives*, 8, 93–115.

Klemperer, P. (1987). The competitiveness of markets with switching costs. *Rand Journal of Economics*, 18, 138–150.

(1995). Competition when customers have switching costs: an overview with applications to industrial organization, macroeconomics and international trade. *Review of Economic Studies*, 62, 515–540.

KPN (1999). Jaarverslag 1998 [Annual report 1998]. The Hague.

Laffont, J. J., and Tirole, J. (1993). *A theory of incentives in regulation and procurement*. Cambridge, MA: MIT Press.

(1994). Access pricing and competition. *European Economic Review*, 38, 1673–1710.

(1996). Creating competition through interconnection: theory and practice. *Journal of Regulatory Economics*, 10, 227–256.

(2000). *Competition in telecommunications*. Cambridge, MA: MIT Press.

Laffont, J. J., Rey, P., and Tirole, J. (1998a). Network competition: I. overview and nondiscriminatory pricing. *Rand Journal of Economics*, 29, 1–37.

(1998b). Network competition: II. price discrimination. *Rand Journal of Economics*, 29, 38–56.

Liston, C. (1993). Price cap versus rate of return regulation. *Journal of Regulatory Economics*, 5, 25–48.

Matutes, C., and Regibeau, P. (1988). Mix and match: product compatibility without network externalities. *Rand Journal of Economics*, 19, 221–234.

McAfee, P., McMillan, J., and Whinston, M. (1989). Multiproduct monopoly, commodity bundling, and correlation of values. *Quarterly Journal of Economics*, 104, 371–384.

Milgrom, P., and Roberts, J. (1990). Rationalizability, learning, and equilibrium in games with strategic complementarities. *Econometrica*, 58, 1255–1277.

Mitchell, B. M., and Vogelsang, I. (1991). *Telecommunications pricing: theory and practice*. Cambridge, UK: Cambridge University Press.

Morgan Stanley Dean Witter (1999). Global telecommunications primer: a guide to the information superhighway. Equity Research/Global Telecommunications.

Nahata, B., Ostaszewski, K., and Sahoo, P. (1999). Buffet pricing. *Journal of Business*, 72, 215–228.

Nalebuff, B. (1999). Bundling. Mimeo, Yale University.

Nera (1999). A price cap model of KPN. Final report for Opta, London.

Noam, E. (2001). Interconnection practices. Forthcoming in M. Cave, S. Majumdar, and I. Vogelsang (eds.), *Handbook of telecommunications economics*. Amsterdam: North-Holland.

Oftel (2000a). Oftel strategy statement: achieving the best deal for telecoms consumers.

(2000b). Consumer switching behavior in the telecommunications market. Report.

(2000c). Review of universal telecommunication services. Consultative document.

(2000d). Consumers' use of fixed telecoms services: summary of Oftel's residential survey.

(2000e). Consultation on future interconnection arrangements for dial-up internet in the United Kingdom.

(2000f). The application of the Competition Act in the telecommunications sector. Guideline.

(2001a). Competition in the provision of fixed telephony services. Consultation document.

(2001b). Market information fixed update Q3 2000/01.

(2001c). Universal service obligation: a statement issued by the Director General of Telecommunications, August 2001.

Opta (1999). Besluit geschil KPN–Enertel [Decision conflict KPN–Enertel]. OPTA/ IBT/99/7686, The Hague.

(2001). Richtsnoeren tariefregulering interconnectie- en bijzondere toegangdiensten [Guidelines tariff regulation interconnection and special access services]. OPTA/IBT/2001/200850, The Hague.

Peitz, M. (1999). Equilibrium uniqueness in oligopoly games with strategic complements. *Economics Letters*, 65, 347–351.

(2001). Asymmetric access price regulation in telecommunications markets. Mimeo, University of Frankfurt.

Perrucci, A., and Cimatoribus, M. (1997). Competition, convergence and asymmetry in telecommunications regulation. *Telecommunications Policy*, 21, 493–512.

Pint, E. M. (1992). Price cap versus rate of return regulation in a stochastic cost model. *Rand Journal of Economics*, 23, 564–578.

Poletti, S., and Wright, J. (1999). Network interconnection with nonlinear retail pricing. Mimeo, University of Auckland.

Ramsey, F. (1927). A contribution to the theory of taxation. *Economic Journal*, 37, 47–61.

Rey, P., and Tirole, J. (1998). A primer on foreclosure. Mimeo, University of Toulouse.

Riordan, M. (2001). Universal residential telephone service. Forthcoming in M. Cave, S. Majumdar, and I. Vogelsang (eds.), *Handbook of telecommunications economics*. Amsterdam: North-Holland.

Rochet, J.-C., and Stole, L. (2002). Nonlinear pricing with random participation. *Review of Economic Studies*, 69, 277–311.

Sappington, D. (2001). Price regulation and incentives. Forthcoming in M. Cave, S. Majumdar, and I. Vogelsang (eds.), *Handbook of telecommunications economics*. Amsterdam: North-Holland.

Sappington, D., and Weisman, D. (1996). *Designing incentive regulation in the telecommunications industry*. Cambridge, MA: MIT Press and Washington, DC: AEI Press.

Schiff, A. (2001). Two-way interconnection with partial consumer participation. University of Auckland Working Paper #223.

Schmalensee, R. (1989). Good regulatory regimes. *Rand Journal of Economics*, 20, 417–436.

Shy, O. (2000). *The economics of network industries*. Cambridge, UK: Cambridge University Press.

Smallwood, D. E., and Conlisk J. (1979). Product quality in markets where consumers are imperfectly informed. *Quarterly Journal of Economics*, 93, 1–23.

Stole, L. (1995). Nonlinear pricing and oligopoly. *Journal of Economics and Management Strategy*, 4, 529–562.

Sutton, J. (1991). *Sunk costs and market structure*. Cambridge, MA: MIT Press.

Tirole, J. (1988). *The theory of industrial organization*. Cambridge, MA: MIT Press.

Tye, W., and Lapuerta C. (1996). The economics of pricing network interconnection: theory and application to the market for telecommunications in New Zealand. *Yale Journal on Regulation*, 13, 419–500.

Valletti, T. (1999). The practice of access pricing: telecoms in the UK, *Utilities Policy*, 8, 83–98.

   (2001). The theory of access pricing and its linkage with investment incentives. Mimeo, Imperial College, London.

Valletti, T., Hoernig, S., and Barros, P. P. (2002). Universal service and entry: the role of uniform pricing and coverage constraints. *Journal of Regulatory Economics*, 21, 169–190.

Van Damme, E. (1999). Competition in the local loop: a study for VECAI, Visions. VECAI, The Hague.

Varian, H. (1996). *Mathematica* for economists. In H. M. Amman, D. A. Kendrick, and J. Rust (eds.), *Handbook of computational economics, volume 1*. Amsterdam: North-Holland.

Vives, X. (1990). Nash equilibrium with strategic complementarities. *Journal of Mathematical Economics*, 19, 305–321.

Vogelsang, I., and Mitchell, B. (1997). *Telecommunications competition: the last ten miles*. Cambridge, MA: MIT Press and Washington, DC: AEI Press.

Wang, R., and Wen, Q. (1998). Strategic invasion in markets with switching costs. *Journal of Economics and Management Strategy*, 7, 521–549.

Watson, L. T. (1979). A globally convergent algorithm for computing fixed points of C^2 maps. *Applied Mathematic and Computation*, 5, 297–311.

Willig, R. (1979). The theory of network access pricing. In H. Trebling (ed.), *Issues in public utility regulation*. East Lansing, MI: Michigan State University Press.

Wilson, R. (1993). *Nonlinear pricing*. Oxford, UK: Oxford University Press.

Wolfram, S. (1996). *The Mathematica Book*. Cambridge, UK: Wolfram Media/ Cambridge University Press.

Wright, J. (2000). Competition and termination in cellular networks. Mimeo, University of Auckland.

Index